# THE
# UNWRITTEN SONG

# THE

# UNWRITTEN SONG

POETRY OF THE PRIMITIVE AND
TRADITIONAL PEOPLES OF THE WORLD
EDITED, IN PART RETRANSLATED,
AND WITH AN INTRODUCTION BY

## WILLARD R. TRASK

---

*VOLUME II*

Micronesia / Polynesia / Asia
North America / Central America
South America

---

THE MACMILLAN COMPANY · NEW YORK

COLLIER-MACMILLAN LTD · LONDON

Library of Congress Catalog Card Number: 66–24053

First Printing

The Macmillan Company, New York
Collier-Macmillan Canada Ltd., Toronto, Ontario

Printed in the United States of America

# SOURCES AND PERMISSIONS

### SYMBOLS USED

(*)    Original text also given in the source cited.
(**)   Original text and melody also given in the source cited.
FROM   English translation taken from the source cited.
AFTER  English translation by the Editor from the language of the source cited.

Sources and permissions are given in accordance with the original material from
which the poems were taken and in accordance with the publisher's requirements.
Every attempt was made to contact the copyright holders of the original material.
Since some of the poems were published a long time ago, and a number of publications have since been suspended, it was not possible to obtain a written release
for every poem in this volume. The phrase "with permission of the publisher"
appears only when its inclusion has been requested.

## MICRONESIA
### Caroline Islands

**Page 3**    "Love Song." AFTER: Augustin Krämer, *Palau*, 5 vols. (Ergebnisse der
Südsee-Expedition, 1908–10, II.B.3) (Hamburg, Friederichsen, De Gruyter & Co.,
1917–29), IV, 282–83. By permission of Cram, de Gruyter & Co., Hamburg.
**Page 3**    "Dance Song of Death." *Ibid.*, pp. 297–98 (*). **Page 4**    "Dance Song on
the Death of a Girl Named Rutenag." AFTER: Wilhelm Müller, *Yap* (Ergebnisse
der Südsee-Expedition, 1908–10, II.B.2) (Hamburg, L. Friederichsen & Co., 1917),
pp. 382–85 (*). By permission of Cram, de Gruyter & Co., Hamburg. **Page 6**
"Boys' Dance Song on the Departure of an Older Girl Named Yiluai." *Ibid.*, pp.
392–94 (*). **Page 7**    "Dance Song." *Ibid.*, pp. 419–22 (*). **Page 9**    "Song of a
Married Woman to Her Lover Yuv." *Ibid.*, pp. 433–37 (*). **Page 12**    "Women's
Ur-Dance Song." FROM: *Flower in My Ear: Arts and Ethos of Ifaluk Atoll*, pp.
140–45, by Edwin Grant Burrows (Seattle, University of Washington Press, 1963).
Copyright © 1963 by University of Washington Press. Reprinted by permission of

the publisher. **Page 16**    "Song of a Navigator's Wife." *Ibid.*, pp. 107–9. Copyright © 1963 by University of Washington Press. Reprinted by permission of the publisher. **Page 18**    "Song of a Widow." *Ibid.*, pp. 138–40. Copyright © 1963 by University of Washington Press. Reprinted by permission of the publisher. **Page 20**    "Song of a Mother for Her Dead Son." *Ibid.*, pp. 297–98. Copyright © 1963 by University of Washington Press. Reprinted by permission of the publisher. **Page 21**    "Girl's Song." *Ibid.*, pp. 207–9. Copyright © 1963 by University of Washington Press. Reprinted by permission of the publisher. **Page 23**    "Girl's Song." *Ibid.*, pp. 228–29. Copyright © 1963 by University of Washington Press. Reprinted by permission of the publisher. **Page 24**    "Love Songs." AFTER: Augustin Krämer, *Truk* (Ergebnisse der Südsee-Expedition, 1908–10, II.B.5) (Hamburg, Friederichsen, De Gruyter & Co., 1932), pp. 379–80 (*). By permission of Cram, de Gruyter & Co., Hamburg. **Page 25**    "The Song of Senia and Monia." AFTER: Paul Hambruch and Annelise Eilers, *Ponape*, 2 vols. (Ergebnisse der Südsee-Expedition, 1908–10, II.B.7) (Hamburg, Friederichsen, De Gruyter & Co., 1932–36), II, 196–98 (*). By permission of Cram, de Gruyter & Co., Hamburg.

## Gilbert Islands

**Page 27**    "Ceremonial Prayer for the Fructification of the Pandanus Tree." FROM: Sir Arthur Grimble, *We Chose the Islands: A Six-Year Adventure in the Gilberts* (New York, William Morrow & Co., 1952; London, John Murray), pp. 169–70. **Page 27**    "Spell Called 'The Lifting of the Head' to Make the Dead Person's Way Straight into the Land of the Ancestors." FROM: Sir Arthur Grimble, *Return to the Islands: Life and Legend in the Gilberts* (New York, William Morrow & Co., 1957), p. 42. **Page 28**    "Invocation of a Poet Seeking Inspiration." *Ibid.*, p. 204. **Page 28**    "Invocation of a Poet Seeking Inspiration." FROM: P. B. Laxton, "A Gilbertese Song," *Journal of the Polynesian Society*, LXII (1953), 344 (*). **Page 29**    "Song of a Fabulous Heroine Whose Lover Has Escaped from Captivity in Tonga." FROM: A. Grimble, *Return . . .*, pp. 200–201. **Page 29**    "Song." AFTER: R. Parkinson, "Beiträge zur Ethnographie der Gilbert-Insulaner," *Internationales Archiv für Ethnographie*, II (1889), 95 (*). **Page 30**    "Satire." FROM: A. Grimble, *Return . . .*, p. 206.

## Marshall Islands

**Page 31**    "Storm Tide on Mejit." AFTER: Augustin Krämer, *Hawaii, Ost-Mikronesien, und Samoa* (Stuttgart, Strecker et Schröder, 1906), pp. 439–40 (*).

# POLYNESIA
## Unspecified Localities

**Page 35**    "Sea Chant." FROM: J. E. Weckler, Jr., *Polynesians: Explorers of the Pacific* (War Background Studies No. 6) (Washington, The Smithsonian Institution, 1943), p. 2. Reprinted by permission from the Smithsonian Institution. **Page 35**    "Lullaby." AFTER: Mme Nordmann-Salmon, in A. Leroi-Gourhan *et al.*, *Ethnologie de l'Union Française (Territoires extérieurs)*, 2 vols. (Paris, Presses Universitaires de France, 1953), II, 827. **Page 36**    "Birth." FROM: J. Frank Stimson, *Songs and Tales of the Sea Kings: Interpretations of the Oral Literature of Polynesia* (Salem, Mass., 1957), p. 11. Reproduced by the courtesy of the Peabody Museum of Salem. **Page 36**    "Marriage." *Ibid.*, p. 24. Reproduced by the courtesy of the Peabody Museum of Salem. **Page 37**    "Passion Spent." *Ibid.*, p. 20. Reproduced by the courtesy of the Peabody Museum of Salem. **Page 38**    "The Four

Winds." *Ibid.*, pp. 53–56. Reproduced by the courtesy of the Peabody Museum of Salem.

## Tikopia

**Page 41**    "Song of a Returning Voyager." FROM: Raymond Firth, *The Work of the Gods in Tikopia*, 2 vols. (Monographs in Social Anthropology, No. 1) (London, The London School of Economics, 1940), II, 247 (*). **Page 41**    "Dirges." FROM: Raymond Firth, *We, the Tikopia: A Sociological Study of Kinship in Primitive Polynesia* (New York: American Book Co., 1936), pp. 290, 298 (*[of I], *ibid.*, p. 289). By permission of George Allen and Unwin, Ltd., London. **Page 42**    "Song of a Girl Cast Off by Her Lover." *Ibid.*, p. 517. **Page 42**    "Ironical Song on the Intolerance of Missionaries and Converts." *Ibid.*, p. 44.

## Uvea

**Page 43**    "Old Funeral Chant." AFTER: Jean Guiart, "Mythes et chants polynésiens d'Ouvéa (Îles Loyalty)," *Journal of the Polynesian Society*, LXII (1953), 101–3 (*).

## Tonga

**Page 45**    "Recitative." Trans. Beatrice Shirley Baker, in Edward Winslow Gifford, *Tongan Myths and Tales* (Bernice P. Bishop Museum Bulletin 8) (Honolulu, Bishop Museum, 1924), p. 18 (*). Thanks are due to Bernice P. Bishop Museum, Honolulu, Hawaii, for its kind permission to reprint materials from its publications. **Page 45**    "Song in Recitative Style." FROM: W. Mariner, *An Account of the Natives of the Tonga Islands*, 2 vols. (London, 1818) (*). (The version given is combined from Mariner's free translation in Vol. I, pp. 293–94, and his literal translation, with the original text, in his "Grammar of the Tonga Language" [unpaged] in Vol. II, with certain corrections from the translations in W. von Humboldt, *Über die Kawi-Sprache auf der Insel Java* [3 vols., Berlin, 1836–39], III, 457–60, and in K. Luomala, *Voices on the Wind* [Honolulu, Bishop Museum Press, 1955], pp. 32–33.) Thanks are due to Bernice P. Bishop Museum, Honolulu, Hawaii, for its kind permission to reprint materials from its publications. **Page 47**    "Praise of Beaches." FROM: E. E. V. Collocott, *Tales and Poems of Tonga* (Bernice P. Bishop Museum Bulletin 46) (Honolulu, Bishop Museum, 1928), pp. 117–18. Thanks are due to Bernice P. Bishop Museum, Honolulu, Hawaii, for its kind permission to reprint materials from its publications. **Page 48**    "Song of Tukulua." *Ibid.*, pp. 77–79 (*). **Page 50**    "Farewell of Warriors of Vavau Going to Fight at Sea." *Ibid.*, p. 123 (**).

## Samoa

**Page 51**    "Kava-Drinking Song." FROM: John Dixon Copp, *The Samoan Dance of Life: An Anthropological Narrative* (Boston, The Beacon Press, 1950), p. 122. Reprinted by permission of The Beacon Press, copyright © 1950 by The Beacon Press. **Page 51**    "Dirge." FROM: E. Schultz, "Proverbial Expressions of the Samoans," *Journal of the Polynesian Society*, LIX (1950), 40 (*). **Page 52**    "Love Song." FROM: J. D. Copp, *op. cit.*, p. 108. Reprinted by permission of The Beacon Press, copyright © 1950 by The Beacon Press. **Page 52**    "Song of a Suitor Dismissed." *Ibid.*, p. 121. Reprinted by permission of The Beacon Press, copyright © 1950 by The Beacon Press.

## Cook Islands

**Page 53**    "Prayer over a Human Sacrifice to Rongo." FROM: William Wyatt Gill, *Myths and Songs from the South Pacific* (London, Henry S. King & Co., 1876), pp. 295–96 (*). **Page 54**    "Prayer for Peace." *Ibid.*, p. 299 (*). **Page 54**    "Tumea's Lament for Her Father Ngakauvarea." FROM: William Wyatt Gill, *From Darkness to Light in Polynesia, with illustrative Clan Songs* (London, Religious Tract Society, 1894), pp. 272–73 (*). **Page 56**    "The Overthrow of Ruanae." FROM: William Wyatt Gill, *Historical Sketches of Savage Life in Polynesia, with illustrative Clan Songs* (Wellington, George Didsbury, Government Printer, 1880), pp. 128–29 (*). With acknowledgment to the Government Printer, New Zealand. **Page 59**    "Final Stanza of the Day-Song for Tenio's Fete." FROM: W. W. Gill, *Myths and Songs . . .* , pp. 96–97 (*). **Page 60**    "The Ghosts Led by Vera Preparing for Their Final Departure." *Ibid.*, pp. 194–98 (*). **Page 64**    " 'Blackened-Face' Dirge-Proper for Atiroa." *Ibid.*, pp. 281–82 (*). **Page 65**    "Song from a Legend." FROM: Te Ariki-tara-are, "History and Traditions of Rarotonga," Part I, *Journal of the Polynesian Society*, VIII (1899), 67–68 (*, *ibid.*, p. 80.)

## Society Islands

**Page 66**    "Priests' Chant to Usher in the Dawn." FROM: Teuira Henry, *Ancient Tahiti, based on material recorded by J. B. Orsmond* (Bernice P. Bishop Museum Bulletin 48) (Honolulu, Bishop Museum, 1928), p. 165 (*). Thanks are due to Bernice P. Bishop Museum, Honolulu, Hawaii, for its kind permission to reprint materials from its publications. **Page 67**    "Tahitian Chant of Creation." FROM: Abraham Fornander, *An Account of the Polynesian Race, Its Origins and Migrations*, 3 vols. (London, Trübner & Co., 1878–85), I, 221–23 (*). **Page 68**    "Aromaiterai's Lament." FROM: *Memoirs of Arii Taimai* (etc.) (Paris, 1901), p. 35 (*). **Page 68** "Lament of Taura Atua." *Ibid.*, p. 37 (*). **Page 69**    "Lament of a Deserted Husband." FROM: W. D. Alexander, "Specimens of Ancient Tahitian Poetry," *Journal of the Polynesian Society*, II (1893), 55–57 (*).

## Tuamotus

**Page 71**    "Greeting of Tane." FROM: Kenneth P. Emory, "Tuamotuan Concepts of Creation," *Journal of the Polynesian Society*, XL (1940), 94 (*). **Page 72**    "Dream Song of a Canoe-Builder." FROM: Teuira Henry, *Ancient Tahiti, based on material recorded by J. B. Orsmond* (Bernice P. Bishop Museum Bulletin 48) (Honolulu, Bishop Museum, 1928), p. 500 (*). Thanks are due to Bernice P. Bishop Museum, Honolulu, Hawaii, for its kind permission to reprint materials from its publications. **Page 72**    "Plaint of a Woman Who Has No Lover but the Post in Her House." FROM: Edwin Grant Burrows, *Native Music of the Tuamotus* (Bernice P. Bishop Museum Bulletin 109) (Honolulu, Bishop Museum, 1933), p. 39 (**). Thanks are due to Bernice P. Bishop Museum, Honolulu, Hawaii, for its kind permission to reprint materials from its publications. **Page 72**    "The Return of the *Marama* from Hiti." FROM: J. Frank Stimson, "Songs of the Polynesian Voyagers," *Journal of the Polynesian Society*, XLI (1932), 190–96 (*). **Page 78**    "Lament." FROM: K. Luomala, *Voices on the Wind: Polynesian Myths and Chants* (Honolulu, Bishop Museum Press, 1955), p. 156. Thanks are due to Bernice P. Bishop Museum, Honolulu, Hawaii, for its kind permission to reprint materials from its publications. **Page 79**    "Creation Chant." FROM: Kenneth P. Emory, "The Tahitian Account of Creation by Mare," *Journal of the Polynesian Society*, XLVII (1938), 50 (*).

**Page 80**    "Lament of Huauri for Her Husband Hema Whose Death Their Son Goes to Avenge." FROM: J. F. Stimson, *Tuamotuan Legends (Island of Anaa)*, Part I (Bernice P. Bishop Museum Bulletin 148) (Honolulu, Bernice P. Bishop Museum, 1937), pp. 74–75 (*). Thanks are due to Bernice P. Bishop Museum, Honolulu, Hawaii, for its kind permission to reprint materials from its publications. **Page 81**    "Chant of Hapai About the Voluptuous Passion of Tahaki." *Ibid.*, p. 93 (*). **Page 82**    "Passion-Song of the Maidens." FROM: J. F. Stimson, *The Legends of Maui and Tahaki* (Bernice P. Bishop Museum Bulletin 127) (Honolulu, Bishop Museum, 1934), pp. 5–6 (*). Thanks are due to Bernice P. Bishop Museum, Honolulu, Hawaii, for its kind permission to reprint materials from its publications. **Page 82**    "Chant of the Hymenal Rupturing of Horohora." *Ibid.*, pp. 61–62 (*). **Page 84**    "Lament of Hapai for Tahaki." *Ibid.*, pp. 76–77 (*). **Page 86**    "Chant of Kororupo." FROM: J. Frank Stimson, *Tuamotuan Religion* (Bernice P. Bishop Museum Bulletin 103) (Honolulu, Bishop Museum, 1933), p. 43 (*). Thanks are due to Bernice P. Bishop Museum, Honolulu, Hawaii, for its kind permission to reprint materials from its publications.

## Mangareva

**Page 87**    "The Mating of Toga." FROM: Te Rangi Hiroa (Peter H. Buck), *Ethnology of Mangareva* (Bernice P. Bishop Museum Bulletin 157) (Honolulu, Bishop Museum, 1938), pp. 346–47 (*). Thanks are due to Bernice P. Bishop Museum, Honolulu, Hawaii, for its kind permission to reprint materials from its publications. **Page 88**    "Lament: Sea-Burial of Toga's Daughter." *Ibid.*, p. 356 (*). **Page 89**    "The Message of the Frigate Birds." *Ibid.*, pp. 330–31 (*). **Page 89**    "Lament." *Ibid.*, pp. 372–73 (*). **Page 90**    "Song at a Funeral." *Ibid.*, p. 486 (*). **Page 90**    "The Karako Bird." *Ibid.*, p. 397 (*). **Page 91**    "Lament for Old Age." *Ibid.*, pp. 390–91 (*). **Page 92**    "The Rich and the Poor." *Ibid.*, pp. 342–43 (*).

## Marquesas Islands

**Page 93**    "*Rari* for O'Otua." FROM: Samuel H. Elbert, "Chants and Love Songs of the Marquesas Islands, French Oceania," *Journal of the Polynesian Society*, L (1941), 79 (*). **Page 93**    "*Rari* About the Faufe'e Bird." *Ibid.*, pp. 83–84 (*). **Page 94**    "*Rari* for the Americans." *Ibid.*, p. 84 (*). **Page 94**    "*Rari*." *Ibid.*, pp. 85–86 (*). **Page 95**    "*Mu*." *Ibid.*, pp. 82–83 (*).

## Hawaii

**Page 96**    "The Fall of Kumuhonua and His Wife." FROM: Abraham Fornander, *Fornander Collection of Hawaiian Antiquities and Folk-Lore*, Third Series (Memoirs of the Bernice Pauahi Bishop Museum, Vol. VI) (Honolulu, Bishop Museum Press, 1919–20), p. 366 (*). Thanks are due to Bernice P. Bishop Museum, Honolulu, Hawaii, for its kind permission to reprint materials from its publications. **Page 96**    "The Water of Kane." FROM: Nathaniel B. Emerson, *Unwritten Literature of Hawaii: The Sacred Songs of the Hula* (Smithsonian Institution, Bureau of American Ethnology, Bulletin 38) (Washington, Government Printing Office, 1909), pp. 258–59 (*). **Page 98**    "House Dedication Prayer." FROM: E. S. Craighill Handy and Mary K. Pukui, "The Polynesian Family System in Ka-'U, Hawaii," Part V, *Journal of the Polynesian Society*, LXI (1952), pp. 280–81 (*). **Page 98**    "The Song of Kualii." FROM: C. J. Lyons, "The Song of Kualii," *Journal of the Polynesian Society*, II (1893), 165–70 (*). **Page 101**    "Song for the Hula Ala'a-papa." FROM: N. B. Emerson, *op. cit.*, p. 59 (*). **Page 102**    "Phases of the Sea." FROM: A. Fornander, *op. cit.*, p. 208 (*). **Page 102**    "Storm Scene." FROM: *Ibid.*, Second

Series (Memoirs of the Bernice Pauahi Bishop Museum, Vol. V, Parts 1, 2) (Honolulu, Bishop Museum Press, 1918–19), pp. 84–87 (*). Thanks are due to Bernice P. Bishop Museum, Honolulu, Hawaii, for its kind permission to reprint materials from its publications. **Page 103**    "Chant of Welcome to a Kinsman or Friend." FROM: Handy and Pukui, *op. cit.*, Part VII, *Journal of the Polynesian Society*, LXII (1953), 307 (*). **Page 103**    "Dirge." Handy and Pukui, *op. cit.*, Part VI, *Journal of the Polynesian Society*, LXII (1953), 164 (*). **Page 104**    "Love Song from a Legend." FROM: A. Fornander, Second Series, p. 254 (*). **Page 104**    "Dawn Song." FROM: David Malo, *Hawaiian Antiquities*, tr. N. B. Emerson (Honolulu, The Bishop Museum, 1951), p. 240 (*). Thanks are due to Bernice P. Bishop Museum, Honolulu, Hawaii, for its kind permission to reprint materials from its publications. **Page 105**    "Taunt Song: A Warrior Replies to His Daughter Who Has Asked Him to Teach Her Husband a Certain Stroke with the War-Club." FROM: Laura C. Green, *The Legend of Kawelo* (Publications of the Folklore Foundation, No. 9) (Poughkeepsie, N.Y., Vassar College, 1929), p. 41 (*).

## New Zealand and Chatham Islands

**Page 106**    "Cosmogony." FROM: Richard Taylor, *Te Ika a Maui; or, New Zealand and its Inhabitants* (London, William MacIntosh, 1870), pp. 109–10 (*). **Page 107**    "The Mating of Hine and Tane-Matua." FROM: S. Percy Smith, *The Lore of the Whare-wānanga; or, Teachings of the Maori College on Religion, Cosmogony, and History*, Part I (New Plymouth, N.Z., The Polynesian Society, 1913), p. 141 (*). **Page 108**    "Charm." FROM: John White, *The Ancient History of the Maori, his Mythology and Traditions*, 6 vols. (Wellington, George Didsbury, Government Printer, 1887–90), II, 32 (original text in Maori part, p. 32). With acknowledgment to the Government Printer, New Zealand. **Page 108**    "The Song of the Aotea Canoe." FROM: James Cowan, *The Maoris of New Zealand* (Christchurch, N.Z., Whitcombe & Tombs, Ltd., 1910), p. 54 (*). **Page 110**    "Old Dance Song, Adapted to Contemporary Incidents in 1885." FROM: Johannes C. Andersen, *Maori Music with Its Polynesian Background* (Memoirs of the Polynesian Society, 10) (New Plymouth, N.Z., Thomas Avery & Sons, 1934), pp. 316–17 (*). **Page 110**    "Vaunt of the Hero Whakatau on Going into Battle." FROM: W. Colenso, "Contributions Towards a Better Knowledge of the Maori Race," Part III, *Transactions and Proceedings of the New Zealand Institute*, XIII (1880), 67–68. **Page 112**    "Taunt Sung to the Impaled Head of an Enemy Chief (*ca.* 1820)." FROM: Barry Mitcalfe, *Poetry of the Maori* (Hamilton and Auckland, Paul's Book Arcade, 1961), pp. 34–35 (*). Reprinted by permission of Blackwood & Janet Paul, Ltd. **Page 113**    "Song of Revenge." FROM: Edward Tregear, *The Maori Race* (Wanganui, N.Z., A. D. Wallis, 1904), p. 76. **Page 113**    "A Joyous Revelling Song Sung by the Wood Rats." FROM: W. Colenso, *op. cit.*, pp. 72–73. **Page 114**    "Choral Songs." FROM: Edward Shortland, *Traditions and Superstitions of the New Zealanders, with illustrations of their manners and customs*, 2nd ed. (London, Longman, Brown, Green, Longmans and Roberts, 1856), pp. 170, 171, 171–72 (*). **Page 114**    "A Lament for His Own Land." FROM: A. T. Ngata, *Nga Moteatea (The Songs): Scattered Pieces from Many Canoe Areas*, Part I (Polynesian Society Maori Texts, No. 1) (Wellington, The Polynesian Society, 1959), p. 93 (*). **Page 115**    "Ihunui's Lament for Her Daughter Rangi." FROM: Elsdon Best, *Games and Pastimes of the Maori . . . including some information concerning their . . . Music* (New Zealand, Dominion Museum, Bulletin No. 8) (Wellington, Whitcombe & Tombs, Ltd., 1925), pp. 110–11 (*). Reprinted by permission of Dominion Museum, Wellington, N.Z. **Page 116**    "Lament for the Chief Te

Kani-a-Takirau (Died 1856)." FROM: S. Percy Smith, "Wars of the Northern Against the Southern Tribes of New Zealand in the Nineteenth Century," Part V, *Journal of the Polynesian Society*, IX (1900), 148 (diction altered) (*). **Page 116**    "Dirge for a Chief." FROM: Peter H. Buck (Te Rangi Hiroa), *Vikings of the Sunrise* (New York, Frederick A. Stokes Co., 1938), pp. 282–83. Copyright, 1938, by J. B. Lippincott and reprinted here by permission of the copyright holder. **Page 117**    "Song of a Widow for Her Dead Husband." FROM: E. Tregear, *op. cit.*, pp. 74–75 (diction altered). **Page 117**    "Lament." *Ibid.*, pp. 75–76. **Page 118**    "Song by an Unnamed Poetess." FROM: E. Shortland, *op. cit.*, pp. 182–83 (*). **Page 118**    "A Song for Te Moana-Papaku." FROM: A. T. Ngata, *op. cit.*, p. 157 (*). **Page 118**    "Song of a Girl Abandoned by Her Lover." FROM: E. Shortland, *op. cit.*, p. 178 (*). **Page 119**    "The Soliloquy of an Invalid." FROM: A. T. Ngata, op. cit., p. 73 (*). **Page 120**    "Incantation Used by Rangitokona to Create Man." FROM: Alexander Shand, "The Moriori People of the Chatham Islands: Their Traditions and History," Chap. 2, *Journal of the Polynesian Society*, III (1894), 121 (*, ibid., p. 129).

# ASIA

## Northern Siberia

**Page 123**    "Songs." FROM: Waldemar Bogoras, *The Eskimo of Siberia* (Memoirs of The American Museum of Natural History, Vol. XII, Part III) (Leiden, E. J. Brill, 1913), pp. 437, 438, 450 (*). Reprinted by the courtesy of the American Museum of Natural History and E. J. Brill, Publishers, Leiden. **Page 123**    "Songs." FROM: Waldemar Bogoras, *Chukchee Mythology* (Memoirs of The American Museum of Natural History, Vol. XII, Part I) (Leiden, E. J. Brill, 1913), pp. 138, 142 (*[and interlinear translations], *ibid.*). Reprinted by the courtesy of the American Museum of Natural History and E. J. Brill, Publishers, Leiden. **Page 124**    "Incantation Used by a Jealous Woman Against Her Rival." FROM: Waldemar Bogoras, *The Chukchee: Religion* (Memoirs of The American Museum of Natural History, Vol. XI, Part II) (Leiden, E. J. Brill, 1907), pp. 507–8. Reprinted by the courtesy of The American Museum of Natural History and E. J. Brill, Publishers, Leiden. **Page 124**    "Prayer to the Sea." FROM: Waldemar Jochelson, *The Koryak* (Memoirs of The American Museum of Natural History, Vol. X, Part I) (New York, G. E. Stechert, 1905), p. 99 (*). **Page 124**    "Prayer to the Creator." *Ibid.*, p. 55 (*[and literal translation], *ibid.*, p. 54). **Page 125**    "Shaman's Address to His Spirits." FROM: Waldemar Jochelson, *Peoples of Asiatic Russia* (n.p., The American Museum of Natural History, 1928), p. 225. **Page 125**    "Songs." *Ibid.*, pp. 224, 225. **Page 126**    "Ceremonial Chant of a Shaman." FROM: M. A. Czaplika, *Aboriginal Siberia: A Study in Social Anthropology* (Oxford, The Clarendon Press, 1914), pp. 235–36 (after W. Sieroszewski). **Page 127**    "Dance Song." AFTER: Artturi Kannisto, *Wogulische Volksdichtung: V. Auffuhrungen beim Bärenfest* (Mémoires de la Société Finno-Ougrienne, 116) (Helsinki, Suomalais-Ugrilainen Seura, 1959), p. 242 (*).

## Central Asia

**Page 128**    "Ceremonial Chants of a Shaman." FROM: M. A. Czaplika, *Aboriginal Siberia: A Study in Social Anthropology* (Oxford, The Clarendon Press, 1914), pp. 300–303 (after W. M. Mikhailowski). **Page 130**    "Improvised Songs." AFTER: W. Radloff, *Proben der Volkslitteratur der Türkischen Stämme Süd-Siberiens*, 10 vols. (St. Petersburg, 1866 ff.), I, 246–47, 249, 259 (originals in the corresponding text volume). **Page 131** "Praise Song of the Wind." *Ibid.*, p. 245 (original in the corresponding text volume). **Page 132** "Songs." *Ibid.*, II, 658, 659 (originals in the corresponding text volume). **Page 133** "The Kalmyk Mourns for His Country." *Ibid.*, III, 66–67 (original in the corresponding text volume). **Page 134** "Song for the Arrival of the Guests and the Bride at the Bridegroom's Door." AFTER: Giuseppe Ruggiero, *Canti popolari dei buriati di Alac* (Naples, E. V. A., 1932), p. 51. **Page 134** "Shaman's Chant at a Wedding." AFTER: A. Bastian, "Die Vorstellungen von Wasser und Feuer," Part II, *Zeitschrift für Ethnologie*, I (1869), 383. By permission of Albert Limbach Verlag, Braunschweig. **Page 135** "Songs." AFTER: Princess Nirgidma de Torhout, *Dix-huit chants et poèmes mongols* (Bibliothèque Musicale du Musée Guimet, Ser. I, Vol. IV) (Paris, Librairie Orientaliste Paul Geuthner, 1937), pp. 10, 17–18 (**).

## Afghanistan, Pakistan, Kashmir

**Page 136** "Couplets." AFTER: James Darmesteter, *Chants populaires des Afghans* (Paris, Imprimerie Nationale, 1888–90), pp. 229, 230 (*). **Page 136** "Dastanghs." FROM: M. Longworth Dames, *Popular Poetry of the Baloches*, 2 vols. (Asiatic Society's Monographs, I) (London, The Royal Asiatic Society, 1907), I, 187, 190 (*, II, 165, 168). **Page 137** "Da-Kudrat Sandre (Songs of Nature)." FROM: Davendra Satyarthi, "Song-Harvest from Pathan Country," *The Modern Review* (Calcutta), LVIII (1935), 516, 518, 518. **Page 138** "Songs." FROM: A. H. Francke, "Ladakhi Songs," *The Indian Antiquary*, XXXI (1902), 94–95, 97, 309 (*).

## India

**Page 139** "Song for a Feast of Krishna." AFTER: Wilhelm Koppers, *Die Bhil in Zentralindien* (Wiener Beiträge zur Kulturgeschichte und Linguistik, VII) (Horn-Wien, Ferdinand Berger, 1948), p. 201. **Page 139** "Bride's Song on the Way to Her Husband's House." FROM: Wilhelm Koppers and Leonhard Jungblut, "Wedding Rites Among the Bhil of North-Western Central India," *Anthropos*, XLVI (1951), 131–32. **Page 140** "Song of a Woman to Her Lover." FROM: T. H. Hendley, "An Account of the Maiwár Bhíls," *Journal of the Asiatic Society of Bengal*, XLIV (1875), 384–85 (*). **Page 140** "Dance Songs." FROM: Shamrao Hivale and Verrier Elwin, *Songs of the Forest: The Folk Poetry of the Gonds* (London, George Allen & Unwin, 1935), pp. 55, 97, 98, 104, 143. **Page 142** "Men's Stick-Dance Songs." *Ibid.*, p. 81. **Page 142** "Songs Sung by Woodcutters or Workers in the Fields." *Ibid.*, pp. 99, 124, 125, 127, 134. **Page 143** "Women's Dance Song." FROM: Verrier Elwin and Shamrao Hivale, *Folk-Songs of the Maikal Hills* (Madras, Oxford University Press, Indian Branch, 1944), p. 34. **Page 143** "Songs and Dance Songs." *Ibid.*, pp. 16, 103, 103, 104, 109, 252. **Page 144** "Fertility." *Ibid.*, p. 246. **Page 145** "Song." FROM: Verrier Elwin, *Folk-Songs of Chhattisgarh* (Bombay, Oxford University Press, Indian Branch, 1946), p. 20. **Page 145** "Dance Songs." FROM: Hivale and Elwin, *op. cit.*, pp. 112, 116, 119. **Page 146** "Dirge." FROM: Shamrao Hivale, *The Pardhans of the Upper Narboda Valley* (Bombay, Oxford University Press, Indian Branch, 1946), p. 177. **Page 146** "Songs." *Ibid.*, pp. 153, 153, 154, 155–56.

**Page 148** "The Birth of the Goddess Jangu Bai." FROM: Christoph von Fürer-Haimendorf, *The Raj Gonds of Adilabad: A Peasant Culture of the Deccan* (The Aboriginal Tribes of Hyderabad, III) (London, Macmillan & Co., 1948), pp. 123–25. **Page 150** "Song." FROM: Verrier Elwin, *The Agaria* (Bombay, Oxford University Press, Indian Branch, 1942), p. 15. **Page 151**    "Women's Dance Song." Hivale and Elwin, *op. cit.*, p. 51. **Page 151**    "Dialogue." FROM: Verrier Elwin, *The Baiga* (London, John Murray, 1939), p. 256. **Page 152**    "Songs and Dance Songs." *Ibid.*, pp. 246, 266, 441, 445, 446, 447, 453, 455. **Page 153**    "A Reaping Song." FROM: V. Elwin, *Folk-Songs . . . Chhattisgarh*, p. 112. **Page 154**    "Song." FROM: S. C. Dube, *Field Songs of Chhattisgarh* (Folk Culture Series, No. 2) (Lucknow, The Universal Publishers, 1947), p. 34. **Page 154**    "Dance Song." *Ibid.* **Page 155**    "Festival Songs." FROM: Gautamansankar Ray, "A Few Songs of the Adibasis of Kolhan," *Man in India*, XXIX (1949), 172, 173. **Page 155**    "Lament." FROM: W. G. Archer, *The Blue Grove: The Poetry of the Uraons* (London, George Allen & Unwin, 1940), pp. 135–36. **Page 156**    "Dialogue Between a Newly Married Couple." *Ibid.*, pp. 53–54. **Page 157**    "Song." FROM: W. G. Archer, "Seventeen Kayesth Poems of the Shahabad District," *Man in India*, XXIII (1943), 17. **Page 157**    "Festival Songs." FROM: W. G. Archer, "Festival Songs," *Man in India*, XXIV (1944), 72–73, 74. **Page 158**    "Jungle Songs." FROM: W. G. Archer, "Santal Poetry," *Man in India*, XXIII (1943), 101, 102, 104, 105. **Page 159**    "Marriage Songs." *Ibid.*, pp. 98, 99, 99. **Page 160**    "Jungle Songs." FROM: W. G. Archer, "More Santal Songs," *Man in India*, XXIV (1944), 141, 143, 143, 143, 144. **Page 161**    "Songs." FROM: W. G. Archer, "The Illegitimate Child in Santal Society," *Man in India*, XXIV (1944), 156, 157, 157, 157.

**Page 162**    "Dance Song." FROM: Rai Bahadur Sarat Chandra Roy, *The Birhors: A little-known Jungle Tribe of Chota Nagpur* (Ranchi, 1925), p. 505 (*). **Page 162**    "Marriage Poems." FROM: W. G. Archer, *Blue Grove*, pp. 107, 116, 130, 138, 142. **Page 163**    "Dance Songs." *Ibid.*, pp. 37, 38, 47–48, 50, 52, 61 (I–VI); and W. G. Archer, *The Dove and the Leopard: More Uraon Poetry* (Bombay, Orient Longmans Ltd., 1948), pp. 71, 108, 109, 111 (VII–X). **Page 165**    "Songs." FROM: Verrier Elwin, "Five Bhattra Songs," *Man in India*, XXIII (1943), 9. **Page 166**    "Songs at a Wedding." FROM: Verrier Elwin, *The Muria and their Ghotul* (Bombay, Oxford University Press, Indian Branch, 1947), pp. 103–4. **Page 168** "Song." FROM: Verrier Elwin, "The Attitude of Indian Aboriginals towards Sexual Impotence," *Man in India*, XXIII (1943), 141. **Page 168**    "Songs." FROM: Verrier Elwin, *Bondo Highlander* (Bombay, Oxford University Press, Indian Branch, 1950), pp. 78, 79. **Page 169**    "Dance Songs." FROM: Verrier Elwin, "Ten Juang Dance Songs," *Man in India*, XXIII (1943), 31–32, 32, 34. **Page 170**    "Song." FROM: V. Elwin: "Attitude . . . Sexual Impotence," p. 144. **Page 170**    "Songs." FROM: Sarat Chandra Roy and Ramesh Chandra Roy, *The Khāriās*, 2 vols. (Ranchi, "*Man in India*" Office, 1937), II, 484, 488, 500 (slightly altered) (*). **Page 171**    "Love Songs." FROM: Bramha Kumar Shukla, *The Daflas of the Subansiri Region* (Shillong, North-East Frontier Agency, Government of India, 1959), pp. 68–69, 69. **Page 172**    "Spring Festival Songs." FROM: P. Goswami, *Bihu Songs of Assam* (Gauhati, India, Lawyer's Bookstall, 1957), pp. 50, 52, 59, 69, 69, 75, 83, 84, 95, 97, 100 (I–XI); and P. Goswami, *Folk-Literature of Assam: An Introductory Survey* (Gauhati, India, Dept. of Historical and Antiquarian Studies, Government of Assam, 1954), pp. 19, 19, 20 (XII–XIV). **Page 174**    "Sad Songs." FROM: P. Goswami, "Bihu Songs . . . ," pp. 115, 114, 34. **Page 174**    "Love Song." FROM: J. P. Mills, *The Ao Nagas* (London, Macmillan & Co., 1926), p. 330. **Page 175**    "Song Contest." *Ibid.*, p. 331 **Page 176**    "Song." FROM: Christoph von Fürer-Haimendorf, "The Role of Songs in Konyak Culture," *Man in India*, XXIII (1943), 73–74. **Page 177**    "Lullaby Sung by a Widow." FROM: J. P. Mills, *The Lhota Nagas* (London, Macmillan & Co., 1922), p. 202 (*).

## Ceylon

**Page 178**    "Lullaby." FROM: C. G. and Brenda Z. Seligmann, *The Veddas* (Cambridge, The University Press, 1911), pp. 367–68 (*). **Page 179**    "Song." *Ibid.*, pp. 369–70 (*).

## Andaman Islands

**Page 180**    "Two Songs Composed on Steamer Voyages." FROM: M. V. Portman, "Andamanese Music, with Notes on Oriental Music and Musical Instruments," *Journal of the Royal Asiatic Society*, N.S., XX (1888), 186, 186 (*, *ibid.*; melodies, *ibid.*, pp. 204–5, 205–7). **Page 180**    "Song on Cutting a Bow." *Ibid.*, p. 188. (*, *ibid.*; melody, *ibid.*, pp. 211–12.) **Page 181**    "Pig-Hunting Song." FROM: M. V. Portman, *Notes on the Languages of the South Andaman Group of Tribes* (Calcutta, 1898), p. 172 (*). **Page 181**    "Song for a Dead Mother." *Ibid.*, pp. 186–87 (*).

## China

**Page 182**    "Improvised Songs Between a Boy and a Girl on Their Way to Commit Suicide for Love." FROM: J. F. Rock, "The Romance of ²K'a-²mä-¹gyu-³mi-²gkyi: A Na-khi Tribal Love Story," *Bulletin de l'École Française d'Extrême-Orient*, XXXIX (1939), pp. 147–52 (*). **Page 185**    "Nature Songs." FROM: David Crockett Graham, *Songs and Stories of the Ch'uan Miao* (Smithsonian Miscellaneous Collections, Vol. 123, No. 1) (Washington, Smithsonian Institution, 1954), pp. 88–89, 89. **Page 186**    "Song of a Young Man About to Be Married." AFTER: Alfred Liétard, *Au Yun-nan. Les Lo-lo p'o, un tribu des aborigènes de la Chine méridionale* (Anthropos-Bibliothek, Vol. I, Issue 5) (Münster i. W., Aschendorffsche Verlagsbuchhandlung, 1913), pp. 114–16 (*). By permission of Aschendorffsche Verlagsbuchhandlung, Münster/Westf. **Page 188**    "Complaint of a New Wife." AFTER: Paul Vial, *Les Lolos: Histoire, religion, moeurs, langue, écriture* (Études Sino-Orientales, Fasc. A) (Shanghai, Imprimerie de la Mission Catholique, 1898), pp. 20–21. [Father Paul Vial was a member of the Paris Foreign Mission.]

## Southeast Asia

**Page 190**    "Song of a War-Band Setting Out." FROM: Harry Ignatius Marshall, *The Karen People of Burma: A Study in Anthropology and Ethnology* (Columbus, Ohio State University, 1922), p. 154. **Page 191**    "Funeral Poem." *Ibid.*, pp. 198–99. **Page 192**    "Dialogue." AFTER: Pierre Lefèvre-Pontalis, *Chansons et fêtes du Laos* (Paris, Ernest Leroux, 1896), pp. 60–61. By permission of Presses Universitaires de France. **Page 192**    "Night Song." AFTER: G. Morechand, in André Leroi-Gourhan et al., *Ethnologie de l'Union Française (Territoires extérieurs)*, 2 vols. (Paris, Presses Universitaires de France, 1953), II, 656–57. **Page 194**    "Song." AFTER: Solange Bernard, "Poèmes populaires," *France-Asie*, No. 37–38 (spring, 1949), pp. 979–80. By permission of René de Berval, ed. **Page 194**    "Lullaby." AFTER: Nguyen Tien Lang, *Les Chansons annamites* (Saigon, Édition de L' "Asie Nouvelle Illustrée," 1937), p. 3 (*, *ibid.*, p. 13). **Page 195**    "Love Song." AFTER: Nguyen Van Huyen, *Les Chants alternés des garçons et des filles en Annam* (Paris, Paul Geuthner, 1933), pp. 165–66. **Page 195**    "Song of Coughing." AFTER: Georges Condominas, "Chansons mnong gar," *France-Asie*, IX (1953), p. 651 (*). By permission of René de Berval, ed. **Page 195**    "Song of a Girl Whose Lover Has Married Another Woman." *Ibid.*, p. 656 (*). **Page 196**    "Song." AFTER: Henri Maître, *Les Régions Moï du Sud Indo-Chinois: Le Plateau de Darlac* (Paris, Plon-Nourrit et Cie. [now

Librairie Plon], 1909), pp. 133–34. **Page 196**    "Prayer at the Sacrifice Before the Coffin." AFTER: Bernard Y. Jouin, *La Mort et la Tombe: L'Abandon de la Tombe* (Université de Paris. Travaux et Mémoires de l'Institut d'Ethnologie, LII) (Paris, Institut d'Ethnologie, 1949), pp. 31–33 (*, *ibid.*, pp. 211–12.)

## Malay Peninsula

**Page 198**    "The Coconut-Monkey." FROM: Walter William Skeat and Charles Otto Blagden, *Pagan Races of the Malay Peninsula*, 2 vols. (London, Macmillan & Co., 1906), I, 645–46, and II, 152–53 (altered) (*). **Page 199**    "The Tiger." *Ibid.*, I, 636–37, and II, 148–49 (altered) (*). **Page 199**    "The Pulai-Tree." *Ibid.*, I, 667–68, and II, 161–62 (altered) (*). **Page 200**    "Fruit Song." *Ibid.*, I, 627 (*). **Page 200**    "Song of the Wild Ginger." *Ibid.*, I, 627–28 (slightly altered) (*). **Page 201**    "Song of the Chinoi as They Come Out of Flowers." AFTER: Paul Schebesta, *Die Negrito Asiens*, 3 vols. (Studia Instituti Anthropos, 6, 12, 13) (Vienna-Mödling, St.-Gabriel-Verlag, 1952–57), II/2, 131. **Page 201**    "Song of a Sunrise Chinoi." FROM: Ivor H. N. Evans, *Studies in Religion, Folk-Lore, and Custom in British North-Borneo and the Malay Peninsula* (Cambridge, The University Press, 1923), p. 171 (*). **Page 202**    "Improvised Song of the Baby Coconut Monkey." AFTER: P. Schebesta, *op. cit.*, pp. 228–29 (*). **Page 202**    "Prayer to the Goddess Ja Pudeu." AFTER: Paul Schebesta, *Orang-utan: Bei den Urwaldmenschen Malayas und Sumatras* (Leipzig: F. A. Brockhaus, 1928), p. 61. **Page 203**    "Pantuns" (I–V). AFTER: W. A. Braasem and E. A. Preyre, "Pantouns: Poésies populaires in-donésiennes," *Les Cahiers du Sud*, No. 303, 1950, pp. 301, 302, 303, 304, 302. **Page 203**    "Pantuns" (VI–VII). AFTER: *Stimme des Wasserbuffels: Malaiische Volksleider* (ed. Prof. Dr. Hans Nevermann; Kassel, Erich Röth-Verlag, 1956), pp. 83, 57. **Page 204**    "Linked Pantuns." *Ibid.*, p. 64. **Page 204**    "Invocation to the Rice Soul at Harvest Time." FROM: R. O. Winstedt, *Shaman Saiva and Sufi: A Study of the Evolution of Malay Magic* (London, Constable & Co., 1925), pp. 84–85. New edition: *The Malay Magician: Being Shaman, Saiva and Sufi* (London, Routledge & Kegan Paul, Ltd.). **Page 205**    "Charm for Striking Fear into a Tiger and Hardening One's Own Heart." FROM: Walter William Skeat, *Malay Magic: Being an Introduction to the Folklore and Popular Religion of the Malay Peninsula* (London, Macmillan & Co., 1900), p. 168 (slightly altered) (*, *ibid.*, p. 604.) **Page 205**    "Love Charm." FROM: R. O. Winstedt, *op. cit.*, p. 61. **Page 206**    "Charm Against the Demon Who Unlooses the Snares of Hunters." FROM: W. W. Skeat, *op. cit.*, p. 105 (slightly altered) (*, *ibid.*, p. 592). **Page 207**    "Charm of the Rice-Reapers When They Start the Day's Work." *Ibid.*, p. 245 (*, *ibid.*, p. 616). **Page 207**    "On the Kelantan Oboe." AFTER: Jeanne Cuisinier, *Le Théâtre d'ombres à Kelantan* (Paris, © Éditions Gallimard, 1957), p. 71 (*). **Page 207**    "Before a Magic Dance, Charm for the *Rebab*." AFTER: Jeanne Cuisinier, *Danses magiques de Kelantan* (Université de Paris. Travaux et Mémoires de l'Institut d'Ethnologie, XXII) (Paris, Institut d'Ethnologie, 1936), pp. 144–45 (*). **Page 208**    "Before a Magic Dance: Charm for the Oil." *Ibid.*, pp. 139–40 (*). **Page 209**    "Magical Chant: Sung by the Chief Musician While the Sorcerer Is Going into Trance." *Ibid.*, pp. 169–75 (*).

# NORTH AMERICA
## The Northwest

**Page 215**    "Song on the Death of an Uncle." FROM: John R. Swanton, *Tlingit Myths and Texts* (*Bulletins of the Bureau of American Ethnology* [hereafter cited as *BBAE*], 39 [1909]), p. 410 (*). Reprinted by permission of the Smithsonian Institution. **Page 215** "Woman's Love Song." *Ibid.*, p. 414 (*). **Page 215** "Song of a Man Whose Sweetheart Had Abandoned Him." *Ibid.*, p. 415 (*). **Page 215** "Mourning Songs." FROM: John R. Swanton, "Haida Songs," in Vol. III, *Publications of the American Ethnological Society* (edited by Franz Boas) (published for the American Ethnological Society by E. J. Brill, Publishers and Printers [Leiden, 1912]), pp. 56, 57, 58, 58, 59. Reprinted with the permission of the University of Washington Press and The American Ethnological Society. **Page 216** "Song for the Thunder Bird Dance." FROM: Franz Boas, "The Social Organization and the Secret Societies of the Kwakiutl Indians" (in *Report of the United States National Museum*, 1895 [pub. 1897]), p. 476 (*[and literal translation], p. 711). Reprinted by permission of the Smithsonian Institution. **Page 216** "Song of a Supernatural Being." *Ibid.*, p. 479 (*[and literal translation], p. 713). **Page 217** "Healing Song." *Ibid.*, p. 612 (*[and literal translation], p. 728). **Page 217** "Mourning Song for Moda'na, Who Was Drowned." FROM: Franz Boas, "Ethnology of the Kwakiutl" (in *35th Annual Report of the Bureau of American Ethnology* [the reports are hereafter cited by number and *ARBAE*], 1913–14 [pub. 1921]), p. 1292 (*). Reprinted by permission of the Smithsonian Institution. **Page 217** "Parting Song." *Ibid.*, pp. 1309–10 (*). **Page 218** "Song of a Warrior for His First-born Son." *Ibid.*, p. 1311 (*). **Page 218** "A Boy's Song (Sung While the Child Is Being Rocked on the Knee)." FROM: Franz Boas, "Songs of the Kwakiutl Indians," *Internationales Archiv für Ethnographie*, IX (1896), Supplement, pp. 1–2 (**). Reprinted by permission of E. J. Brill, Ltd., Publishers, Leiden. **Page 218** "War Song of the Kwakiutl." *Ibid.*, p. 9 (*). **Page 219** "Love Songs." *Ibid.*, pp. 3–4, 5–6 (*). **Page 219** "Love Song of the Dead." FROM: F. Boas, "Ethnology . . . ," pp. 1306–7 (*). Reprinted by permission of the Smithsonian Institution. **Page 220** "Girl's Song." FROM: Frances Densmore, *Nootka and Quileute Music* (*BBAE*, 124 [1939]), p. 172 (melody, *ibid.*, p. 171). Reprinted by permission of the Smithsonian Institution. **Page 220** "Love Song." FROM: Helen H. Roberts and Herman K. Haeberlin, "Some Songs of the Puget Sound Salish," *Journal of American Folk-Lore*, XXXI (1918), p. 496 (*). Reprinted by permission of the American Folklore Society. **Page 220** "Responsive Song for the Dead Child of a Chief." FROM: Franz Boas, "Poetry and Music of Some North American Tribes," *Science*, Vol. IX, 22 April, 1887, p. 385.

## The East and the Great Lakes

**Page 221** "The Song of the Stars." FROM: Charles Godfrey Leland and John Dyneley Prince, *Kulóskap the Master and Other Algonkin Poems* (New York and London, Funk & Wagnalls Co., 1902), pp. 312–13 (*). **Page 221** "Girl's Song from a Legend." FROM: John Reade, "Some Wabanaki Songs," *Proceedings and Transactions, Royal Society of Canada*, I (1887), Section II, p. 6 (*, p. 7). Reprinted by kind permission of the Royal Society of Canada, Ottawa. **Page 222** "Love Song." *Ibid.*, pp. 6–7 (*, pp. 7–8). **Page 223** "Love Song." FROM: Henry R. Schoolcraft, *Information Respecting the History, Condition and Prospects of the Indian Tribes of the United States*, Part V (Philadelphia, J. B. Lippincott & Co., 1855), p. 559 (*). **Page 223** "Hunting Song." FROM: Frances Densmore, *Chippewa Music* (*BBAE*, 53 [1910]), p. 84 (**). Reprinted by permission of the Smithsonian Institution. **Page 223** "Love-Charm Songs." *Ibid.*, pp. 89, 90 (**). **Page 224** "Mǐdé Song." *Ibid.*, p. 110 (**). **Page 224** "Dream Songs." *Ibid.*, pp. 129, 129, 134 (**). **Page 225** "Love Songs." *Ibid.*, pp. 150, 153, 154, 184 (**). **Page 226** "Woman's-Dance Song." *Ibid.*, p. 193 (**). **Page 226** "Death Song of a

Warrior." FROM: Frances Densmore: *Chippewa Music—II* (*BBAE*, 45 [1913]), p. 114 (**). Reprinted by permission of the Smithsonian Institution. **Page 226**   "Song After a Battle with the Sioux." *Ibid.*, p. 115 (**). **Page 226**   "Song After a Victory." *Ibid.*, p. 122 (**). **Page 227**   "War Song on a Brave Woman." *Ibid.*, p. 131 (**). **Page 227**   "Song of a Man Urged to Join the Warriors." *Ibid.*, p. 185 (**). **Page 227**   "Love Song." *Ibid.*, p. 218 (**). **Page 227**   "Song of One Whose Lover Is Dead." *Ibid.*, p. 219 (**). **Page 228**   "Dream Song: Spring." *Ibid.*, p. 254 (**). **Page 228**   "Dawn Song." FROM: Frederick R. Burton, *American Primitive Music: With Especial Attention to the Songs of the Ojibways* (New York, Moffat, Yard & Co., 1909), p. 221. **Page 228**   "Song of a Woman When Her Lover Went on a Journey." FROM: Ruth Landes, *The Ojibwa Woman* (New York, Columbia University Press, 1938), pp. 129–30. **Page 229**   "On the Iroquois League." FROM: Horatio Hale, *The Iroquois Book of Rites* (Brinton's Library of Aboriginal American Literature, No. 2) (Philadelphia, D. G. Brinton, 1883, p. 153 (*). **Page 229**   "From the New Year's Ceremony (February)." FROM: Arthur C. Parker, *The Code of Handsome Lake, the Seneca Prophet* (New York State Museum Bulletin, 163) (Albany, 1912), pp. 87–89. Courtesy of New York State Museum and Science Service. **Page 231**   "From the [Seneca] Medicine Lodge Initiation Ceremony." FROM: Harriet Maxwell Converse, *Myths and Legends of the New York State Iroquois* (New York State Museum Bulletin, 125) (Albany, 1908), pp. 180–81, 181. Courtesy of New York State Museum and Science Service. **Page 232**   "Love Incantations." FROM: Jack Frederick Kilpatrick and Anna Gritts Kilpatrick, *Walk in Your Soul: Love Incantations of the Oklahoma Cherokees* (Dallas, Southern Methodist University Press, 1965), pp. 86–87, 115, © 1965 by Southern Methodist University Press, Dallas, Texas. Reprinted by permission. **Page 233**   "Song Concerning the Removal of the Seminole to Oklahoma (1836–1840)." FROM: Frances Densmore, *Seminole Music* (*BBAE*, 161 [1956]), p. 201 (melody, *ibid.*). Reprinted by permission of the Smithsonian Institution.

# The Plains

**Page 234**   "Dancing Song of the Skunk." FROM: Frances Densmore, *Mandan and Hidatsa Music* (*BBAE*, 80 [1923]), p. 93 (**). Reprinted by permission of the Smithsonian Institution. **Page 234**   "Song of a Scout Remembering Home." *Ibid.*, p. 154 (**). **Page 234**   "Black Mouth Society Song." *Ibid.*, p. 50 (**). **Page 235**   "Song of the Pasque Flower." AFTER: Hartley Burr Alexander, *L'Art et la philosophie des Indiens de l'Amérique du Nord* (Paris, Éditions Ernest Leroux, 1926), p. 88. By permission of Presses Universitaires de France. **Page 235**   "Song of the Final Visit to the Vapor Lodge Before the Sun Dance." FROM: Frances Densmore, *Teton Sioux Music* (*BBAE*, 61 [1918]), p. 124 (**). Reprinted by permission of the Smithsonian Institution. **Page 235**   "Song Commemorating a Dead Sioux Warrior." *Ibid.*, p. 137 (**). **Page 236**   "Song of a Medicine Man." *Ibid.*, p. 276 (**). **Page 236**   "Song of the Horse Society." *Ibid.*, p. 300 (**). **Page 236**   "War Songs." *Ibid.*, pp. 335, 346 (**). **Page 237**   "Song Sung During or After a Fight." *Ibid.*, p. 357 (**). **Page 237**   "Songs of a Mother Mourning Her Sons Killed in Battle." *Ibid.*, pp. 365, 366–67 (**). **Page 238**   "Song in Honor of a Prominent Warrior." *Ibid.*, p. 369 (**). **Page 238**   "Old Love Songs Connected with War." *Ibid.*, pp. 370–71, 372, 373 (**). **Page 239**   "Praise Song." *Ibid.*, p. 384 (**). **Page 239**   "Song of the Maiden's Leap." *Ibid.*, p. 495 (**). **Page 239**   "Song of a Ghost." *Ibid.*, p. 497 (**). **Page 240**   "Modern Love Song." *Ibid.*, p. 510 (**). **Page 240**   "Song Concerning a Message from Washington." *Ibid.*, p. 517 (**). **Page 240**   "War Songs." FROM: Robert H. Lowie, *The*

*Crow Indians* (New York, Farrar and Rinehart, 1935), pp. 114, 114. Reprinted by permission of Holt, Rinehart & Winston, Inc. **Page 241**    "Ghost-Dance Songs." FROM: James Mooney, "The Ghost-Dance Religion and the Sioux Outbreak of 1890" (in *14th ARBAE*, 1892–93, Part II [pub. 1896]), pp. 961, 966 (*). Reprinted by permission of the Smithsonian Institution. **Page 241**    "Old War Song." FROM: Frances Densmore, *Cheyenne and Arapaho Music* (Southwest Museum Papers, No. 10, Los Angeles, 1936), p. 35 (melody, *ibid.*). Courtesy Southwest Museum. **Page 242**    "Song of the Wolf Society." FROM: Frances Densmore, *Pawnee Music* (*BBAE*, 93 [1929]), p. 57 (**). Reprinted by permission of the Smithsonian Institution. **Page 242**    "Song of a Woman Welcoming Victorious Warriors." *Ibid.*, p. 64 (**).

**Page 242**    "Litany to the High Gods." FROM: R. F. Fortune, *Omaha Secret Societies* (Columbia University Contributions to Anthropology, Vol. XIV) (New York, Columbia University Press, 1932), p. 48. **Page 243**    "Song of Two Ghosts." *Ibid.*, p. 78. **Page 243**    "Death-Dance Song." *Ibid.*, p. 130. **Page 243**    "Love-Magic Song." *Ibid.*, p. 168. **Page 244**    "Victory Song." FROM: Alice C. Fletcher and Francis La Flesche, "The Omaha Tribe" (in *27th ARBAE*, 1905–06 [pub. 1911]), p. 433 (**). Reprinted by permission of the Smithsonian Institution. **Page 244**    "Woman Song." *Ibid.*, p. 323 (**[and literal translation], *ibid.*, pp. 321–23). **Page 244**    "Ritual Recitation: The Symbolic Painting." FROM: Francis La Flesche, "The Osage Tribe: The Rite of Vigil" (in *39th ARBAE*, 1917–18 [pub. 1925], pp. 75–76 (*[and literal translation], pp. 388, 529). Reprinted by permission of the Smithsonian Institution. **Page 246**    "Little Song of the Sun." FROM: Francis La Flesche, "The Osage Tribe: Rite of the Wa-xo'-be" (in *45th ARBAE*, 1927–28 [pub. 1930]), p. 605 (**). Reprinted by permission of the Smithsonian Institution. **Page 246**    "Hunting Song." *Ibid.*, p. 633 (**). **Page 247**    "War Song." FROM: F. La Flesche, "The Osage Tribe: The Rite of Vigil," pp. 191–92 (**[and literal translation], pp. 191–92, 447, 578). Reprinted by permission of the Smithsonian Institution. **Page 247**    "Woman's Song of Corn Growing." FROM: *Ibid.*, p. 639 (**).

## California and the Southwest

**Page 248**    "Song of the Spirit of the Pole Star." FROM: Jeremiah Curtin, *Creation Myths of Primitive America in Relation to the Religious History and Mental Development of Mankind* (Boston, Little, Brown & Co., 1903), p. 516. **Page 248**    "Dream Songs." FROM: D. Demetracopoulou, "Wintu Songs," *Anthropos*, XXX (1935), 485, 487, 487. **Page 249**    "Rattlesnake Ceremony Song." FROM: A. L. Kroeber, *Handbook of the Indians of California* (*BBAE*, 78 [1925]), p. 506. Reprinted by permission of the Smithsonian Institution. **Page 250**    "Song of the Red Cloud." FROM: Stephen Powers, *Tribes of California* (U.S. Geographical and Geological Survey of the Rocky Mountain Region, Contributions to North American Ethnology, Vol. III) (Washington, 1877), p. 307 (*). **Page 250**    "Prayer to Dsilyi Neyani." FROM: Washington Matthews, "The Mountain Chant: A Navajo Ceremony" (in *5th ARBAE*, 1883–84 [pub. 1887]), p. 420 (*, *ibid.*, p. 465). Reprinted by permission of the Smithsonian Institution. **Page 251**    "Song of the Prophet to the San Juan River." *Ibid.*, p. 393 (*, *ibid.*, p. 464). **Page 251**    "Song of the Thunder." *Ibid.*, p. 459 (*, *ibid.*). **Page 251**    "Processional Song from the Night Chant." FROM: Washington Matthews, *The Night Chant: A Navaho Ceremony* (Memoirs of the American Museum of Natural History, Vol. VI) (New York, 1902), p. 76 (*, *ibid.*, pp. 275–76). **Page 252**    "Song of a Bear." FROM: Pliny Earle Goddard, *Navajo Texts* (Anthropological Papers of the American Museum of Natural History, Vol. XXXIV, Part 1) (New York, 1933), p. 178. **Page 252** "Gambling Songs." FROM: Washington Matthews, "Navajo Gambling Songs," *The*

*American Anthropologist*, II (1889), 9, 13, 15 (*). Reprinted by permission of the American Anthropological Association. **Page 253**    "Trading Song." FROM: W. W. Hill, "Navaho Trading and Trading Ritual: A Study of Cultural Dynamics," *The Southwestern Journal of Anthropology*, IV (1948), 384–86. **Page 254**    "From a Seasonal Prayer." FROM: Ruth L. Bunzel, "Introduction to Zuñi Ceremonialism" (in *47th ARBAE*, 1929–30 [pub. 1932]), p. 74. Reprinted by permission of the Smithsonian Institution. **Page 255**    "Prayer at an Offering of Food to the Ancestors." FROM: Ruth L. Bunzel, "Zuñi Ritual Poetry," *Ibid.*, pp. 621–23 (*). **Page 256**    "Song of the Sky Loom." FROM: Herbert Joseph Spinden, *Songs of the Tewa: Preceded by an Essay on American Indian Poetry* (New York, The Exposition of Indian Tribal Arts, Inc., 1933), p. 94. **Page 256**    "Prayer for Long Life." *Ibid.*, p. 106. **Page 257**    "At the Grave of a Warrior." *Ibid.*, p. 108. **Page 257**    "Love Song." *Ibid.*, p. 73. **Page 257**    "Corn-grinding Songs." FROM: Frances Densmore: *Music of Acoma, Isleta, Cochiti and Zuñi Pueblos* (*BBAE*, 165 [1957]), pp. 60, 67 (melodies, *ibid.*, pp. 61, 67). Reprinted by permission of the Smithsonian Institution. **Page 258**    "Hunting Song." *Ibid.*, p. 22 (melody, *ibid.*, p. 21). **Page 259**    "Winter Dance Song." *Ibid.*, p. 33 (melody, *ibid.*). **Page 259**    "Flower Dance Song." *Ibid.*, p. 38 (melody, *ibid.*, p. 37). **Page 259**    "Ouwe Dance Song for Good Crops." *Ibid.*, p. 90 (melody, *ibid.*).

**Page 260**    "Song of a Departed Spirit." FROM: Frances Densmore, *Music of Santo Domingo Pueblo, New Mexico* (Southwest Museum Papers, No. 12) (Los Angeles, 1938), p. 69 (melody, *ibid.*). Courtesy Southwest Museum. **Page 261**    "Closing Song of a Ceremony to Procure Abundance." *Ibid.*, pp. 86–87 (melody, *ibid.*). **Page 261**    "Song Concerning the Corn Harvest." *Ibid.*, pp. 110–11. **Page 263**    "Song at the Painting of Ceremonial Dancers." FROM: Morris Edward Opler, *An Apache Life-Way: The Economic, Social and Religious Institutions of the Chiricahua Indians* (Chicago, University of Chicago Press, 1941), p. 108. **Page 263**    "Love Song." *Ibid.*, p. 125. **Page 263**    "Song of Rejection." *Ibid.*, p. 125. **Page 264**    "Song at Sunrise on the Last Day of the Gotal Ceremony." FROM: Pliny Earle Goddard, "Gotal—A Mescalero Apache Ceremony" (in *Putnam Anniversary Volume: Anthropological Essays Addressed to Frederic Ward Putnam* [New York, Gustav E. Stechert, 1909]), p. 397. **Page 264**    "Songs from the Deer Ceremony." FROM: Pliny Earle Goddard, *Myths and Tales from the San Carlos Apache* (Anthropological Papers of the American Museum of Natural History, Vol. XXIV, Part 1) (New York, 1918), pp. 57, 59. **Page 265**    "Festal Song." FROM: Frank Russell, "The Pima Indians" (in *26th ARBAE*, 1904–05 [pub. 1908]), pp. 283–84 (*[and literal translation], *ibid.*). Reprinted by permission of the Smithsonian Institution. **Page 266**    "Dance Song of the Swallow." *Ibid.*, pp. 292–95 (*[and literal translation], *ibid.*). **Page 267**    "Medicine Songs." *Ibid.*, pp. 314–15, 324–25 (*[and literal translation], *ibid.*). **Page 269**    "War Song." *Ibid.*, p. 335 (*[and literal translation], *ibid.*). **Page 269**    "Invitation to Drink Cactus Liquor at a Rain-bringing Ceremony." FROM: Ruth Murray Underhill, *Singing for Power: The Song Magic of the Papago Indians of Southern Arizona* (Berkeley, University of California Press, 1938), pp. 29–31. **Page 270**    "Dreaming Liquor Songs." FROM: Ruth Murray Underhill, *Papago Indian Religion* (Columbia University Contributions to Anthropology, No. 33) (New York, Columbia University Press, 1946), p. 47. **Page 271**    "Liquor Song." *Ibid.*, p. 64. **Page 271**    "Hunting Song." *Ibid.*, p. 93. **Page 271**    "Railroad Rails." *Ibid.*, p. 311. **Page 272**    "Telegraph Wires." *Ibid.*, p. 312. **Page 272**    "Distant Train." *Ibid.*, p. 312. **Page 272**    "Songs of the Light Women." *Ibid.*, pp. 66, 66. **Page 273**    "Songs Received in Dreams." FROM: Frances Densmore, *Papago Music* (*BBAE*, 90 [1929]), pp. 140, 141 (melodies, *ibid.*, p. 142). Reprinted by permission of the Smithsonian Institution. **Page 273** "Song at a Ceremony for Securing Good Crops." *Ibid.*, p. 142 (melody, *ibid.*). **Page 273** "Song Sung on an Expedition to Obtain Salt." *Ibid.*, p. 173 (melody, *ibid.*).

# CENTRAL AMERICA

**Page 277** "Hymn to the Mother of the Gods." AFTER: Eduard Seler, *Gesammelte Abhandlungen zur Amerikanischen Sprach- und Alterthumskunde,* 5 vols. (Berlin, A. Asher & Co., 1902–15), II, 994–96 (\*). **Page 278** "This Is the Song They Sang at the Fast Every Eight Years." *Ibid.*, pp. 1059–61 (\*). **Page 279** "Prayer." AFTER: Angel María Garibay K., "Panorama de la poesía de Anáhuac," *México en el Arte,* No. 9 (1950), p. 32. **Page 280** "Warrior's Song." AFTER: A. M. Garibay K., *Poesía indígena de la altiplanicie: Divulgación literaria* (Mexico, Ediciones de la Universidad Nacional Autónoma, 1940), p. 172. By permission of Universidad Nacional Autónoma de México. **Page 280** "War Song." AFTER: A. M. Garibay K., *Historia de la Literatura Nahuatl,* 2 vols. (Mexico, Editorial Porrua, 1953–54), I, 219. By permission of Editorial Porrua. **Page 281** "Song: The Bird and the Butterfly." AFTER: A. M. Garibay K., "Panorama . . . ," pp. 32–33. **Page 281** "The Poet's Mission." AFTER: A. M. Garibay K., *Poesía indígena . . . ,* p. 173 (I), and *id.,* "Panorama . . . ," p. 32 (II). By permission of Universidad Nacional Autónoma de México and of Instituto Nacional de Bellas Artes. **Page 282** "The Origin of Songs." AFTER: A. M. Garibay K., *Poesía indígena . . . ,* pp. 67–70. By permission of Universidad Nacional Autónoma de México. **Page 284** "One Poet Praises Another." AFTER: A. M. Garibay K., "Panorama . . . ," p. 33.

**Page 285** "Our Father the Sun." AFTER: Konrad Theodor Preuss, *Die Religion der Cora-Indianer* (Die Nayarit-Expedition. Textaufnahmen und Beobachtungen unter mexikanischen Indianern. I) (Leipzig, B. G. Teubner, 1912), pp. 1–3 (\*). **Page 285** "The Eagle Above Us." *Ibid.*, p. 43 (\*). **Page 286** "The Morning Star in the North." *Ibid.*, p. 230 (\*). **Page 287** "Dance Song of a Shaman." FROM: C. Lumholtz, *Unknown Mexico: A Record of Five Years' Exploration,* 2 vols. (New York, Charles Scribner's Sons, 1902), I, 338–39 (\*\*). **Page 287** "Love Song." FROM: C. Napier Bell, *Tangweera* (etc.) (London, Edward Arnold Ltd., Publishers, 1899), p. 89 (\*, p. 312). **Page 288** "The Song of the Birds." FROM: Nils M. Holmer, *Cuna Chrestomathy* (Göteborg, Etnografiska Museet, Series: Etnologiska Studier, 18) (Göteborg, 1951), pp. 94–103 (\*). **Page 291** "Olowilasop Visits the Morning Star." FROM: N. M. Holmer, *Inatoipippiler or the Adventures of Three Cuna Boys, according to Maninibigdinapi* (Göteborg, Etnografiska Museet, Series: Etnologiska Studier, 20) (Göteborg, 1952), pp. 71–75 (\*). **Page 292** "Song Before Gathering Medicinal Herbs for the Treatment of Sick Children." FROM: Frances Densmore, *Music of the Tule Indians of Panama* (Smithsonian Miscellaneous Collections, Vol. LXXVII, No. 11) (Washington, 1926), pp. 16–17 (melody, *ibid.*). Reprinted by permission of the Smithsonian Institution. **Page 293** "Song After a Man Dies." *Ibid.*, pp. 18–20 (melody, *ibid.*). Reprinted by permission of the Smithsonian Institution. **Page 294** "Conversation Between a Boy and Two Girls Looking Through a Spyglass." *Ibid.*, pp. 31–32 (melody, *ibid.*). Reprinted by permission of the Smithsonian Institution. **Page 295** "Love Song." *Ibid.*, p. 34 (melody, *ibid.*). Reprinted by permission of the Smithsonian Institution.

# SOUTH AMERICA

**Page 299** "Hymn of an Inca to the God Viracocha." FROM: Philip Ainsworth Means, *Ancient Civilizations of the Andes* (New York, Charles Scribner's Sons, 1931), pp. 437–38. Reprinted with permission of Gordion Press, Inc. **Page 300**    "Verses of an Inca Poet and Astrologer." AFTER: Garcilaso de la Vega, *Primera parte de los commentarios reales, que tratan de los Incas*, 2nd ed. (Madrid, 1723), p. 68 (*). **Page 301**    "To a Traitor." FROM: Richard Pietschmann, "Some Account of the Illustrated Chronicle by . . . D. Felipe Huaman Poma de Ayala," International Congress of Americanists, *Proceedings of the XVIII. Session, London, 1912*, p. 511 (slightly altered) (*). **Page 301**    "Song of an Imprisoned Prince." *Ibid.*, p. 517 (slightly altered) (*). **Page 301**    "Song." *Ibid.*, p. 518 (slightly altered) (*). **Page 301**    "Song." AFTER: Garcilaso de la Vega, *op. cit.*, p. 67 (*). **Page 302**    "Song of the Victim at a Cannibal Feast." AFTER: Konrad Theodor Preuss, *Religion und Mythologie der Uitoto: Textaufnahmen und Beobachtungen bei einem Indianerstamm in Kolumbien, Südamerika*, 2 vols. (Quellen der Religionsgeschichte, Gruppe 11, Bd. 10–11) (Göttingen, Vandenhoeck & Rupprecht, 1921–23), II, 675 (*). **Page 302**    "Song of the Sweet-smelling Love Charm." *Ibid.*, pp. 669–70 (*). **Page 302**    "Song of the Priestess at a Victory Feast." FROM: Rafael Karsten, *The Head-Hunters of Western Amazonas: The Life and Culture of the Jibaro Indians of Eastern Ecuador and Peru* (Societas Scientiarum Fennica. Commentationes Humanarum Litterarum. VII. 1) (Helsingfors, 1935), p. 355 (*). **Page 303**    "Planting Song of Women to the Earth-Mother." *Ibid.*, p. 128 (**, *ibid.*, p. 135). **Page 303**    "Invocation Sung by a Hunter Setting Out." AFTER: Mario Forno, "Credenze spirituali presso i Ghivaro (Ecuador e Peru)," *Rivista di Etnografia* (Naples), XVII (1963), p. 88. **Page 303**    "Songs of Dancing Women Personifying Birds." FROM: R. Karsten, *op. cit.*, pp. 497–98, 498 (**).

**Page 304**    "Dance Song." AFTER: R. and M. d'Harcourt, *La Musique des Incas et ses survivances* (Paris, Librairie Orientaliste Paul Geuthner, 1925), p. 484 (**). **Page 305**    "Lullaby." FROM: Clements R. Markham, *Cuzco: A Journey to the Ancient Capital of Peru; . . . and Lima . . .* (London, Chapman & Hall, 1856), p. 195. **Page 305**    "Song." *Ibid.*, p. 196. **Page 306**    "Girl's Song." AFTER: R. and M. d'Harcourt, *op. cit.*, p. 291 (**). **Page 306**    "Song." AFTER: José Maria Arguedas, *Canciones y Cuentos del Pueblo Quechua* (Lima, Editorial Huascaran, 1949), p. 37. **Page 307**    "Song." *Ibid.*, p. 27. **Page 307**    "Elegy." AFTER: Jesus Lara, *La Poesia Quechua: Ensayo y Antologia* (Cochabamba, Universidad Mayor de San Simón, 1947), pp. 188–89 (*). Used by the kind permission of Mr. Jesus Lara. **Page 308**    "Assembly Songs." FROM: Mischa Titiev, *Social Singing Among the Mapuche* (Anthropological Papers, Museum of Anthropology, University of Michigan, No. 2) (Ann Arbor, University of Michigan Press, 1949), pp. 6–7 (*). **Page 308**    "Man's Assembly Song." *Ibid.*, p. 12 (*). **Page 309**    "Song of a Visitor to a Strange Village." AFTER: Erland Nordenskiöld, *Indianlif. I. El Gran Chaco (Syd-Amerika)* (Stockholm, Albert Bonners Förlag, 1910), p. 131 (*). **Page 309**    "Keening." FROM: Jules Henry, *Jungle People: A Kaingáng Tribe of the Highlands of Brazil* (Locust Valley, N.Y., J. J. Augustin, Inc., Publisher, 1941), p. 189. **Page 310**    "Word of the Thunder." FROM: A. P. and T. E. Penard, "Popular Notions Pertaining to Primitive Stone Artifacts in Surinam," *Journal of American Folk-Lore*, XXX (1917), p. 259 (*). **Page 310**    "Love Songs." FROM: Morton C. Kahn, *Djuka: The Bush Negroes of Dutch Guiana* (New York, The Viking Press, 1931), p. 59 (*). **Page 310**    "Religious Songs." FROM: Melville J. and Frances S. Herskovits, *Suriname Folk-Lore* (Columbia University Contributions to Anthropology, XXVII) (New York, Columbia University Press, 1936), pp. 641, 663 (**).

# Table of Contents

# ASIA

# NORTH AMERICA

# CENTRAL AMERICA

# SOUTH AMERICA

# Introduction

In presenting the indigenous background of the poetry of primitive and traditional peoples—that is, of peoples whose cultures have been without writing—the Introduction to the previous volume of this anthology\* stressed the difference between it and the poetry of the written literatures. The present Introduction will even the scales by dwelling on aspects that the two bodies of poetry have in common.

I

Recognition of the kinship between them, together with appreciation of "unwritten" poetry, began early. By 1579, only twenty years after the first publication of an American Indian poem in Europe, Montaigne was praising another American Indian poem as "the perfection of the Anacreontic."[1]†

This kind of appreciation was but natural in a culture whose literary aesthetic was, at least in theory, based on the Greek and Roman classics. It continued for some time and, in occasional instances, has survived even down to the present.

Touching at Huahine and Raiatea in May, 1774, during his second voyage in the Pacific, Captain James Cook and his party were regaled with two "dramatic entertainments" put on by the inhabitants. Cook merely describes the performances. But the anonymous early nineteenth-century editor of an abridged version of *Cook's Voyages* was reminded by the first of the play scene in *Hamlet* and by the second of a scene in Terence.[2]

On a diplomatic mission to Ashanti (now Ghana) in 1817, T. Edward Bowdich witnessed several choral performances of a song in

---

\* Willard R. Trask, *The Unwritten Song: Poetry of the Primitive and Traditional Peoples of the World*, Vol. I: *The Far North, Africa, Indonesia, Melanesia, Australia* (New York and London, The Macmillan Company and Collier-Macmillan Ltd., 1966) (hereafter cited as: *The Unwritten Song*, I). Definitions of the terms "primitive" and "traditional" and discussion of the criterion "without writing," *ibid.*, pp. ix–x.

† Numbered notes will be found at the end of the Introduction.

dialogue. In his account of the mission, published two years later, he commented, "I never heard this sung without its recalling Horace's beautiful little dialogue ode . . . *Donec gratus eram tibi.*"[3]

In our own day, Angel María Garibay Kintana still finds a "Horatian coloring" in many Nahuatl poems. "Tomorrow," says one of them, "day after tomorrow perhaps, we shall be gone; let us enjoy ourselves."[4] But Horace's famous "Strain the wine; enjoy today" also appears in songs of peoples as far from Mexico in space as they are from Augustan Rome in time: "I say: The drinks you drank, the pleasure of them goes with you" (Dahomey); "Enjoy this one lifetime" (Kashmir); "Buy a sari while you can for the body you love" (Hyderabad); "It may only be today" (Bihar).[5]

In our own time, again, R. F. Fortune has compared a Dobuan song of mourning for the dead with a passage in Euripides.[6]

An African chant which was "old" when it was collected more than a hundred years ago runs (in part) : "In the days when Dendid created all things, he created the sun, and the sun is born, and dies, and comes again. He created man, and man is born, and dies, and never comes again." Even in our time of decline in classical studies, there will be many who, reading this, will inevitably be reminded of Catullus: "Suns may set and rise again; for us, when the short light has once set, there is the sleep of an endless night."[7]

So, too, a Dyak chant of "Evening Quietness," with its evening star, its pigs and chicks and fowl that have gone to sty or roost, its children who have ended their games, inevitably suggests Sappho's evening star that "brings back all that dawn has scattered, the sheep, the goat, the child."[8]

II

A poetess of the Caribou Eskimos is at one with poets of Papua and Mangareva in lamenting the infirmities of old age. "I shall never move again from my place on the bench, though I feel the old wish to go out and away," she sings. "I am too old and worn out," comes the echo from Papua, in a song by a poet who himself entitled it "Of Old Age and a White Head." And the poet of Mangareva mourns, "Alas! when our bodies grow old and thin, like a flat-fish resting on the bottom."[1] Villon's Belle Heaulmiere, with her "when I think what I was, what I have become—poor, dried up, thin, shrunken," is but the most celebrated of many examples in European literature. Indeed, the tradition of which it is a part goes back at least to the ninth-century Irish "Lament of the Old Woman of Beare." She begins, "Ebb-tide has come to me."[2]

In a similar vein—though prompted by sickness instead of old age— a Maori poet sings, "I look down and regard myself, see how twisted are the sinews"; and a poet of Tonga, "I who am fallen down, who am cast aside."[3] "I who lie flat on this bed," wrote John Donne in a poem composed "in my sickness." And William Dunbar's famous "Lament for the Makers When He Was Sick" begins, "I that in health was and gladness am feebled with infirmity."[4]

To the compelling force of the theme of the death which inevitably follows after sickness and old age, the number of "Dirges" and "Threnodies" in the two volumes of this anthology bears sufficient witness. Outstanding, perhaps, in their somber intensity are a dance song from Palau which begins, "We people are skilful, but death has only one speech," and a song from Ghana which ends, "To be in the hands of death is to be in the hands of someone indeed."[5] It seems unnecessary to quote Western parallels; such poems as Shakespeare's "Fear no more the heat o' the sun" and Shirley's "The glories of our blood and state" (both of them songs in the strictest sense of the word), as Malherbe's "Consolation à Monsieur Du Périer" and Jorge Manrique's stanzas on the death of his father, are in every anthology, if not in every memory.

### III

As for that widespread (though not universal) type of poetry, the love song:

My own investigations for a number of years have concentrated on the subdivision of the love song known as the "girl's song." In it the speaker is a girl. Its authorship, however, is not always as simple as that: the composer may be the girl herself, but may also be a man or a woman putting words into a girl's mouth. It occurs in written literatures from Ancient Egyptian and Chinese through the medieval Germanic and Romance literatures of Europe (most notably and charmingly in Galician-Portuguese) and on down to Robert Burns and beyond. As for the "unwritten" literatures, it is plentifully represented in both volumes of this anthology; it is rife in European and Asiatic folk song; in our day, it still forms the mainstay of improvised "blues." I have in preparation a study of it; the following parallels are drawn from the material I have so far collected.

A famous poem by Walther von der Vogelweide, the greatest of the German medieval lyric poets, begins, "Under the linden on the heath." The speaker is a girl, and she is describing a meeting with her lover. "There," she goes on, "We made our bed. . . . Anyone passing that way now could tell it from the broken flowers and grass." A song from Ifaluk, in Micronesia, by an unnamed singer of the present century, begins, "The name of my house is Ligurang." The speaker is a girl, and she is describing her meetings with her lover. She goes on, "There is a place . . . deep in the woods. . . . My lover and I used to have it to ourselves. . . . His red paint would come off on the leaves; the paint showed that we had been there."[1]

An Ahir song which begins with a newly married couple "doubting if they will like each other and ends with the girl's excitement at her husband" has a parallel in a French ballad about an English king and a French princess. The ballad ends: " 'Turn that way and I'll turn this way, accursed Englishman, when I feel you near me my heart fails.' And when it was almost midnight the fair girl waked. 'Turn over toward me, King of England! Since we are married we must love each other.' "[2]

Songs in which a bride bemoans the necessity of marriage are found in Africa ("No one gets used to unhappiness. No, I don't want to go") and among the Niassans ("Why do you give me away to serve strangers?"), the Bhil, the Uraon ("My mind is dying in the rocky uplands"), the Lolos. The same note of regret is sounded in French medieval poetry and in Portuguese folk songs.[3]

The Clayoquot girl who refuses a suitor "because he is too old" has equally reluctant sisters in Berber, in Norman and medieval French, Middle English, Irish, Lapp, Serbian, and other languages.[4]

The Baiswari girl who sings, "I am young and lovely; what more can anyone do for me?" has her counterparts in the girl speakers in a nineteenth-dynasty Egyptian love song ("that I may let thee see my beauty"), in girls' songs by the thirteenth-century Portuguese poets King Dinis ("He may well die for me who has seen my beauty") and Joan de Guilhade ("God made me beautiful"), and in the girl's dance song which, in charming summary of the medieval tradition, Boccaccio put into Emilia's mouth to end the first "Day" of his *Decameron*: "I am so much in love with my beauty."[5]

The Baganda girl who asks passing travelers for news of her absent lover ("You who are going by, stop and I'll ask you: What about my beloved Ndawula?") has hers in the girl of Ophelia's famous song

"How should I your true love know" and in Spanish and other European folk songs.[6]

The Uraon girl who comes home with her basket empty (the implication being that, instead of picking flowers, she has dallied with her lover) has sisters as far apart in time as a girl in the sixth-century Chinese *Book of Songs* ("Even a shallow basket I did not fill") and girls in French folk songs.[7] There is this difference: the Uraon girl consults her mother, the French girls are afraid of theirs. They all have at least cousins in the girl in Sappho who is so overwhelmed with love that she "cannot weave her web."[8]

Another subdivision of the love song is the dawn song. In it a pair of lovers who have spent the night together are forced to part by the coming of dawn. The dawn is often announced by the singing of some bird—swallow, lark, the domestic cock. The most famous example of the situation in English literature, perhaps in world literature, is the scene of the newly married lovers' parting after their one night together in Shakespeare's *Romeo and Juliet*, with its "It was the nightingale and not the lark. . . . It was the lark, the herald of the morn . . . for she divideth us."[9] In its lyric form the dawn poem was practiced by early Chinese poets and, in Europe, by the Provençal troubadours and their disciples in Italy, Austria, Germany, and elsewhere; it also occurs in European and Asiatic folk poetry.

But it is also known among peoples with whom this anthology is concerned. Here are two examples. The first is from Dobu:

> The cook is crowing
> my sweetheart embrace me
> dawn breaks hitherward
> your embraces are sweet to me
> my sweetheart embrace me.[10]

The second is from Ceram:

> It is morning, morning, the cock crows,
> It is already morning, turn and give me another kiss.[11]

Further examples will be found in various sections of this volume.[12]

Love songs—be they dawn songs, girls' songs, women's songs, men's songs—more often than not are unhappy. To end with happiness:

A French ballad of the Middle Ages has the refrain: "Guy loves Aigline, Aigline loves Guy." A Kassonke ballad collected toward the end of the nineteenth century in West Africa has the refrain: "Sega loves Diudi, Diudi loves Sega."[13]

IV

Technical accomplishments can be properly judged only on the basis of original texts. Yet even in their absence, some indications of achievement are possible.

That boast of Western poetry, the Homeric simile—the simile in which one term of the comparison is developed far beyond the point of what the two terms have in common, so that it leads, as it were, a brief life of its own—argues a degree of literary sophistication at least as great as Homer's. I have not found many examples of it. But two are included in this anthology, one in a poem of the Aandonga,[1] the other in a song from Somalia in praise of a horse. The Somalian example is at once so ingenious and so unexpected that I repeat it from Volume I: "His four hoofs clatter over the ground, like a grown girl who has been given her husband and has received great flocks, who, with most costly robe, and silken raiment and dress, has clothed herself, and at the time of mid-day shadows to her sleeping husband brings his food, as with shoes of cow's hide she clatters."[2]

Milton practiced the Homeric simile. But even more "Miltonic" is his use of proper names for the associations they evoke. Commenting on two songs of the Bondo, Verrier Elwin wrote: "Another song follows the same technique of using a large number of proper names which presumably have romantic associations to the hearers."[3] The same use of proper names for their associations is found all over Polynesia. Examples from Tonga and Hawaii and from Maori poetry are included in this anthology. Indeed, Maori poets are so fond of using the device that some of their finest efforts have had to be excluded; the amount of commentary necessary to elucidate the proper names would extinguish the poetry. And no wonder—for, as one student of such songs has well said, in them "the Maori plays on history as on a huge organ."[4]

Prose is not included in this anthology. But any literature which has been historically studied shows that accomplished prose does not arise until after a long practice of accomplished verse. Any reader of the early French and English accounts of the settlement of North America must have been struck by the wonder with which the settlers heard the oratory of Indian envoys. Such qualities as "naturalness," "simplicity," "enthusiasm," "impassioned delivery" have been suggested, both in colonial times and ours, as accounting for Indian eloquence.[5] But "impassioned delivery" is itself an art. And in the age of Massillon and

Jonathan Edwards in the pulpit, of the two Pitts and Edmund Burke in Parliament, no amount of the other qualities would have sufficed for admiration without an accomplished use of technical rhetorical devices. Jefferson knew better:

> Of their [the Indians'] eminence in oratory we have fewer examples, because it is displayed chiefly in their councils. Some, however, we have of very superior lustre. I may challenge the whole orations of Demosthenes and Cicero, and of any more eminent orator, if Europe has furnished more eminent, to produce a single passage, superior to the speech of Logan, a Mingo chief, to Lord Dunmore, when governor of this state.[6]

## V

Many of the poems in this anthology are known to have been recorded not long after they were composed. Others, more especially (but not exclusively) poems with ritual connections, claim a relative antiquity.[1] It has been asked: What fidelity can be attributed to texts which have been orally transmitted, sometimes for many generations?

Four testimonials, from as many different parts of the world, may serve to indicate the answer.

From Africa:

> The method [oral transmission by singers] has, however, a safeguard. I refer to the really extraordinary memory of the singers. . . . I know Kabyles who can recite verses through a whole day without repeating themselves and without hesitating. I have several times tested them by making them repeat songs written from their dictation a year or two earlier, and I have never found them making a mistake.[2]

From Fiji:

> [Poets] teach their compositions to bands of youths who master every detail of the poem in a single evening. It is then as permanent and unalterable as if it had been set up in type. I had a curious instance of the remarkable verbal memory of the Fijians in a long poem taken down from the lips of an old woman in 1893. The poem had been published by Waterhouse twenty-seven years earlier, and on comparison only one verbal discrepancy between the two versions was found.[3]

From South America:

> All the extremely long songs, with their many and irregular repetitions of verses and parts of verses, are preserved from generation to generation by oral tradition. The youths study first to learn the text, with its occult meaning, then the rhythm and the intonations, and finally the accompaniment with two calabashes. To this end they very commonly employ . . . plants

believed capable of helping the mind to learn and remember songs and of strengthening the voice to sing them.[4]

From Australia:

Each singer, building on the remembered phrases of others, adds something of his or her own experience and emotion. . . . It is this feature of Bathurst-Melville Islands culture which makes it possible to record songs that were actually "composed" some years ago. There is of course a margin of error resulting from the informants' need to rely upon unaided memory; but the presence of a number of older people who remember vividly the occasions on which the various songs were sung supplies some check, which is reinforced by the desire not to anger the spirit of a dead man or woman by distorting one of his or her songs.[5]

I find no better way to end this Introduction than with the hope and the wish with which I concluded the first. I hope that the poems that follow will show what the poetry of the written literatures and of the oral literatures has in common, both on the plane of inspiration and on the plane of accomplishment. May this gathering of "unwritten songs," in its small way, prove to be a contribution to human solidarity.*

*Brooklyn, New York*
*January 1967*

---

* In addition to presenting material of general literary interest, I have again also sought to serve some of the needs of scholars. Specifically, in every case where the collector has given either the original text or the melody of a poem (or both) I have indicated the fact in the Sources and Permissions. The symbols used for the purpose are explained therein.

# Notes to Introduction

## I

1. *The Unwritten Song*, I, viii.

2. James Cook, *A Voyage Towards the South Pole and Around the World* [etc.], 2 vols. (London, 1777), I, 356, 366; *Captain Cook's Voyages of Discovery* (London, 1906), pp. 174, 175.

3. *Mission from Cape Coast Castle to Ashantee* (London, 1819), pp. 368–69. (The poem is given in *The Unwritten Song*, I, 48).

4. "Panorama de la poesía de Anáhuac," *México en el Arte*, No. 9, 1950, p. 33.

5. Horace, *Odes*, I, xi; *The Unwritten Song*, I, 55; this volume, pp. 138 (I), 147 (II), 160 (III).

6. *Sorcerers of Dobu: The Social Anthropology of the Dobu Islanders of the Western Pacific* (New York, 1932), pp. 187, 257.

7. *The Unwritten Song*, I, 110; Catullus, *Carmina*, v.

8. *The Unwritten Song*, I, 148–51; Sappho, fr. 95.

## II

1. *The Unwritten Song*, I, 14, 193; this volume, p. 91. See also p. 144 (VI).

2. "Regretz de la Belle Heaulmiere," François Villon, *Oeuvres*, ed. A. Jeanroy (Paris, 1934), pp. 33–36; "Lament of the Old Woman of Beare," *Early Irish Lyrics, Eighth to Twelfth Century*, ed. Gerald Murphy (Oxford, 1956), pp. 74–75.

3. This volume, pp. 120, 48.

4. John Donne, *Complete Poetry and Selected Prose*, ed. J. Hayward (Bloomsbury, 1929), p. 320; William Dunbar, *Poems*, ed. W. M. Mackenzie (Edinburgh, 1932), p. 20.

5. This volume, pp. 3–4; *The Unwritten Song*, I, 47 (II).

## III

1. *Walther von der Vogelweide*, ed. F. Pfeiffer and K. Bartsch (Leipzig, 1911), pp. 15–17; Edwin Grant Burrows, *Flower in My Ear: Arts and Ethos of Ifaluk Atoll*, University of Washington Publications in Anthropology XIV (Seattle, University of Washington Press, 1963), pp. 115–16. For the same situation in "real life"—this time in New Guinea in 1961: "At a place along the trail the grass was crushed and flattened; Asukwan laughed. He poked the forefinger of one hand back and forth between the second and third fingers of the other, and Weakelek grinned" (Peter Matthiessen, *Under the Mountain Wall: A Chronicle of Two Seasons in the Stone Age* [New York, The Viking Press, 1962], p. 142).

2. This volume, p. 156; Charles Beauquier, *Chansons populaires recueillis en Franche-Comté* (Paris, 1894–96), p. 379.

3. *The Unwritten Song*, I, 99, 161; this volume, pp. 139, 162 (III), 188; the other references in my forthcoming study of the girl's song. Cf. W. G. Archer's explana-

tion of the "feeling of grief" in Uraon marriage poems in his *The Blue Grove: The Poetry of the Uraons* (London, 1940), pp. 96–97.

4. Clayoquot, this volume, p. 220; Berber, *The Unwritten Song*, I, 128; the other references in my forthcoming study.

5. W. Irvine, "Baiswárí Folk Songs," *Journal of the Royal Asiatic Society of Bengal*, LIII (1884), 258; Adolf Erman, *The Literature of the Ancient Egyptians*, tr. A. A. Blackman (New York, n.d.), p. 243; J. J. Nunes, *Cantigas d'Amigo dos Trovadores Gallego-Portugueses*, 3 vols. (Coimbra, 1926–28), II, No. 42 (p. 42), No. 178 (p. 161); Boccaccio, *Il Decameron*, 2 vols. (Leipzig, 1877), I, 65–66.

6. *The Unwritten Song*, I, 102; *Hamlet*, Act IV, scene 5; the other references in my forthcoming study.

7. This volume, p. 164 (VII); Arthur Waley, *The Book of Songs* (2nd ed., London, 1954), No. 40 (p. 45); other references in my forthcoming study.

8. Sappho, fr. 90.

9. *Romeo and Juliet*, Act III, scene 5.

10. *The Unwritten Song*, I, 199 (I).

11. Odo Deodatus Tauern, *Patasiwa und Patalima: Vom Molukkeneiland Seran und seinen Bewohnern* (Leipzig, 1918), p. 78 (translated).

12. E.g., pp. 42, 90, 104 (spoken by an equivalent of the Provençal watchman), 146, 153, 172, 228 (American Indian).

*Eos: An Enquiry into the Theme of Lovers' Meetings and Partings at Dawn in Poetry*, edited by Arthur T. Hatto with the collaboration of forty-odd scholars (The Hague, Mouton & Co., 1965), was published too late for me to use it in compiling this anthology. So far as my knowledge goes, it is the only really cross-cultural study of a poetic genre, and as such I welcome and salute it. I add that, though its large-octavo size, its eight-hundred-odd pages, and its extensive critical apparatus may make it seem a book only for specialists, any lover of poetry will find it most rewarding. Yet even it gives short shrift to the literatures of peoples without letters. In addition to examples from some fifty written languages, of the languages with which this anthology is concerned it gives examples from twelve (seven of them Indian tribal languages). To these my own researches, though not particularly directed to this end, have added: in India itself, examples from Pardhan and Assamese; in Indonesia, an example from Ceram; in Polynesia (represented in *Eos* only by the Marquesas) examples from Tikopia, Hawaii, and Mangareva; in Micronesia (unrepresented in *Eos*) an example from Dobu. (Specific references in notes 10 and 11, above, and at the beginning of this note.)

13. Karl Bartsch, *Altfranzösische Romanzen und Pastourellen* (Leipzig, 1870), p. 17; Laurent J. B. Bérenger-Féraud, *Recueil de contes populaires de la Sénégambie* (Paris, 1885), pp. 28–38.

I V

1. *The Unwritten Song*, I, 69–70 (simile of the ombimbo-root).

2. *Ibid.*, p. 115.

3. *Bondo Highlander* (Bombay, Oxford University Press, Indian Branch, 1950), p. 78.

4. For example, this volume, pp. 47–50, 103, 115; J. P. Johansen, *The Maori and His Religion in its Non-Ritualistic Aspects* (Copenhagen, 1954), p. 157. On the difficulty of translating Maori poetry in general, see Elsdon Best, *The Maori* (Memoirs of the Polynesian Society, V), 2 vols. (Wellington, 1924), p. 136.

5. Cf. Louis Thomas Jones, *Aboriginal American Oratory: The Tradition of Eloquence Among the Indians of the United States* (Los Angeles, Southwest Museum, 1965), *passim*.

6. Thomas Jefferson, *Notes on the State of Virginia*, ed. William Peden (Chapel Hill, University of North Carolina Press, 1955), p. 62. Logan's speech was delivered in 1774.

V

1. For example: *The Unwritten Song*, I, 110 (Dinka: "Chant"); *ibid.*, p. 228 (Fijian: "On the Pestilence"); this volume, p. 115 (Maori: "Ihunui's Lament"); *ibid.*, pp. 53, 54 (Mangaian: "Prayer over a Human Sacrifice," "Prayer for Peace").

2. A. Hanoteau, *Poésies Populaires de la Kabylie du Jurjura: Texte kabyle et traduction* (Paris, Imprimerie Impériale, 1867), p. v.

3. Basil Thomson, *The Fijians: A Study of the Decay of Custom* (London, William Heinemann, 1908), p. 315.

4. Antonio Colbacchini and Cesar Albisetti, *Os Boróros Orientais: Orarimodogue do Planalto Oriental de Mato Grosso* (Brasiliana, Series 5, Vol. 4) (São Paulo, Companhia Editora Nacional, 1942), p. 361.

5. Catherine H. Berndt, "Expressions of Grief Among Aboriginal Women," *Oceania*, XX (1949–50), 290.

# Acknowledgments

The good offices of the Bollingen Foundation and of the Widener and Peabody Museum Libraries at Harvard (already gratefully acknowledged in Volume I) have been of equal assistance to me in the preparation of Volume II.

I now have to express my indebtedness to the Library of the Museum of the American Indian (New York), and there especially to Miss Nancy Strawbridge.

In addition to the individuals whose interest and assistance have been acknowledged in Volume I, I am grateful to Mr. Arthur Gregor, at The Macmillan Company, for several helpful suggestions (not the least of which was his *trouvaille* of the title "The Unwritten Song"); to Mr. William McGuire for a number of references; and to Miss Katharine Tousey for continued help of many kinds.

Acknowledgments to publishers and authors for permissions to reprint are made in the Sources and Permissions.

# MICRONESIA

# Caroline Islands

PALAU

## LOVE SONG

Boxes from Tereked and Keremong,
Piled on each other,
Pelevai leans against you.

When you go eastward, Pelevai,
I go up on Ketund Hill
And I stand and watch your sail disappear.

## DANCE SONG OF DEATH

### 1

We people are skilful,
we set right what has grown too long,
we take away from what is big,
and what is too long we shorten
and make it as it should be,
but when it is too little and too short
death has only one speech,
there is no remedy.

### 2

When I was a young shoot and curious
my heart was set on this world;
my evil deeds will make me die soon,
only death remains.

If death were a man, so that we could see him,
we would twist cords for his outrigger,
we would tie up the world.
This house and the gapdui-trees in the plain are alike.
Who gets loose from him?
Now a man goes here, now he goes there
to escape death;
and when we go in a circle,
death knocks us down.

### 3

These mothers of ours, who bore us,
whose only care is to feed us in vain—
but we cannot be men,
we all die of disease,
only death remains.
If death were a man whom we saw,
we would twist cords for his outrigger,
we would tie up the world.
This house and the gapdui-trees in the plain are alike.
Who gets loose from him?
Now a man goes here, now he goes there
to escape death;
and when we go in a circle,
death knocks us down.


YAP


## DANCE SONG ON THE DEATH OF A GIRL
## NAMED RUTENAG

### 1

Now open your ears,
we tell our grief,
the grief of us who are young men.
We grieve for a girl who is good,
who is very beautiful, a wonder.

She has been taken up to the sky,
she has been chosen from among us.
No one spoke again.
Lug has cut off this hand.
Always they dance for you
in the house Folroman,
always you watch them.

2

Something has broken in the mouths
of the young men on earth.
Our thoughts fail us, we are made poor.
We are tired from performing incantations.
The god looked away,
our will-power is extinguished.
Both Lug and Yelogaf came
to bind the woman,
they have pillaged us.

3

Happy the young men in the sky.
The two together chose the young shoot
of our hearts, the best of the dearest.
They took her up from among us,
they carried her in their hands,
they took her by the road of the guor-bird to the sky.
They have come to their houses Moroiilan and Moroijitsig
and it is shouted in the house,
in Folroman.

4

The loud shout roars in the house,
in Folroman,
and they come from the house Vuger,
Yelafath comes at the head of the procession
and in the middle walks Yelogaf;
Lugalan follows far behind
for he is angry with the youth of Vuger,
he walks with none of them.

5

No one speaks in the sky.
She is oil trickling from her eyebrows,
her brightness flickers in the sky.
A rainbow falls
between those two houses.
Yelafath rises and tells of our condition:
"You have stricken the young men of the earth."
Confused are our thoughts.

6

Our minds are confused,
we are broken
over the rugod of the earth.
It is as if all girls had been put in a row by the height of their heads.
"Never before in the sky has there been such a fruit of the earth.
Here at last is the true one."
You have taken a dream from us!

## BOYS' DANCE SONG ON THE DEPARTURE OF AN OLDER GIRL NAMED YILUAI[1]

. . . Girl,
We want to touch our tongues to yours, we bite your mouth,
your mouth which is beautifully carved.
Beautifully carved is your eyelid,
beautiful are your eyebrows,
high-curved in your face.
You roll your eyes,
you twitch your eyebrows,
which are beautifully curved in your face.
They are shaped like the string of luminous spots on a luod-cuttlefish.
Like prongs are your gums,
like a red rar-fruit.

You make brightness
with your hair-knot,

*Lug:* the god of death.    *This hand:* Rutenag herself.    *Folroman:* the "club-house" of the sky people.    *Incantations:* by which they tried to prevent her death. *Yelogaf:* a god.    *The Woman:* Rutenag.    *The two:* Lug and Yelogaf.    *Vuger:* the house of the god Yelafath.    *Rugod:* (not explained).

[1] Second half. The boys belong to a younger age-group than the girl, but in this part of the song they imagine that they are old enough to court her.

which is as if it were smoothed with a plane.
Then you twist it,
you turn the ends back into the thick mass of your hair.
Our thoughts dwell on it.
A girl is going from us,
a wonder, who is ours.
You are stubborn,
you wear out our lungs, girl,
you break our mouths.

Ended the song that we have carved,
the song of Yiluai.
Now we will perform it, then our song will be known,
which is a song of sorrow within us.
We enter the house
beside the beach.
When we touch you there
in the deep darkness
you must not speak to us,
or our older companions
would recognize us.

## DANCE SONG

### 1

Open your ears,
we tell what is happening
in our two age-groups.
Evil are our hands
for we have seen
things not good:
the dead
who have broken
the young shoots of our minds.

### 2

What kind of dead are these
who come first to us
who are young?

What sickness is this
from abroad
whose spell we suffer?

### 3

O Lug, what spell is this?
The young go to death first.
O Lug, what spell of the dead is this?
Men no longer reach due age.

### 4

No longer do they reach
our due age;
for us in Yap here
this has gone wrong.
Now love us,
Lug, transform yourself,
then come as a dream,
speak,
so that we may know what you intend, O Lug.
How could you be brought to love us?

### 5

On the day of the full moon
Lugala'n net-fishes
for our souls.
But you cloud the moon,
the sky weeps
and you come with the fine drizzle
and carry off our souls.
But we call to you aloud,
O Lug.
He has carried off our souls.
Now sweep them together and go up to the sky.

### 6

A beautiful wonder is your brightness,
like moonlight.
The moonlight floods our minds,

girl whom we love, announcing the time
for us both.
The first red streaks of dawn glimmer,
the first bird tells that he is here
in the early morning.
He speaks once,
the bird, and the cicada
in the wood.

7

We will speak our dance.
What has befallen us?
These two children have left us.
They have gone from our hands,
our thoughts follow after them.
Fear coils in us, alas!
On the day when you hastened away, girl,
when you went into the south,
you are there, with our thoughts
which have gone beside you.
You did not turn and look back.

## SONG OF A MARRIED WOMAN TO HER LOVER YUV

It is all over
what we did in the bush together as lovers.
It was only once
that you came.
No one must know that we are lovers,
we will not tell it;
lower
your voice.
My lover, lower your voice,
watch my lips,
then I will tell you the thoughts I had
when I was still little.
Nothing can break the ear-ornament.
(*Yuv answers*:) "Do not be afraid,

my lover,
I will do as you wish,
then it will be well."
I am sad, but you are far away;
come closer, come here
to me, to the sign.
Let us separate, Yuv, let us go!
Go now, then come back,
crook your fingers
and show them to me so that I see them.
But I say, when three moons
have been in the sky,
I will go to the grass-field
beyond the peak of Thauenifan.
And I will come, I will stay, Yuv!
Then we will separate, Yuv!
One day in the morning
I will come from the west
to the grass-field,
to the head of the brook in Difad. . . .
I will climb down, I will climb up, and I will bring blood.
Fear has driven me
to the blood-house.
There I know a something
by the fito-tree in the south,
in the thicket
of young uouai
under the kal-tree and the vid-tree.
But you have not come yet and I stand up
and I think of what you said to me.
It is impossible now that I should leave you.
And I seek,
seek, seek
around our meeting place
and I hear the click of your footsteps.
You go about
behind the dwelling place of the spirit,
the rtsalai-tree.
You could prick yourself on it.
Come, sit down,

sharpen your ears,
and I will tell you
about the point of Map
which stretches toward the south. . . .
Kiss me!
He will not know,
if he knew he would go to the official!
Then they will come and beat you beside me.
Let us separate, Yuv.
Only when the bell
rings there
is our time for meeting.
And when it rings in my thoughts
I go mad.
My leg is in his hand,
it is held fast there,
and he keeps me by talking,
and I know you are in the grass-field,
at the meeting-place
under the orovol-tree and the otsonol-tree
with many branches.
You stay, you are waiting.
If I could send you
a go-between!
I stay, I am tired,
I am tired, tired.
I beg you,
lie with me, pour out your semen.
Then go;
but I go to the grass-field
to the slope in the thicket of grass,
and my spirit seeks in the thicket
for the snap, the snap of your fire.
Come, I will stay on your legs,
when the sun is low
in the branches of the pandanus;
we two are under
the trunk of the mathei-tree
which leans toward the south.
Come, let us smoke.

But in the colony they are blowing for the end of the day's work.
Let us separate,
Yuv, let us go!

IFALUK ATOLL

## WOMEN'S *UR*-DANCE SONG

In the southern sky make ready the canoe,
We are going away to the north.
The captain is sad; the sailors are weary, and cry
For the people in their mountain home.
Ho! At least they are not dead!

The wind is in the north;
We are ready to go.
Now we reach land; they lie down in the canoe house
Beside the southern seas.
The canoe drifted off its course.
The rest of the flotilla is out of sight.
The father and mother of one sailor are lost.
Ho! Keep up your spirits.
At least we are still afloat.

She reaches the pass,
Comes into the lagoon,
And approaches shore.
Going around the point
We reach the fine sands of Fauiau.
Ho! We have been guided by the god Mware.
The god has descended to earth.
Hail, Angi!

*Nothing can break the ear-ornament:* symbolically, "I cannot give you up."
*The sign:* a twisted leaf, a stone painted red, or the like, to indicate the meeting
place.    *Crook your fingers:* the number of fingers that he leaves unbent shows the
number of days until he can meet her again.    *Three moons:* not three months,
but the third day after the new moon.    *A something:* the place where they are to
meet.    *The point of Map:* she will tell him that her husband has gone there.
*The bell:* the angelus from the Catholic mission.    *His hand:* her husband's hand.
*The snap of your fire:* as he strikes a match or a flint and steel.

Fair is the morning sky;
The canoe prepares to sail again.
Leaving the land of Vatarai
The captain speaks to the people.
He sings an incantation as he stands beside the mast,
Calling upon the god to look after him.
Great king of gods, Angelabw,
Make winds and waves and currents favor us.

They go to Ulithi, and come ashore.
They take a vessel with oil for the god,
And go to Lategi, the god's house.
The captain cries before the god
For his dead father.
The god descends upon him.

In sleep he remembers
When he and his father were together.
He stays at home now, thinking of his days at sea.
*Uya uya hei!* Must we die? We are not dead!

The sunrise is fair; they launch a canoe
In the little northern bay.
A single canoe puts out to sea.
Ahead he sees a bird, harbinger of land,
Draws near, and catches sight of it.
Going through the pass, he turns northward,
And seeks the shade of the leafy wut-tree.
Looking about him he sees an uninhabited islet.
Going ashore, he finds houses on the western side,
And mog-trees giving shade.
He stoops to pass under the pandanus leaves
And stops to rest there a while.

The sun rises, and he stops to watch it.
All right. We will not leave yet.
*Uya uya hei!* Must we die? I am not dead!

Finally he makes ready to go,
For his mother mourns his absence.
The captain is eager to go.
She remembers she can write

And urges him not to go.
She cries and calls upon the god.

The wind blows hard
And she fears for the sailor.
She sits down and cries.

Seeking the shade of the canoe platform,
The captain calculates how far he has to go.
He follows the guiding star until he sees a bird,
Then knows he is close to land.
He swings the canoe to allow for the current,
When about to drop anchor.
He thinks of the pass, where there is no current.
He furls the sail. The people throng to see.
He thinks about his farther course.
*Uya uya hei!* Must we die? I am not dead!

Nearing another land, an uninhabited island,
He sees a bird to lead him ashore.
The captains of two canoes consult together.
He who saw the bird knows the way,
But sees the waves rising high.
He turns the canoe aside,
For surf is breaking on a rock.
He bemoans the strong wind
And cries, calling upon his two gods.
They come to help him,
And he asks them to bring him ashore.
So he lands safely. Hail! All is well!
*Uya uya hei!* We are not dead yet!

A typhoon blows up, and the waves rise high.
The seas strike amidships, smashing against the canoe.
Then the god speaks, sending a token
That there is land to westward.

The other canoe is not far away.
But one is fast, the other slow, in sailing.
The captains consult: "Which way are you going now?"
"To which land?"
He puts in at the nearest shore,

By the house called Rek, in Yap.
Hail! The god comes! Where shall the people gather?

The throng is dancing
Under the flowering trees
Beside the fragrant turmeric of Yap,
Beloved of all the people.

Beside the channel they see, in the distance,
A ghost departing toward the bare southern sands.
All the people watch the ghost.
Departing toward the bare southern sands,
There on the beach it stops.
The ghost enters his canoe, and all the people sing.
He paddles, crying aloud.
The wind springs up, and blows him overboard.
He cannot see land.
He soars to the clouds,
Thinking of one he left behind,
A woman of earth.
He steals away her breath
And she joins him in the skies.
He seizes upon her spirit,
And picks flowers for a garland,
Flowers of wut and gabwilier.
Seeing the garlands the new ghost wears,
Many other ghosts gather
Beneath a flowering tree
Whose fragrance reaches even to earth below.
Ho! The ghost from the southern sky.
Hail! The god descends from heaven.
Down from the southern sky. *Uya uya hei!*

They launch the canoe, the canoe of the god,
To carry the departing soul.
The star Itr brings fair weather
Over the seas between Yap and Ulithi.
The waves strike the canoe,
They break over it,
Driving two canoes together,
Driving them together.

A rock rises from the sea,
And the voyagers watch it with joy.
Hail! The red canoe comes ashore.
Ho! The canoe has landed safely.
*Nga ho i! Uya uya hei!*

From far away in the sky,
The southern sky, not overhead,
The people await his coming.
Fragrant coconut oil for her,
The mother of the god, to anoint her.
Jorulimwar descends!
*Nga he he! Wai ei! Nga ho ho! Ya!*


## SONG OF A NAVIGATOR'S WIFE

Flower strung about my neck,
Fragrant flower of the ragues-tree.

He could not sleep at night.
As I lay by him, he said, "I must go away."
I have no heart for work,
I lie and think of him,
I think, "If only he could have stayed."

I think of my beloved gone to Yap.
While my body sleeps here, can I go to him in a dream?
Can I go to him like rain falling?
Oh, there I see him!
He is lost at sea!
No, I cannot leave this house.
But in my heart I am with him.

I don't want to see anybody else;
I see others going about but he is not there;
He is far away.
If he were only here so I could see him!
Only the sight of him would delight me.
I am weary with longing.
Along the path that leads to our house,
My beloved might come.

I don't want others to use it.
Just before he went, on a hot night,
After going out to cool himself in the breeze,
He came back and talked to me.
"When I go, don't let anybody else come to you.
Whoever entices you, pay no heed.
If they say, 'Leave him, he is gone,' refuse them.
Tell them to stop their talk, send them away."

In my heart I love him only.
I do not heed someone who speaks from the woods.
"Leave your husband,
I want you for my wife." — "Go away!"
Whoever could look in my heart would see him there.

What if I were to go and see him?
Go out to the canoe,
When it was put into the water,
And sail away to where he is!
When he was here, his boy would come to him,
With face paint mixed in oil in a coconut shell.
Son and daughter would decorate their father,
Putting the paint on his cheeks,
And above his eyes,
Making his mouth fine;
Then how they would admire their gay father!
He is like a bird, always flying away.
His hair adorned with oil and comb.

I told him, "If you go, be strong.
Put iron in your entrails.
If you must go, I'll not object,
No matter how far it is.
Some canoes that put out for Yap were lost!
Still, if you can't rest here, you must go."

"You want to see the great island of Yap;
The mountain that towers there,
Its long slopes rising, rising . . .
You want to see all there is in that land.

The coral reef beside the sea,
All the length of the island."

When he had seen Yap, he thought of me:
"If only Ifaluk were not so far away!
If it were close in to the reef here;
If the reefs of Ifaluk and Yap were nearly touching;
Then I could see my family.
We could all go about together;
Together in my home."

Flower I wear . . .
Flower strung about my neck
And in my heart.

## SONG OF A WIDOW

I am lost in grief,
Worn out with sorrow.
I love my husband dearly;
When shall I see him again?

For a long time I have been waiting;
A year passed by,
A new year has begun,
Still he does not appear.

I am always thinking of him.
For a while I forget, then suddenly remember.
I have not put him out of my heart.
It is long since I saw him.
How handsome he was,
With his finely curved eyebrows
And dark glowing eyes.
I cherish his memory;
If he is dead, what shall I do?
Who could ever take his place?
News of his death would be a heavy blow.
I am afraid of the sharks
That gather about canoes at sea.

What if a shark should come,
Seize him and tear him.
Oh, my dear husband!
Everybody admired him,
Tall and straight like a tree.
When he left, I told him: "Be strong,
So the long journey won't tire you;
You can stay in the canoe, and still be fresh.
Be hard as if you had eaten stone!
As if you had stone inside you,
Or were made of iron!
That way you can endure a long voyage!"

I am afraid the canoe has been lost;
That it drifted far beyond its goal,
Out where they cannot see the birds that betoken land.
Where even the birds never fly,
The birds of our islands.
In seas that border on some other land
At the other end of the world,
In the salt spaces where no land is.
If food gives out, he will be near death,
He will lie down, too weak to move.
Oh, is my dear husband dead?

So fine his face was;
So shapely and strong his body.
On what sea does he wander now?

A year has passed without him;
Another comes, and I do not see him.
Another comes, and I do not see him.
No other man is my lover.
For a long time I have not known where he is;
For a long time he has not come to the house,
Here where he belongs.
Oh, my sorrow overwhelms me!

I understand now; he will not come back.
I cannot talk about him.
No matter what wind blows, he does not come.

## SONG OF A MOTHER FOR
## HER DEAD SON

We all lived together here
Beside the channel between the islands—

I am worn and weary
All through my body.
It is like a fire burning inside me,
A sickness that rises into my head,
A soreness all over me
That wears me down.
Every bit of me is weary.

I picked up my little boy when he was sick;
He said, "Good-bye, I think I must die tonight."
His brother, whose name is like his,
Is here with me still.
They used to play together.
If only both could be here now!
When I see the one, I think of the other;
It nearly drives me mad!
I walk about like a crazy woman.
This house where we all used to live
Reminds me of him too.

If people could see inside me,
If they could know how worn out I am.
People come and go, but I think only of him.
I think I will gird the place about
With coconut leaves for a taboo sign,
So they will not come here all the time,
Stepping in his footprints.
I am always thinking of him.
If only he could come back
And be close beside me, as he used to!

I will go and lie inside his body,
Go down in the sea where they buried him,
And stay with him there,

Wrapped about in the kilts that form his bed,
Fashioned with patient skill,
Of the finest weave and dye.

Everything I have I would give to him;
I would only be sorry if anything were left.
Every day I remember that he will never come back.

Flower in my ear . . .
We all lived together here . . .
My precious ointment.


## GIRL'S SONG

I am happy in my love,
I want to find my beloved.
He is happy too;
I from Elato, he from Ifaluk.

By night he comes to me
Where I lie on the mat,
Pulls aside the wall mats,
Takes off two of them and comes in—
Bold lover, heedless of who may be there.
I call out, "Who is that?"
He is like my sweetheart—
Then I know that it is he.
I know the strong, firm body
Tattooed black like a man-of-war bird,
A bird from far Ifaluk.

He came to Elato to find me.
"That is the woman I want for my love."
"Do you love me?" — "If you love me I do."
He pulls me to the tattooing on his collarbone
And the tattooing of his arm.
He lays my head on the tattooing of his chest.
I say, "No! I will not stay here!"
(I lie, for I love him well.)
I say, "How much will you give me?
It is money I want; lots of it."

(I am lying; I love him dearly.)
Then he loves me fiercely;
Our bodies melt into one.

At night we go out from the house,
Walk around on the sand,
And find a beautiful place
In the woods on a bed of coconut leaves.
There we lie down together,
Where the fragrant lamul-tree grows.
He takes off his loincloth,
He pulls me to him,
He hugs me tight,
He puts me on his thighs
(Strong young thighs they are).
He says to me,
"I want to sleep in your house every night."
I say, "I am afraid. You are too fierce."
He is a fine man in face and body.
At last I say, "I am not afraid. We two will sleep together."
He sits up. "I am telling you the truth.
I was lying when I said I was afraid."

He is like the black ura-fish,
His thighs are as fresh as sea water.
He looks only at me.
All the women come and dance, but he likes me best.
They all paint their cheeks with turmeric
And put on fine new skirts;
He cannot rest until he finds me.

In the evening he bathes and anoints himself for me,
Puts on a new loincloth and a wreath,
And comes by night to find me.
We meet in another place now!
He comes into the house. When he sees me:
"I love you." — "I have not forgotten,
Black fish of Ifaluk!"
Like the swift perang-fish he comes.
His home is far away,

But he covers the distance in a flash.
"Never mind what the people say,
The people of Elato are not gossiping.
They think it is right for us to marry.
Like two trees growing straight together,
Though you come from a distant island,
Tattooed like the black Ifaluk fish."
He has come, and I belong to him;
We love each other well,
Each feels the other as part of himself.

### GIRL'S SONG

Glance over your shoulder,
So I'll know where to meet you!
I'll rub between my hands
Leaves of the turmeric,
Fragrant in the afternoon.
If you come to me, move quietly!

He came and whispered to me.
"Come with me," he pleaded,
"Let's go to the other islet."

We waded across the channel
And went into the woods on the other side.
We spread remag-leaves on the ground
In a place open to the breeze,
Making it smooth as a bed,
Over there in Ievang.

There we lay down
And he held me tight
Under the pandanus trees.
He took off my skirt
And looked underneath;
"Sweeter than ever," he said,
"Because it's mine now."
The dark place inside me

*I want to sleep in your house:* This is a proposal of marriage.

He sees every night
Over there in Ievang.

Flower in my ear . . .


TRUK


## LOVE SONGS

### I

I go walking, I look up
at the beautiful breadfruit tree,
I see the shadow of the man
on the beautiful breadfruit tree.

### II

Man, do not wake me,
for I am drunk with sleep;
I came from the beautiful sea.
But now, go away
for I want to hear
the morning song of the birds.

### III

See now, my love is bent
on a man of my clan,
my heart loves him.
I came on the man
at the beautiful crossroad
and felt pain in my heart.
See now, I wish
I could drink
water from his beautiful mouth;
but I see nothing
because the tears in my eyes
are falling into the beautiful sea.

## THE SONG OF SENIA AND MONIA

Who, tell me, knows the old times?
Two children set out,
They found the sky-reaching rock together,
A cliff. You jumped up, and now it grew
Till it touched the sky.—Good.

Quickly with his knife
He cuts out a piece of the stone,
So that he had a foothold, then he climbed up
On Tol en iap, to which they came.—Good.

They rubbed fire. "We will cook
Our fish, which are squirming."
There was taro there too,
Its flowers shone bright.—Good.

The fish is ready, it does not hold back,
When one side is eaten
The flesh grows again on the other.
The skin stays on its head.
And so too the taro.

How are we to get down?
The younger, the braver, he jumps first,
He rests on the aiau-twigs and waits
For the elder to jump, he comes down,
Falls and does not move again,
He is dead.—Good.

He rubbed his body, he did not move.
"Come to life now, we are late,
Look at the house into which we jumped."—Good.

Many villages appear,
But the villages are without people.—Good.

He entered a thousand-fathom house.
"Now let us perform our leaf-charm,
The oracle of Nan pes and of Nan mualan,
The oracle on the heads of the posts,
There beyond the door-sills."

Three spirits hurry past,
Three cried out, and four,
Then they counted ten or twenty,
Then thirty, forty, fifty,
Finally there were a hundred,
Thousands danced their dance there.—Good.

A line is formed, the first song begins,
The notes of the song rise.
They wanted to capture them.—Good.

The spirits flew up, they flew away
And now they dance no more.—Good.

"Where do you come from, boys?"
"We are born of a line of princes."
"Then take the notes of the song.
And fear not the song of your uncle."—Good.

Then they came quickly down and seized it.
"Are you two spirits or men?"
"We are Senia and Monia."—Good.

# Gilbert Islands

## CEREMONIAL PRAYER FOR THE FRUCTIFICATION OF THE PANDANUS TREE

This is the planting of our emblem of a tree, Au-forever-rising-o-o!
This is the planting of our emblem of a tree, Au-forever-turning-
over-o-o!
This is our planting of our emblem of a tree, Au-forever setting-o-o!
I have spread the branches of our tree of fruitfulness, our tree of the
Sun and the Moon.
The lightning flashes, the thunder and the rain descend, even the
fructifiers of the tree,
The virgin tree, the pandanus of Abatoa and Abaiti,
Thy tree, thy mother, Au of the Northern Solstice, Au of the Southern
Solstice!
Spirit of the Crest, son of the tree, Au-forever-rising,
Spirits of Matang, Tituaabine, Tabuariki, Tewenei, Riiki,
I call to you, I call only to you:
Bless us under our tree of fruitfulness, fructify our pandanus trees, I
beg you.
I beg you-o-o! I, Kirewa.
Blessings and peace are ours. Blessings and peace.

## SPELL CALLED "THE LIFTING OF THE HEAD" TO MAKE THE DEAD PERSON'S WAY STRAIGHT INTO THE LAND OF THE ANCESTORS

I lift your head, I straighten your way, for you are going home, Marawa,
Marawa,
Home to Innang and Mwaiku, Roro and Bouru.

*Au:* sun god.

You will pass over the sea of Manra in your canoe with pandanus fruit
    for food;
You will find harbour under the lee of Matang and Atiia and Abaiti in
    the west,
Even the homes of your ancestors.
Return not to your body; leave it never to return, for you are going
    home, Marawa, Marawa.
And so, farewell for a moon or two, a season or two.
Farewell! Your way is straight; you shall not be led astray.
Blessings and peace go with you. Blessings and peace.

## INVOCATION OF A POET SEEKING INSPIRATION [2]

O Sun, thou art reborn out of darkness;
Thou comest out of deep places, thou comest out of the terrible
    shadows;
Thou wast dead, thou art alive again.
O Sun, behold me, help me:
The word of power died in my heart,
Let it be reborn again as thou,
Let it fill me with light as thou,
Let it soar above the shadows,
Let it live!
So shall I be eloquent.

## INVOCATION OF A POET SEEKING INSPIRATION

O-ho, for I seize the leaf of the tree, the leaf of the tree the Ocean-One,
    the Ocean-One,
Come down to me, come to me my inspiration verse,
Come forth and be drawn forth from below, for I begin above, under
    the blowing wind of the south-east,
It is finished the tune . . . It is finished its begetting.

---

[2] Literal translation. The poet "will enter the sea before dawn and swim beyond
the ocean reef, a feat in itself involving no little danger. There, just beyond the line
of breakers he will lie and swing up and down in the rollers as they pile themselves
to crash on the reef and chant his *tabunea* or invocation. . . . The words and the
music then come to him" (P. B. Laxton, as cited, pp. 343–44. See Sources and Permissions) .

## SONG OF A FABULOUS HEROINE WHOSE LOVER HAS ESCAPED FROM CAPTIVITY IN TONGA

Haste, ah, haste thee from the East, my beloved.
Thou hast come out of bondage in Tonga,
Thou art gone like a tempest over the land;
Even the waves of the sea shrink back before thy wrath.
Thou comest in anger, thou Terrible One, yet I fear thee not.

Haste, ah, haste thee from the East, my beloved.
Thou art exalted in thine anger, thou art exalted in Tonga;
Thou treadest upon the clouds—they are tangled about thy feet;
Thou pluckest down with thy fingers the mountains of Samoa;
Yet thy hand upon my breast will be as gentle as a child's.

Haste, ah, haste thee from the East, my beloved,
Thy feet are swifter in the East than the feet of the wind and the rain;
The noise of thy coming is the tumult of falling skies;
So that in the face of all men thou art terrible,
Save only in my sight, who love thee, therefore fear not.


## SONG

People have heard it,
It is all over Einei
and makes a stir in Arorai.
Shall I deny it?
It is breaking my heart.
His oil smells so beautiful
and he is beautiful and good!
I love him so much! And he seems to love me.
Now he is standing under that tree,
I will call to him. Ngo, Ngo, Ngo.
I must go where I find rest,
north over the deep water. Ngo, Ngo, Ngo.
Now I see him standing on the beach,
he takes his canoe and sails

off between Tarawa and Apaiang.
There he drops anchor, he has found her again.
O, there comes the kabane-bird.
O kabane, O kabane, O kabane!

## SATIRE

That man came shouting, "I am a chief."
Certainly he looks lazy enough for the title;
He also has the appetite of a king's son,
And a very royal waddle.
But he shouts, "I am a chief":
Therefore I know he is not one.

# Marshall Islands

MEJIT (NEW YEAR ISLAND)

### STORM TIDE ON MEJIT

The wind's spine is broken,
It blows less,
We perform the wind-tabu.
It grows still, still, still,
Wholly still,
The calm, the calm.
The wind-tabu, *e,*
Makes calm, calm, calm.
The surf, surf, surf,
The surf, surf, surf,
The surf, surf, surf,
Plunges, roars,
Plunges, roars,
Plunges, roars.
It flows up,
The sea covers the beach with foam,
It is full of the finest sand,
Stirring up the ground, stirring up the ground.
It slaps, slaps, slaps,
Slaps, slaps, slaps
On the beach, and roars.

# POLYNESIA

# Polynesia*

## SEA CHANT

The handle of my steering paddle thrills to action,
My paddle named Kautu-ki-te-rangi.
It guides to the horizon but dimly discerned.
To the horizon that lifts before us,
To the horizon that ever recedes,
To the horizon that ever draws near,
To the horizon that causes doubt,
To the horizon that instills dread,
To the horizon with unknown power,
To the horizon not hitherto pierced.
The lowering skies above,
The raging seas below,
Oppose the untraced path
Our ship must go.

## LULLABY

Sleep, little one, sleep. Mama has gone to get fish for you. Papa has gone to the valley for wild bananas to make poipoi for baby. You are beautiful as a puahinano-flower this evening.

Sleep, little one, sleep. Drink your milk. You smell as good as a puahinano-flower this evening.

Sleep, little one, sleep. Mama has gone to get fish, papa has gone to the valley to get fei.

* Unspecified localities.

## BIRTH

Slowly the unborn babe distends life's pathway,
　　　torn by the child's head;
Now the living child,
　　　long cherished by the mother beneath her heart,
Fills the gateway of life.

There is room to pass safely through;—
　　　The child slips downward,
　　　It becomes visible,
　　　It bursts forth into the light of day,—
The waters of childbirth flow away.


## MARRIAGE

Your two smoothly voluptuous and comely bodies
　　　have been united in wedlock upon this day,
To be bedded together this first night,
Now tightly intertwined, like a warrior's topknot
　　　pierced by a thorn—the urgent thorn of the husband.
The rounded cheeks of your buttocks, O fortunate wife,
　　　have been tattooed red, red as the ripe mountain apple;
And your hair is deeply waved,
　　　like the fronds of the curly-leaved mountain fern;
Your teeth are white as the heron;
And you are both patterned with bands in black and white,
　　　like the striped fish of the lagoon,
And your whole body, O Wife! is covered with dotted designs,
　　　like the eel called Two-lords-gliding-through-the-ocean.

O thou the Sacred One!
O Protector of lovers!

How rapturous are the joys of marriage!

　　　Honor to your mother!
　　　Honor to your father!

## PASSION SPENT

At the core of my being, in the pale light of early dawn,
    Your spear advances in flaming ardor.

    Now it has withdrawn.

Our bodies are like the tiny leaved mint in fragrance;
They have been anointed with the sweet scented sap
    of the wild ginger root,
Gathered on the bold promontory, Hill-of-the-children,
    jutting into the blue reflection of the lagoon,
From the western flank of the mountain called Life-giving-creator.
The secluded nook, Land-crab-scuttling-over-the-flowering-dell,
    is our trysting place,
Where the plover twitters as it snatches small fry
    from the brook, Clamoring-waters.
Oh, deep is our rapture in our secret retreat,
While ever the great temple—
Primordial-abyss-within-the-dark-rim-of-the-rock-base-of-the-world,
    the flaming body of woman—
Gleams in the flickering light of moving torches;
A temple consecrated to the two thighs of the Earth-mother
Ever bringing forth children into this world of light.

    Behold! The divine goddess!

    O Urgent desire—
    Assuaged in the cup-of-life!
O Adored Cup-of-life—
    Enfolding the flame of desire!
O Ecstasy!

    Rapturous is the union of the gods!

## THE FOUR WINDS

### i *North Wind*

O North Wind!
Evoked from the abyss,
Driving the scudding clouds over unsailed horizons.
A Wind,
Made known in the onrush of cloud banks
    fleeing before the fury of the blast,
Whose tempestuous breath
    swells the surging chaos of the sea.

O North Wind!
You come from the Primeval Source
    trembling in the first throes of creation,
While the divine seed of life, there—far below,
Impregnates the womb of the winds!

You come, red-washed in the streamers of the sunset,
Trailing cloud banners
    torn in the consummation of your desire.
Evoke your rapture till the oceans seethe and toss!
    Oh, divine ecstasy!

### ii *East Wind*

O East Wind!
Born of the abyss,
Conceived in the womb of the universe
    pregnant with the winds.
A Wind,
Holding steadily over wide wastes of remote oceans,
And revealed in the tempest
    of storm-heads and scurrying rain.

O East Wind!
You burst forth into the world of light,
While, far below,
The life generating waters
    explore the primeval source of the divine surge of life.

O East Wind!
O visible rapture of the Towering One
        mated with the Eternal Goddess!
You come from the age-old realm of the noble dead.

You have carried out your life bestowing labors
        upon the wide spread, welcoming Earth,
While ever your winds strive together
        in the primordial cup of life,
Convulsed in the sacred union of the gods.

        Oh, assuagement of divine desire!


III    *South Wind*


O South Wind!
'Mighty-Wind-of-the-South' was the name
        of your bleak and frigid breath in times of old,
Holding steadily over diminishing ranges
        reaching to far horizons.


O South Wind!
Of you it was said, in ancient times:
*"The south wind is the breath*
        *of him who leans upon the lightning!"*

You are the wind honored in song
        by the young women of our clan, chanting:
*"O Mighty-wind-of-the-south!*
*How bitterly cold is your breath!*
*How bleak is the wind*
        *fingering the crowded peaks,*
        *and frosting the pathway winding along the shore!"*
You are the wind arousing the wife
        to the warmth of love, as she sings:
*"O my husband!*
*Now build a fire upon our hearth*
        *to warm us this night;*
*Come to my straining arms—wrapped in your patterned quilt*
        *stained with yellow turmeric designs,*

*And fragrant with blossoms of the creeping vine,—*
*While we cling together, O my lover!*
*Embracing, flaming with ardor.—*


*Swooning in the sacred fire!"*


### IV   *West Wind*


O West Wind!
You dwell in the deep caverns of the realm of night;
Sharp is your chilly breath
Coming from ocean wastes, beyond the setting sun,
        where storm clouds gather.


O West Wind!
Ever you abide in the primeval chasm,
Roiling the tidal flow with white sands
        flung up from your ocean bed.


A Wind,
Dying down into the gentle, westerly breeze,
        wafted from the cloudless vault of the sky,
And sighing to the seething murmurs of the Ancient One—
Primordial Source of life wherein the winds were born.


A Wind,
Blowing across desolate waters
Skimmed by the tripping feet of sea birds
        winging over lonely oceans.


O West Wind!
Dwelling in the abyss of the Dark Goddess;
You evoke the storm imprisoned in the bowl of night,
And, in the prodigious consummation
        of the passion of the gods,
You cast forth the hurricane
        into the trembling light world here above!


Oh, divine and immortal rapture!

# Tikopia

## SONG OF A RETURNING VOYAGER

The dawn broke in the east, O!
To me appeared
Reani then, O!
Risen in the sea.
The crests of the mountains
Which were formerly buried
By the swollen tide.

Ai-e! Crests of the mountains
Buried
By the swollen tide.
Riele, riele!
Mounting, and now to be reached.
Reani has flown and stands on high.

## DIRGES

### I *For a Father Drowned in a Storm*

Your sky, Father,
Stands in the ocean
Your canoe will be buried in the sea
Blanketed by the waves
Of the ocean wastes it will be buried.

Broken is the shelter
Of my father
Lost to sight
You were the true *maru*, generous to common folk

His mind also
*Nevaianevaia!*

His mind has become untied while I
Am living orphaned.

11   *For a Sister Who Committed Suicide*

My sister, my nourisher, you have leapt into the ocean
And you did not turn your head to shore

You formed your idea, your foolish thought
You went away that you might die.


## SONG OF A GIRL
## CAST OFF BY
## HER LOVER

I shall sever O!
I shall sever my mind
I was consumed by the talk
This is the young man
Whom I let sleep with me.

Part then in the dawning
But let there be affection
I shall arise
But I desire still
You to sleep with me.


## IRONICAL SONG ON THE
## INTOLERANCE OF
## MISSIONARIES AND
## CONVERTS

My dwelling is evil
I dwell in darkness;
My mind is dark.
Why don't I abandon it?

It is good that I should die
Die with the mind
Of one who dwells in darkness.

Stupid practices to which I have clung;
Let them be pulled down and caused to slip away.

# Uvea

## OLD FUNERAL CHANT[1]

### 1

Be it heard, the road of my song.
the song that comes out of the ground
is your song Sungida
I am standing against the amejo-tree
it is dripping on my head drop by drop.
I raise my arm
with my arm raised I weep.
yet I sing the road of my song.
the song of the ledena-tree
is your song Sungida
Sungida has gone to the fields.
leaf of the walei and leaf of the meli-tree
give the drink for my song.
the song coming out of the ground.

### 2

It is past noon.
I do not know the flight of the stone
it comes flying from Germany.
it strikes my face.
I fall to the ground
I ask for help in vain
help from whom?
there is no one
alas for me!
now among the boys

---

[1] "This old chant was revived and brought up to date on the occasion of the death of a volunteer in the war of 1914–1918. The speaker is the dead man; he describes his death, the funeral ceremonies, and his departure for the underworld" (J. Guiart, as cited, p. 103. See Sources and Permissions).

of our marching squad.
where they make each other laugh
I shall be gone from among you.

### 3

The sound of mourning must be heard.
it is the chief's servant
who will weep for me first
who will weep saying: alas! my child.
do not sleep, think: there is the country
the country in the ground, the country of joy.

### 4

Alas! my mother and my father,
alas! the son of you both
is lost forever
he is no longer with you
it is good that my death
today does not come from my mother,
but that it comes from strangers
woe to them.

### 5

Morning is soon come, I have no road.
I break the walei-leaf
my road to the ground
and I must go on
here is your skirt, leaf of the sea
my skirt for the song
with the daughters of Soihnyilit
the girls who live in Oijone
evening is come
I am standing under the u-tree
I hear the sound of a word
it is the long leaf saying to me:
come to us
as I go I gather walei-leaf
I crown myself with it for the song
with the girls of the land of Oijone.

*The stone:* the bullet.    *Oijone:* the underworld.

# Tonga

## RECITATIVE

Listen, O poet,
While I tell of the skies:
First sky and second sky
Pushed by Maui to be high
So that I could walk stately;
Our lands are two,
The sky and the underworld.
Third sky and fourth sky,
Dwell there the covered and inclouded,
The different sky, the sky that rains
And that hides the cloudless sky.
Fifth and sixth sky,
Dwells there the sun, who dies in crimson,
The little stars moving in succession
Like a string of walking-sticks;
And look up to them the dwellers on earth.
Seventh sky and eighth sky,
Dwell there Hina and Sinilau;
The sky of the thunder
With a great loud voice,
When angry or giving omen of war.
The ninth sky and the tenth,
The sky feathery like herons,
The sky of uncertain rumbling,
Perhaps telling of parting.

## SONG IN RECITATIVE STYLE

We were sitting talking about the weather shore of Vavau when the
women said to us:

"Let us take a walk to the weather shore to watch the sun go down; we will listen to the singing of the birds and the lament of the wood pigeon.

We will pick flowers near the precipice at Matawto.

We will stay there and share out the provisions brought to us from Likuone.

We will bathe in the sea and rinse in the Vau-Aka and anoint ourselves with sweet-smelling oil; we will string flowers and plait the *chi* which we pick at Matawto.

While we stand on the precipice at Ana Manu we will look down breathless on the sea far below.

As our minds are reflecting, the great wind whistles toward us from the tall toa-trees inland on the plains.

My mind grows large, watching the surf below, trying in vain to tear away the firm rocks.

Our state then will indeed be happy compared with the state of those engaged in the common tasks of life.

It is evening. Let us go to the village. Hark! I hear the band of singers. Are they practicing a hula to perform tonight at the malae at Tanea?

Let us go there.

We shall think of our former state, when the war had not yet torn our land.

Alas! it is a terrible thing, the war! See how the land is overgrown with bushes and weeds; and, alas! many men are dead.

Our chiefs are unsettled; they will not often wander alone by moonlight to their mistresses.

Enough of reflecting! How can it be helped that our land is at war?

The land of Fiji has brought the war to our land of Tonga, so let us act like Fijians.

Enough of melancholy! We shall perhaps be dead tomorrow.

Let us decorate ourselves with red dye and gird our waists with fine white tapa. We will plait wreaths of gardenias for our heads, and prepare strings of hooni-flowers to show off our sun-coloured skins.

Listen to the applause of the crowd!

Now the hula has ended, and they are distributing the feast food. Let us go to the village tomorrow.

The young men are eagerly begging for our wreaths of flowers, and they flatter us, saying.

'They are very beautiful, these young women from the weather side,

their sun-coloured skins are very beautiful; their fragrance is like the
flowers at the precipice, at the look-out place.'

I am anxious to go to the weather side. Let us go tomorrow."

## PRAISE OF BEACHES

Give heed to me, our festive throng,
I shall tell the row of beaches,
The gathering place of the fleets of boats
When they plan to meet together.
I shall praise the strand Longonoa,
When the calm evening falls
Like a bird with fluttering wing
The dear shade of the crest of the land.
Strand Tukulolo we shall praise,
Alakifonua and Hilatali,
The dear standing of the great banyan-tree,
The Shade-of-Fulilangi.
I shall praise the strand of Leolava,
A thing of all to delight the gaze,
Like the deck of a boat that is crowded
Dear stand of the town that is pleasing.
I shall praise our sacred beach,
Early morn of a dewy night
A thing most lovely to me
Is to gaze at Kolongahau,
That is hid in clinging mist,
Like a chief's head crowned with lime.
I shall praise the strand Metevae
That lies spread hither and yon,
A thing most lovely it is,
Its dear standing shame-faced
Like a wrong-doer discovered,
Ensnared by its loveliness.
I shall praise the strand Foiaka,
In the place of Niutao the pleasing,
Sweet sunafea-ni with its blooming,
And the smooth white sand with its gleaming.
I shall praise the eastern strand,

The quarreling waves of the Tauafanga;
Best of all beautiful things
Is to stand and look towards 'Onevai,
Which dear appears in the mist
Like a face upturned with smiling.
I shall praise the strand of fragrant flowers,
And the standing of Motu-tabu;
Lovely it is to me
When the wind is fair from the north,
Like the sounding of a flute
The dear murmur of swaying palms.

### Chorus

Youth, let us pace the dance,
And dance in unison;
And look upon our line of strands,
Lovely its appearance.
*Aue,* youth, let us dance,
And dance in unison,
And look upon our line of strands.


## SONG OF TUKULUA[2]

When the calm mists fall I am filled with yearning,
With welling desire for the forest huni;
Smiling are the wreaths of siale,
I think of you, I who am fallen down.
The boat has not yet come to land,
But I cannot escape this fate that is planned;
Calm has been left behind,
Through a day of storm must her way be steered.
Lo, our boat is at sea,
And snapped is the mainsheet
Of the boat that must beat up, but will come to shore,
And embark my dear desire.
Oh night when the songs are chanted

*The Shade-of-Fulilangi:* name of a famous banyan-tree.

[2] Composed during the poet's illness.

Think kindly of me who am cast aside,
Who have been desired for forgetfulness.
There works in me the desire not to be absent.
Not to leave Onevao,
And walks on the cape of Niutao,
Plucking hala and hingano.
Would it were a boat that was mended again,
Made all new to sail about
With me who am fallen down.
*Angi-a-he*
Alas, how 'tis cheerless.
What wonder that the thunder mutters.
*Angi-a-he*
The lightning darts flashing through,
But I just lie and gaze.
*Angi-a-he*
The chief of the voyage had gone aboard,
And I shall go to unfriendly Pulotu,
*Angi-a-he*
And leave the land of light.
Farewell flocks of tern,
*Angi-a-he*
And another shall sit in my place
When there is fullness of oil and garland,
*Angi-a-he*
In the rivalry of the dance and song.
Do not blame me overmuch;
If there be one with a friendly thought,
Then weave the heilala,
Bring pebbles of Fatailangalanga
When I have gone on my lonely voyage;
Treat kindly my body and character
When fate hath desired me,
*Ho-he*
Like a prairie of dried grass.
The boat is putting out,
Breakers engirdle the Sacred Reef,
White is the surf on Tuila and Huangalau.
I love the cluster of Tongan hea trees.
Thicket of makai farewell, I am going,

Lolohea prepared for oil and mingled
Taken that they may bathe—
They do this or that, stand here and there,
Light on the place where ivory is carved,
Blow the conch, beat the drum.
'Twas such a day that we were here,
How I love their sitting about,
Frequenting of those who come to the games,
The chief with necklace of puleoto,
And they gather amongst the motelolo.
Blow hither, blow, *he, he'ia,*
Choir of women farewell.


## FAREWELL OF
## WARRIORS OF VAVAU
## GOING TO FIGHT
## AT PEA

Hill of Kafoa, Aloitalau,
This my parting is, I shall go.
And if perchance I come not again,
Mingled is my dust with Tongatabu.


*Pulotu:* in the afterworld.

# Samoa

## KAVA-DRINKING SONG

Kava, calling out kava;
My kava tree stands sideways;
It is forbidden to a boy,
But only for a girl with eyes like a flower,
Who can't stand still, but who runs
With her mouth open like a crack in the lava.
My kava is forbidden to be uprooted,
But only its branches can be cut.
It is forbidden to pound it,
But only to chew it soft,
And squeeze its juice inside a bowl
For us to drink and wonder.

## DIRGE[3]

Sina ma Tinae!
I, Sina i Fa'ananu
Dipped water to refresh you,
But you were neither relieved nor refreshed.
The tide was low and the rocks were uncovered;
There was no squall to bring a cooling shower;
Only a few drops fell from the heavens.
Besides, the path was difficult;
It was covered with sharp stones,
The sun was scorching hot.
That is why I was late.
Alas, my poor mother.

[3] "Sina ma Tinae, an old woman of Asau, Savai'i, ate some breadfruit that were too hot. Her daughter Sina i Fa'ananu hurried to get her a cooling drink, but Tinae had already burned her throat and was dead" (E. Schultz, as cited. See Sources and Permissions).

## LOVE SONG

Blessed are the billows of the ocean,
Which roll eastward and roll westward;
But you do not see my body growing lifeless,
And my broken heart . . .

## SONG OF A SUITOR
## DISMISSED

My pearl, and my partner, I am willing;
Come, I cannot do anything;
My boat must turn in and rest,
And anchor by land,
Because the dark of the night is come.

# Cook Islands

MANGAIA

## PRAYER OVER A HUMAN SACRIFICE TO RONGO[4]

Stately, noble priest!
Sweet peace, pleasant offering!
Securely fastened and well-tied.
These human hands and human form,
Devoted to this fate by the gods:
Doomed to sacrifice by the god Rongo.

Great Vatea is the guardian of the ocean.
By him it is ruffled:
By him it is calmed.

Here is iron-wood of noble growth—
A most graceful tree,
With numerous branches.
Fell this iron-wood tree;
Divide its trunk;
Split it with wedges,
For the making of spears.

In every age the iron-wood has yielded
Death-dealing spears
For the use of warriors only—
From time immemorial.
And bravely have *we* wielded them!
The wild ti-root of the hills was our food.

[4] "Of unknown antiquity" (W. W. Gill, as cited. See Sources and Permissions).

But now we shall enjoy plenty.
This day we heartily rejoice.

Lately we hid in the rocks—
The refuge of the conquered.
But now we shall enjoy plenty,
This day we heartily rejoice.

### PRAYER FOR PEACE[5]

*The single voice of the "praying king":*
A bleeding victim has been chosen for our altar.
By it are weeded out the evils of the land
Which spring up from nether-world.

*All the drums and all the voices:*
Let peace begin. May the sky be cloudless!
Let peace begin. May the sky be cloudless!
Weed out all evils. Weed them out!
Weed, weed them out; utterly and for ever!
Aye, let each threatening cloud entirely disappear!

## TUMEA'S LAMENT FOR HER FATHER NGAKAUVAREA

### 1

A daughter is seeking for her cave-dwelling father.
Where, oh, where is Ngakauvarea?
He who guarded the cave of Tautua.

### 2

Asleep there, his hands were stealthily grasped:
Cruelly seized and dragged was he,
And slain with the white man's axe!

### 3

It was the white man's axe that slew thee—
So utterly unlike all others!
Why did not the wooden spear lay thee low?

[5] "Of unknown antiquity" (W. W. Gill, as cited. See Sources and Permissions).

### 4

Oh, that white man's axe! Alas for thy brother,
Alas for Uruata! Oh, that cruel stratagem!
That fearful blow! Oh, that I too had died!

### 5

Kaarau saved his own skin.
Was not Kaku his father? But thou,
Ngakauvarea, wast pitilessly hurled to those below.

### 6

Pitilessly hurled down! Who now will fill up the ranks?
Would that these three warriors had been saved!
Why did the babblers oppose thy wish to fight?

### 7

They opposed thy wish. The foes beneath
Kept shouting, "Come out and fight."
"Wait, that we may for awhile gaze at the light of day,"
Said his death-fearing friends.

### 8

Death! Dance the war-dance: send a message of defiance.
Fight the cave-dwellers. Will they venture out?
No, they will not. There they are doomed to perish.

### 9

Ay, doomed to perish! The sun is setting.
Come, let us go and greet our father
In his miserable abode.

### 10

Alas, that wretched abode!
Let us go to Butoa to collect and cook
His repast of wild leaves.

### 11

Yes, a repast of cooked leaves was ready for our father.
He was not killed by hunger.
Our approach to the cave was prevented.

12

Our approach was prevented. We heard a report,
"The fight is over; Ngakauvarea is slain."
His corpse lies exposed at Tamarua.

13

Lies exposed at Tamarua; sad resting-place!
Exposed on a rock! Ah, my brother,
O Tuturi, why didst thou not save him?

14

Why was he not saved? He was dragged and slain.
Such was your pity for your sister!
Kurakaau is left utterly desolate.

## THE OVERTHROW OF RUANAE[6]

### INTRODUCTION

*Solo*

The tribe of Ruanae has perished!
As the reef covered with dead fish
Is the ground where they fought.

*Chorus*

Let the dead rot there!

### FOUNDATION

*Solo*

Ruanae lies low in the dust,
Where he rushed on to his fate
In the vain hope of victory.
Akapautus pressed behind:
"Come on, stand shoulder to shoulder,
That we may die together."

*Chorus*

Both warriors lie in one place!

*Kurakaau:* Ngakauvarea's wife.

[6] Composed by Potiki, *ca.* 1791.

### FIRST OFFSHOOT

#### *Solo*

The tribe of Ruanae
Has perished!

#### *Chorus*

By the purling brook the fight took place.
Ay, by yon purling brook the fight took place.

#### *Solo*

"Should the worst come to the worst,
Should we be overpowered by our foes,
Our bodies shall lie on the field of battle."
As the reef covered with dead fish
Is the ground where they fought.

#### *Chorus*

Let the dead rot there!

### SECOND OFFSHOOT

#### *Solo*

Waiting for a sign
Of advancing foes,—
Of any advancing foe.

#### *Chorus*

Ngako climbed the mountain top,
        And long watched there
To get notice of their approach,—

#### *Solo*

Ay, for the faintest token of their approach.
The priest-leader gave the fatal command,
"Climb the trees and bare them of their fruit."
As the reef covered with dead fish
Is the ground where they fought.

#### *Chorus*

Let the dead rot there!

### THIRD OFFSHOOT

*Solo*

The only thought was

*Chorus*

—now of flight,—
Of mere flight!
Shall it be by Teone, the path to the sea?
Or by the hill Paeru, overlooking the battle-field,—

*Solo*

Ay, overlooking the battle-field?
Dare thy utmost to live;
'Tis hard to escape.
As the reef covered with dead fish
Is the ground where they fought.

*Chorus*

Let the dead rot there!

### FOURTH OFFSHOOT

*Solo*

Ask the road

*Chorus*

—by which to fly,—
To fly for one's life!
Ruanae's home had been in the rocks,
Where a solitary Barringtonia grows,—

*Solo*

Yes, where a solitary Barringtonia grows.
He subsisted on pandanus berries,
And the sour fruits found in the wilds.
For none befriended him!
As the reef covered with dead fish
Is the ground where they fought.

*Chorus*

Let the dead rot there!

FINALE

*Ai a ruaoo! E rangai e!*


# FINAL STANZA OF THE DAY-SONG
## FOR TENIO'S FETE[7]

*Solo*

The stars have all set
Behind the western hills.

*Chorus*

Like a tall solitary tree is the fairy
Who committed herself to the winds.
Ina invoked the aid of many fish
To bear her gaily on their backs;—
The lordly shark to convey her safely
To the royal Tinirau o'er the sea.
Alas, the bruised head of the angry monster,
Who hitherto had obeyed the trembling maid,
Who opened a cocoa-nut
On her voyage to the Sacred Isle.
    Softly she beats the drum.
    Tinirau is enchanted
    By the music of the lovely one.


Our sport is over: the visit of Tautiti is ended,
The guests from spirit-world are gone!


[7] Composed by Koroa, *ca.* 1814. The stanza refers to the journey of Ina, a legendary heroine ("fairy"), to rejoin her husband Tinirau on the Sacred Isle, to which she is finally carried on the backs of fish.

*Tautiti:* "Tautiti was supposed to be present at the particular dance of which he was the originator. As soon as it was over, he returned to the shades" (W. W. Gill, as cited, p. 186, n. 1. See Sources and Permissions) .

## THE GHOSTS LED BY VERA PREPARING FOR THEIR FINAL DEPARTURE[8]

### INTRODUCTION

*Solo*

List, Vera, to the music of the sea.
Beyond yon dwarfed pandanus trees
The billows are dashing o'er the rocks.
'Tis time, friends, to depart;

*Chorus*

Our garments are mourning weeds and flowers.

### FOUNDATION

*Solo*

Advance to yonder level rock;
There to await the favouring wind
That will bear thee o'er the sea.
Thy father Mitimiti looks sorrowfully on

*Chorus*

The departing band led by thee.

### FIRST OFFSHOOT

*Solo*

List, dear Vera,

*Chorus*

to the music of the sea.
Thou art a wretched wanderer,
Almost arrived at Iva—

---

[8] Composed by Uanuku, *ca.* 1770. Vera was the nephew of Ngara, paramount chief of the island before its discovery by Cook in 1777. "In this 'lament' it is supposed that the spirits of the dead have been marshalled by Vera on the eastern shore of Mangaia, and then . . . led by him over the rocks and through the thickets of the southern half of the island, until reaching the point due west, where the entire troop take their departure for the shades. . . . The father, Mitimiti [is] represented as chasing the spirit of his beloved Vera in this mournful journey of ghosts round half the island" (W. W. Gill, as cited, p. 199. See Sources and Permissions).

*Solo*

yes, at Iva;
Once from Tahiti, then from Tonga;
Now bound to the land of ghosts,
Entered through the gaping grave.
'Tis time, friends, to depart;

*Chorus*

Our garments are mourning weeds and flowers.

### SECOND OFFSHOOT

*Solo*

I turn my eyes

*Chorus*

to another land.
In some other region may my spirit rest!
On this trembling stone, at the edge of the chasm I stand—

*Solo*

At the entrance

*Chorus*

of this dark chasm.
My path is over yon black rocks near the sea.
Over the roughest and sharpest stones
I lead this feeble troop of ghosts.
Whence come we? We are awaiting
The long-hoped-for

*Solo*

south-eastern

*Chorus*

breeze
To waft us over the far-reaching ocean.
We have wandered hither and thither,
Stepping lightly on the sea-washed sandstone.
Over thickly studded rocks we have come.
Overtaken by darkness we sit down to weep,

*Solo*

A tearful band, under the guidance of Vera.
At one time a drizzling shower

Hides from view the heights of the interior;
At another we are besprinkled with ocean spray.
'Tis time, friends, to depart;

### Chorus

Our garments are mourning weeds and flowers.


### THIRD OFFSHOOT

#### Solo

Press forwards

#### Chorus

on our journey!
Take care that we miss not the way.

#### Solo

Yonder is the landing-place,

#### Chorus

Auveo,
The entrance of which is so difficult to find.
There, too, is my father,

#### Solo

watching our course.
The sun is low; rest we awhile.

#### Chorus

Our feet are worn out over these stones;
Yonder is the gloomy cave Raupa.
Let us move slowly on our way.
We friendless ghosts have reached Auneke.
Look eastward; look westward;
Gaze at the setting sun.

#### Solo

Ah! Mitimiti is following hard behind,
Beckoning me to return.
Here let us halt awhile.
'Tis time, friends, to depart;

#### Chorus

Our garments are mourning weeds and flowers.

### FOURTH OFFSHOOT

*Solo*

Thy feet, Vera,

*Chorus*

      are entangled with wild vines.
Art thou bound for Vavau, the home of ghosts?
Over

*Solo*

  the foaming billows

*Chorus*

      wilt thou voyage?
Thread now thy way through groves of pandanus,
The favourite haunt of disembodied spirits;
Near where the royal Utakea landed,

*Solo*

A level beach laved by the sea.
The cricket-god is chirping to direct thy path,
Through the thickets to the shore
Where the spirits of the dead wander.
Bathe thy streaming locks, Vera.
Grant me a new life, O light of the morning!
'Tis time, friends, to depart;

*Chorus*

Our garments are mourning weeds and flowers.

### FIFTH OFFSHOOT

*Solo*

Descendant of the kings

*Chorus*

    of Mauke;
Favoured one, led by a prosperous wind
From the root of the skies to these shores,
Ere taking a long farewell, turn back!
Idol of my dwelling, remain awhile,

*Solo*

Decked with the buds of sweet-scented flowers
And fragrant leaves brought from Tutuila.
'Tis time, friends, to depart;

*Chorus*

Our garments are mourning weeds and flowers.

### FINALE

*Ai e ruaoo e! E rangai e!*


## "BLACKENED-FACE" DIRGE-PROPER
## FOR ATIROA[9]

*Solo*

Alas, Pangeivi! The case is hopeless.
The canoe is lost;

*Chorus*

Oh, my god Tane thou hast failed me!
Thou didst promise life;
Thy worshippers were to be as a forest,
To fall only by the axe in battle
Had it been the god Turanga—
That liar! I would not have trusted him.
Like him, you are a man-eater!
May thy mouth be covered with dung:
Slush it over and over!
This god is but a man after all!

*Solo*

Plaster him well, friends. Ha! Ha!!

*Chorus*

Dung is fit food for such gods!
We parents are in deep mourning,
Like that first used by Tiki.
We mourn for our beloved first-born.
Oh, that one could stir up the gods,
And cause the very dead to awake!
Yonder stands thy weeping mother.
Thy spirit wanders about One-makenukenu,
Inquiring the reason
Why his poor body was devoured by the gods.

9 Composed by Atiroa's father Koroneu, *ca.* 1820.

Fairy of the axe! cleave open
The secret road to spirit-land; and
Compel Vatea to give up the dead!

*Solo*

Fart, Tiki, a fart such as only ghosts can!

*Chorus*

Wait a moment.

*Solo*

Fart, fart away!
(*Chorus* of pretended farts)

*Chorus*

A curse upon thee, priest Pangeivi.
Thou hast destroyed my boy.

RAROTONGA

## SONG FROM A LEGEND [10]

Uenga was encountered;
Why take heed of Taranga,
Pleasant is the water,
A drinking spring of chiefs,
A very delightful stream,
She was encountered up above—
Above on the upper bank
She was found, on the lower bank
They came together and they slept,
The woman and the man,
At the chief-like bathing place,
O pleasant is the water,
A drinking spring of chiefs,
A stream very delightful,
A drinking spring of chiefs,
A bathing stream indeed.

---

[10] "[Tangaroa] saw the wife of Ataranga . . . coming to the water to bathe at noonday. He . . . took hold of her, and when he had succeeded, they went to the head of the stream, and there they slept. He now composed a song . . ." (Te Ariki-tara-are, as cited, p. 67. See Sources and Permissions).

# Society Islands

### PRIESTS' CHANT TO USHER IN THE DAWN

The clouds are bordering the sky,
The clouds are awake!
There are the rising clouds
That ascend in the morning,
Clouds that are wafted—
Wafted are those dark clouds,
Made perfect,
And lifted from 'Oro-pa'a,
Lord of the ocean.
In the shades of night
The clouds that arise embank,
The clouds condense, and
Form an archway for the sun.
The clouds are wafted,
Perfected betimes,
And lifted from 'Oro-pa'a,
The lord of the ocean.
In the shades of night
The clouds do rise, and part,
Condense, and reunite
Into an arch of red clouds,
For the sun as it rises
From 'Oro-pa'a of the ocean.

TAHITI

## TAHITIAN CHANT OF CREATION[11]

He abides—Taaroa by name—
In the immensity of space.
There was no earth, there was no heaven,
There was no sea, there was no mankind.
Taaroa calls on high;
He changed himself fully . . .
Taaroa is the root;
The rocks [or foundation];
Taaroa is the sands;
Taaroa stretches out the branches [is wide-spreading].
Taaroa is the light;
Taaroa is within;
Taaroa is . . .
Taaroa is below;
Taaroa is enduring;
Taaroa is wise;
He created the land of Hawaii;
Hawaii great and sacred,
As a crust [or shell] for Taaroa.
The earth is dancing [moving].
O foundations, O rocks,
O sands! here, here.
Brought hither, press together the earth;
Press, press again!
They do not. . . .
Stretch out the seven heavens; let ignorance cease.
Create the heavens, let darkness cease.
Let anxiety cease within; . . .
Let repose [immobility] cease;
Let the period of messengers cease;
It is the time of the speaker.
Fill up [complete] the foundations,

[11] Collected by Moerenhout *ca.* 1835.

Fill up the rocks,
Fill up the sands.
The heavens are enclosing [surrounding],
And hung up are the heavens
In the depths;
Finished be the world of Hawaii.

## AROMAITERAI'S LAMENT

From Mataoae I look toward my land Tetianina, the mount
Tearatapu, the valley Temaite, my drove of pigs on Mourahi, the
great mountain. Mist hides the mountain. My cloak is spread. Oh that
the rain clear away, that I may see the great mountain! Aue! alas! the
wall of Mapuhi, dear land of mine!

The drums that sound above Faraeura draw to me the winds of the
south for a fan to fan the chief Aromaiterai. I long for the sight of my
home.

## LAMENT OF TAURA ATUA[12]

Taura atua lives at the terrace of the paepaeroa
The little Uriri flies to the Ruaroa, for him the loved:
"Come back to Papara, the heavy-leaved;
Come back to Teva, your home, your Parpara, the golden land;
Your Moua, the Moua Tamaiti above;
Your Outu, the Outu Manomano on the shore,
The throne of Teriirere of Tooarai."

Then let me go and bend aside the leaves of the Ruaroa
That I may see those two buds of Marae-ura on the shore.

---

*Drove of pigs:* name of a straggling line of trees on Mourahi.

[12] "The young chief [Taura atua] was in love with a girl of lower rank, who lived
at the Ruaroa. . . . He calls his mistress Marae-ura in the song. . . . The messenger,
called the bird Uriri, had come to the Ruaroa, where Taura was living with his
mistress, and brought the order for him to return to Papara" (*Memoirs of Arii
Taimai*, as cited, pp. 36–37. See Sources and Permissions).

RAIATEA

## LAMENT OF A DESERTED HUSBAND [13]

Come back from Toa, O Aitofa,
O my beautiful erring spouse!
As the rapid flow of the current at Onoiau,
And as the swollen torrent from the valley,
So flows my yearning heart after thee.
O Aitofa, have compassion on thy lover lest he die!

The promontory of Tainuu has become beautified by thee.
The husband will fear, will shrink, will faint at the reappearance,
At the return of the love of the cherished wife,
Of that face so bright and beautiful.
Look whichever way he will, she seems to be still down there.

The moon sinking into the western shades is the image of the husband,
The image of Moanarai at this moment.
As a great cloud obscuring the sky is his grief,
The grief of the husband mourning for his estranged wife,
And like the sky darkened by its rising is my distress for her.

Alas for me! Alas for me! my little wife,
My darling has gone astray!
My little beautiful wayward spouse,
My friend who made my heart brave,
My friend in the storm has been stolen away.
A wreath of the fara-tree, a garland of pandanus-blossoms I have
    gathered for thee,
O Aitofa, and lo! thou art flown.

Ah, woe is me! Is it thus that thou shouldst treat me?
Lo, thou art drifting away over the ripples in the Aoa shallows,

---

[13] Collected in 1824. "Chanted by one Moanarai, whose wife has deserted him.
Standing on the south-west point of Raiatea—called Tainuu—he watches the canoe
that is carrying his wife, Aitofa, past Tahaa, to the neighbouring island of Borabora"
(W. D. Alexander, as cited, p. 55. See Sources and Permissions).

Thou art passing the fragrant vale of Vavaara,
And leaving Mt. Rotui, the upper jaw of Hades, behind thee.
Thou hast forsaken thy favourite bathing place with its clear water,
And thy tiare-bush that blossoms without ceasing.
Alas for thee, Aitofa! Thou art a little toy canoe that the wind carries
    away.

Alas for my anguish and the rage of my heart!
Ah me! I despair and think of suicide.
I am possessed with frenzy. Alas for us both!
The mind of the husband gives up the effort to win back thy love.

Alas for my darling! Thy fair face is lost from sight.
There is no benefit from the home.
A piercing thorn to me, a pretty thorn to me art thou.
What is my fault for which thou art vexed,
For which thou hast disdained me?
Why hast thou cut the cord of love, and deserted me?
An evil-working woman.

As a long continued storm is my anger,
At the throbbing within, within me,
My bowels yearn, my heart flows out after thee.
I am chilled with lingering affection for thee, O Aitofa, return!

Here is a bunch of red feathers for thee,
Here is a wreath of scarlet feathers for thee,
Here is a necklace of beautiful pearls for thee,
Here is thy home,
I am Moanarai, thy husband.

# Tuamotus

## GREETING OF TANE

Hail my chief, Tane!
There is not a god travelling the region of the skies,
Only one, Tane!
      Tane-thundering-on-the-land,
      Tane-thundering-in-the-skies,
      Tane-the-thunderer,
      Tane-the-cloud,
      Tane-standing-at-the-temple,
      Tane-standing-within,
      Tane-the-braider,
      Tane-the-torch-bearer,
      Tane with blood inspiring sympathy, that he be given sympathy
         by Rongo-and-Tutavake.
He is the beloved one, the teacher of chiefs,
The whirlwind on the land,
The crimson of the sky,
The glowing red of the sky,
The scarlet of the sky,
The clearness of the sky.
It is the sacred sky of Tane.
Tane here is the supreme ruler of the skies.
Hail to Tane!
It is the highest acclaim!
He is the trumpet, the drum, the leaves-of-kava.
The maker of chiefs.
Come forth,
Emerge encircled by the rainbow, with the flashing of lightning in the
  sky, with the crowding round of the multitude!
Hail to the chief,
Hail to the ancestor of chiefs!

## DREAM SONG OF A CANOE-BUILDER

Oh, mine eyes did close!
My dream is to stand, to be a champion;
My dream is to demolish,
Demolish by the master in 'ura feathers, Tane,

This is Tane's evening.
My sleep is amid boards, amid awakening by the song

Of the nightly thrush,
That records in the day, records at night,
Chirps, and spreads out its wings;
And the fountains flow in the dreams of night.
It is the gods, O it is the gods,
That excite in sleep.

## PLAINT OF A WOMAN WHO HAS NO LOVER BUT THE POST IN HER HOUSE

Who? Who is my friend there?
The post in my house is my friend.
I sleep here in the night,
I dream here.
The house lifts up the edge of my *pareu*.

## THE RETURN OF THE *MARAMA* FROM HITI[14]

*Characters of the Chant*
*Fariua-Mahinui a Papa-te-rangi,* High Chief
*Teata,* his elder brother
*Puatoro, Tuhimata,* his daughters

---

[14] "An account of the return voyage . . . from a successful war-expedition in which the High-Chief, Fariua, complains that the winds will not blow to bring him back to his two daughters. Apparently . . . on the way back . . . the *Marama* was driven, high and dry, upon a bar, where much difficulty was experienced in getting her launched again" (J. F. Stimson, as cited, pp. 183–84. See Sources and Permissions).

*Tama-hiri-atea,* the High Priest
*Marumaru-aitu,* captured Princess of Hiti
*Fariki,* navigator of the *Marama*
*Marama,* the larger of the two ships composing the catamaran
*Teivi,* the smaller, said to be scarcely more than an outrigger
to the mighty *Marama*

PROLOGUE

*First Voice*
*Fariua*

Inland my mast is stepped.
Ever my daughters lament the long separation.

*Second Voice*

Blows not the gentle easterly—

*Chorus*
—breeze,
While my dear children remain hidden from my sight.

*Teata*

Let *Marama* be launched upon the sea.
Shouting and clamour rise in tumult on the shore,
Beneath the grinding keel of *Marama* crunches the coral reef at
Tariahea.

*Refrain*
*Fariua*

*Ceaselessly my daughters weep.*

STANZAS

1

*First Voice*

Blows not the soughing easterly breeze
While my loved children are hidden from my straining eyes.

*Second Voice*
*Teata*

There, beside you, lie those two—

*Chorus*
—great ships,

Those dauntless ships!
Ho! His own—
His very own—are these two prized and splendid ships!

*Fariua*

It must be *Marama* resting high and dry upon the jutting ledge of
coral.

*Teata*

She will not move, indeed,
Even should thousands—or tens of thousands—give a hand.

*Fariua*

The mighty cavalla strikes in the shoal of mullet!
The tiny mullet break and scatter!

*Teata*

*Marama* has driven swiftly on the land,
She has indeed grounded high upon the bar.

*Refrain*
*Fariua*

*Ceaselessly my daughters weep.*

2

*First Voice*

Blows not the sighing easterly breeze
While my dear children stay hidden from my longing gaze.

*Second Voice*
*Teata*

Hauled—dragged sideways over the coral fragments of the reef—

*Chorus*

The ship lies on the very spot where she was first constructed,
Poised there on the land where she was fashioned into final form.
Let *Marama* be launched upon the wave
While cheers break out in shout and clamour on the shore!

*Fariua*

Long-plumed frigate-birds of lustrous black dive and mount—
White seagulls, white-tailed phaetons, and gray gulls dip and scatter.

*Teata*

*Marama* has settled in a deep depression.
Now, Fariua! Regain thy laboring breath upon the rising ground!

*Refrain*
*Fariua*

*Ceaselessly my daughters weep.*


3


*First Voice*

Blows not the gusting northerly breeze ruffling the still surface of the
    sea
While ever my beloved children lie hidden from my searching eyes.

*Second Voice*
*Teata*

Drawn round and round about you—
There, wrapped round you, are those two—

*Chorus*
                    —girdles,

They are the royal girdles—
Ah! Belonging to him—to Fariua.
His very own are those two girdles of the looped-weave called
    "Carrier-of-sacred-crimson-plumes"  and  "Glimpse-of-blue-sky-seen-
    through-rifted-clouds."
Let the mighty Chief—let Fariua—be invested with the royal girdles!
Let the hand of the High Priest, of Tama-hiri-atea, be uplifted in
    sacred invocation to the heavens!

*Fariua*

Seven waves had passed.
Colliding seas broke in flying bursts of spray—
While *Marama* drove on to Hiti in the teeth of the gale.

*Teata*

Marumaru-aitu, called "Deep-shade-of-the-gods"—Princess of Hiti—was
    taken, bound by the wrists,
Slain was her great fish named "Multitude-of-monsters-of-the-deep"
That thy fame—O *Marama!*—might attain even to far Maurua-of-
    the-heavens!

*Refrain*
*Fariua*

*Ceaselessly my daughters weep.*


### 4

*First Voice*

Blows not the boisterous, turbulent wind out of the south
While my dear children remain hidden from my questing eyes.

*Second Voice*
*Teata*

Swept along—circling above!

*Chorus*
*Fariua*

Moving—drifting along,
Ah! Drifting above,
Remotely high sail by the footsteps of the gods.
Here, on the earth below, transiently go the footsteps of men.

*Teata*

Swine grunt, dogs bark, tails wag—in Maurua-of-the-heavens!

*Refrain*
*Fariua*

*Ceaselessly my daughters weep.*


### 5

*First Voice*

Blows not the raging tempest of the south
While my loved children are hidden from my roving eyes.

*Second Voice*
*Teata*

Wrapped round and round about you—
There, wrapped round you, are those two—

*Chorus*

—garments,

They are the royal robes—
Ah! His very own,

These two robes—the royal robes of Fariua!
Let them float in the gale, fluttering above the foaming wake, and
trailing lightly on the deck!

### *Fariua*

Blow—angrily blow! O vehement wind of the west—
Slapping the clinging garments on Fariki's back!

### *Teata*

Blow—till the foam-flecked breath of Mahinui whips past the blade of
the churning oar!
Held—pressed firmly down—shall ride the shaft of the steering sweep!

### *Refrain*
### *Fariua*

*Ceaselessly my daughters weep.*

### 6

### *First Voice*

Blows not the favouring northerly breeze
While my dear children lie hidden from my eager gaze.

### *Second Voice*
### *Teata*

Caught up in the wind—darting hither and yon—
There, round about you, flock those—

### *Chorus*

—birds,
The graceful tern—white as the flying foam, the wheeling albatross,
even the woodland pigeon—
Invoked by the magic incantations of the priest.
Ah! By him invoked,
These birds—the birds of Fariua!

### *Fariua*

Let *Marama* be launched—let her ride free—
So may she win at last to Mata-henua-kura—called "High-headland-
of-the-sacred-land."

### *Teata*

May drenched girdles hang on swinging hooks to dry in the breeze!

*Refrain*

*Fariua*

*Ceaselessly my daughters weep.*

### EPILOGUE

*First Voice*

Alas! *Marama* will not be caught up by favouring winds.
The while my beloved children stay hidden from my straining eyes.

*Second Voice*

The prow of *Marama* swings uncertainly.
The splendid vessel lies becalmed.

*Refrain*

*Chorus*

*Fariua*

*Ceaselessly my comrades of the House-of-Nobles weep.*

## LAMENT

*Huauri*

The son is a castaway, who wanders far and wide.
I am an old woman, an aged mother, alas.

*Tahaki*

The son weeps for his parent, the old woman.
Ah, the son is a castaway, who wanders far and wide.
Oh, wildly calling out his love,
That he will not see Huauri when she dies.

*Refrain*

Wandering, alas, wandering.

*Huauri*

I am an old woman, an aged mother, alas.

*Tahaki*

The son weeps for his parent, the old woman.
For me there will be the sacred land, the sacred land.
For me there will be Vaerota,
I shall be weeping where the sun rises.

*Refrain*

Wandering, alas, wandering.


*Huauri*

I am an old woman, just an aged mother, alas.


*Tahaki*

The son weeps for his parent,
And here I am in the dark night of misery, alas, alas.


TAKAROA


## CREATION CHANT

Life appears in the world,
Life springs up in Havaiki.
The Source-of-night sleeps below
      in the void of the world;
      in the taking-form of the world,
      in the growth of the world,
      the life of the world,
      the leafing of the world,
      the unfolding of the world,
      the darkening of the world,
      the branching of the world,
      the bending-down of the world.
Waves swerve aside,
With the tide rising inland,
With the tide rising seaward.
The tide rises till it touches Atea,
A sea below
      in the narrowness, in the confinement;
      in this, in that.
That gods may appear,
That people may issue forth,—
Atea produces above,
Fakahotu produces below,
Through whom life was born into the world.

ANAA

# LAMENT OF HUAURI FOR HER HUSBAND HEMA WHOSE DEATH THEIR SON GOES TO AVENGE

### PROLOGUE

*First Voice*

The sky!

*Second Voice*

It is a portentous sky—a sky threatening rain!
It is a sky dark with violent storm-winds.

### STANZAS

1

*First Voice*

My bird—my cherished son—flies away!

*Second Voice*

It flies to Havaiki.

*Chorus*

My bird flies away to Havaiki-of-the-nether-world.
It is a bird flying with beating wings over the pathway to Havaiki-of-
the-twilight-shades.

*Refrain*

The father has long since vanished on a journey without returning.
Oh, the adored husband!
A bitter cold chills the heart of Huauri, filled with anxious compassion
for the lost husband now sleeping in the arms of death.
Now my bird flies afar—

2

*First Voice*

My bird—my beloved son—now flies afar!

*Second Voice*

It flies through the sky—

*Chorus*

My bird flies away through the blue firmament above.
It is the bird ever flying over the highways of the vaulted skies.

*Refrain (as above)*

Now my bird flies afar—

3

*First Voice*

My bird—my cherished son—now flies away!

*Second Voice*

It flies to the Netherworld—

*Chorus*

My bird flies away to the remote World-of-night below,
It is the bird ever flying with flashing wings over the dark pathways
    of the night-realm of Rau, God-of-multitudes.

*Refrain*

The father has long since vanished on a journey without a returning,
Oh, the adored husband!
A bitter cold chills the heart of Huauri filled with anxious compassion
    for the lost husband now sleeping in the arms of death.
Oh, alas! Alas!


# CHANT OF HAPAI ABOUT THE VOLUPTUOUS
## PASSION OF TAHAKI

Thy voluptuous passion consummated in the house, now consummated
    by Tahaki—
By thy voluptuous passion the Maiden Hapai is stirred to ecstasy.
Oh, thy god-like passion!

Thy voluptuous passion consummated in the house, now consummated
    by Tahaki—
By thy voluptuous passion the Maiden Hapai is stirred to ecstasy.
Oh, thy god-like passion!

Thou hast penetrated—completely penetrated,
        Oh, ecstasy!

FAGATAU


## PASSION-SONG OF THE MAIDENS

*First voice:*
The difficult entrance, the veiled gateway
*Second voice:*
Now is stormed, is carried by assault.
*Chorus:*
The intruder thrusts against the nub of desire.
Here is a maid; there below is the cleft portal.
Perhaps it is Tu-of-the-long-blade who has flung her upon the ground.
Extended by the finger nails,
A net lies open; it has found a handle.
Drawn tightly, the net is drawn tightly,
O rapturous little evoker of delight!
O lusty fellow probing the slippery wound!
The fount of passion gushes forth,
The blade plies in and out,
Anon brought sharply up against the inner gate.
Elsewhere a sudden flow escapes;
The lovers are united in vigorous interplay, made audible in mutual
   embraces.


## CHANT OF THE HYMENAL RUPTURING OF HORAHORA

### PROLOGUE

*First Voice*

Tahaki is the lover—

*Second Voice*

Tahaki is the lover,

*Chorus*

Horahora is the maiden.
You two shall dwell together upon the sacred temple, Mata-aru-ahau,
   called First-tender-wooing.

*Refrain*

Ho! The sacred temple!
There shall sleep—

I

*First Voice*

There, you shall sleep together—

*Second Voice*

—within the sacred enclosure of
the Temple.

*Chorus*

Tahaki shall kneel over the maiden on the field of Nuku-roa, called
Long-sustained-impulsions.

*Refrain*

Ho! The sacred field-of-strife!
A radiant Princess—

II

*First Voice*

A radiant Princess, nobly born, is the maiden—

—Horahora,

*Chorus*

Yielding her virginal guerdon to the lover at the place called The
Stronghold, at Taka-mura, land of swirling flame.

*Refrain*

Freely shall gush forth the ichor of her maidenhood!
Shall dwell together—

III

*First Voice*

You two shall dwell together—

*Second Voice*

—within Ahu-tu, house of the Gods,

*Chorus*

Till the day comes when the surface of the sea is broken into rippling
  wavelets by the wind—
Till the lover departs,
While the maiden remains behind.

### EPILOGUE

You shall dwell in the night-realm of Kiho,
The last haven of repose.


## LAMENT OF HAPAI FOR TAHAKI

### PROLOGUE

*First Voice*

Indeed, this is the first time that I have been deserted by my lover.

*Second Voice*

Came hither—

*Chorus*

              —an evil witch who stole you from me,
Then was my heart consumed with grief.

*Refrain*

Alone I returned to my house, Kapenu—to our home.
Truly, never before have I been cast away.
The North-wind blows bitterly within my breast.
Will you not—

I

*First Voice*

Will you not sometimes think of me with longing?
With regret?

*Second Voice*

Will you not weep for your dear mistress—

*Chorus*

                        —at Tamatahoa, upon this
  further shore? Alas!
Came hither a cruel witch—stealing you from me.
Then was my heart devoured with anguish.

*Refrain*

Alone, I returned to my house, Kapenu—to our home.
I am indeed destitute—


## II

*First Voice*

I am now utterly destitute,

*Second Voice*

For naught is left me.

*Chorus*

—I am bereft, in hopeless misery, a misery unconcealed—
Revealed—when you deserted me—to all who had eyes to see.
A tress of my hair was completely severed—torn away by that evil
　woman.

*Refrain*

Alone I returned to my house, Kapenu—to our home.
I returned—


## III

*First Voice*

Alone, I returned for one full circuit of the Moon.

*Second Voice*

A fallen leaf—

*Chorus*

　　　　　　　—blown afar in the wind,—thou art
　lamented by me.
For I have been torn away from the rapturous embrace of my lover,
　alas!
An evil witch came hither—stealing you from me,
Devouring my heart with inconsolable grief.

*Refrain*

Alone I returned to my house, Kapenu—to our deserted home.


### EPILOGUE

You have gone far away to the night-realm of Kiho,
The last haven of repose.

VAHITAHI

## CHANT OF KORORUPO

The portal of Kororupo,—
Stretch forth thy hand within, extend thy groping hand—
    My soul is a wild pigeon—
    A petrel, a stormy petrel!
Bitter-cold is the far journey.
Thou art gate-keeper at the portal of Havaiki—
    A pigeon, a wild pigeon,
    My soul is a wild pigeon!
A sand-piper, twittering at the portal of Kororupo.
Uttering a plaintive note, suddenly my soul starts up—
    The soul—it is the soul!
There beside you lingers the spirit, like a bird pausing at the Gate of
  Havaiki.
It begins to ruffle up its feathers—to spread them out—
    My soul, wending its long way hither!
A heron, voicing its mournful cry at the portal of Kororupo,
Over and over repeating its nocturnal cry—
    A pigeon, a wild pigeon!
Speed hither to the sky above, to the Dawnlight-realm—to the
  World-of-light!

*Kororupo:* the entrance abyss leading to the Night-realm.

# Mangareva

## THE MATING OF TOGA

*Refrain*
Close your eyes in sleep,
The eyes of Toga close,
Close, close in sleep.

Who will open
The eyes of Toga-tea?
Te Tapu-a-roko will open
The eyes of Toga-tea.

Who will press
The nose of Toga-tea?
Te Tapu-a-roko will press
The nose of Toga-tea.

For whom will speak
The mouth of Toga-tea?
For Te Tapu-a-roko will speak
The mouth of Toga-tea.

Who will form a pillow
With the arm for Toga-tea?
Te Tapu-a-roko will make a pillow
With her arm for Toga-tea.

Who will provide a body
For the embraces of Toga-tea?
Te Tapu-a-roko will provide a body
For the embraces of Toga-tea.

Who will unite
In love with Toga-tea?
Te Tapu-a-roko will unite
In love with Toga-tea.

Whose are the hips
That will sway with joy for Toga-tea?
Te Tapu-a-roko will sway
Her hips in joy for Toga-tea.

Who will clasp the limbs
In love for Toga-tea?
Te Tapu-a-roko will clasp
The limbs in love for Toga-tea.


## LAMENT: SEA-BURIAL OF TOGA'S DAUGHTER

*Refrain*

I lowered thee down.

Thou hast been lowered down to the deep,
Down to the depths, my loved one,
And I lowered thee down.

Our daughter, the Princess-who-plaited-precious-things,
She died on the open sea.
My darling, I lowered thee down.

A deep-sea fisherman I,
Storm-bound at night,
But the way was too long
For the gods to hear,
So thy body, my dear one,
I lowered thee down.

## THE MESSAGE OF THE
## FRIGATE BIRDS

*Refrain*
O son, O son of mine, O son!

Attend, O bird that flyeth above,
Hast thou seen my beloved son dead,
Who sojourned amidst the myriads of Tahiti?
Feathers on thy legs,
Feathers on thy wings,
Thy beak bends low.
O son!

As a torea-bird wert thou flitting along the shore
On the coast of distant Tahiti.
O son!

The canoe did I provide
In which the son embarked,
The son so dear to me,
Cast up on a distant land.
O son!

Thou art a moon
That will not rise again.
O son, O son of mine, O son!
The chill dawn breaks without thee,
O son, O son of mine, O son!

## LAMENT

*Refrain*
Beloved, I am left alone,
O Te Matererea, my dear one.
The odor of the death of the beloved assails me,
I am left alone.

The waves flow o'er thee,
The waves recede,
The waves lift up thy body,
The waves lave Te Matererea.
I am left alone.

Thou wert borne in
By the waves of Pua-ragahia.
We two are now parted,
O beloved, I am left alone.
Washed up on the strand was the precious one of Aiuragi.
O beloved, I am left alone.

## SONG AT A FUNERAL

Hill of Paueki the ancient,
      it is sweet.
Whence comes the sweet sound of song,
      it is sweet.
Borne from that windy site,
      it is sweet.

## THE KARAKO BIRD

*Refrain*
Rising is the dawn,
Crying is the karako,
My handsome lover will now move on.

Many are the garments
Of the departing loved one.

He will stay seaward of Nukuroa,
My handsome lover—ah.

He will stay at Aorere,
My absent handsome lover—ah.

He will stay at Taravai,
My absent handsome lover—ah.


## LAMENT FOR OLD AGE

*Refrain*
Alas! We grow old, O beloved,
We two.

We two indeed together, O beloved,
When we two were little
When we played together in the sea.

We two indeed together, O beloved,
When we took our walks together
As we were growing up.

We two indeed together, O beloved,
When your breasts were firm and round,
When your breasts drooped in motherhood.

We two indeed together, O beloved,
When your hair floated down your back,
When your body was strong and virile.

We two indeed together, O beloved,
When our bodies grew old and thin,
Like a flat-fish resting on the bottom.

We two indeed together, O beloved,
When so feeble we but sat apart,
So feeble we could but rest the hours away.

We two indeed together, O beloved,
When our dim eyes gaze at the misty skies,
When vision fails to see their splendor.
Ah, whither doth God draw me?

*Karako:* a sea bird which gives an early morning call and so awakens people.

## THE RICH AND THE POOR

*Refrain*
The well-beloved has been rejected,
So I shall haste me afar
And beyond to my mother, ah me!
The well-beloved has been rejected.

Sit on the high stone seat,
Sit with high-held head,
The one with a wealthy father.

Put on the feathered headdress,
Sit with haughty glancing eyes,
The one with a wealthy father.

Hang round thy neck the ivory jewel,
Sit with proudly heaving breast,
The one with a wealthy father.

Grasp in thy hand the chiefly staff,
Sit with imposing dignity,
The one with a wealthy father.

Gird round thy waist the barkcloth kilt,
Sit with chiefly arrogance,
The one with a wealthy father.

Sit on the corner of the low house platform,
Sit with downcast head,
The one with a father in poverty.

Hold in thy hand the menial staff,
Sit with drooping shoulders,
The one with a father in poverty.

Tie round thy loins the ti-leaf kilt,
Sit with shame-bent back,
The one with a father in poverty.

# Marquesas Islands

## *RARI* FOR O'OTUA[15]

With the climbing of the hot, burning sun high overhead,
Come back deep within me the thoughts of my love,
As though sailing on a surf-board and landing on your shores, o To'a.
And my soul would walk to you, stop, and startle you.
Then at night it is good for man to be unwed,
Then we are enlaced together until dawn is on the sea.
We weep the last day when I leave you.
I cannot take my eyes from the tattooing of Iki-o-'ani.
My garlands and potent fruit-plucking-pole are taken to the shadows.
You are the virile one, you are perfumed with oils, lover of the girl,
Tari-atua.
Pick my flower, O'otua.
Kiss the superb eight-petalled flower,
It is love burning in my heart.
Cut it . . . tear up the path!
My hand crushes by accident the whiteness of love.
Thus were torn asunder the clasps on my unfettered clothes.

## *RARI* ABOUT THE FAUFE'E
## BIRD[16]

The faufe'e flies in the sunlight, wings motionless,
The tempestuous booby dives into the waters.
The wild pigeon and the ku'a claw
In changing sea and rain and hot sunshine,

*Rari:* "love-spell-to-hibiscus-batons" (S. H. Elbert, as cited, p. 76. See Sources and Permissions) .

[15] By Mahana, Tahuata.
[16] By Puko'i, Tahuata. "Girls singing this *rari* gracefully imitate the flight of the various birds, the raging sea, rain, sunshine, thunder, and winds, with their hands and arms" (S. H. Elbert, as cited, p. 83. See Sources and Permissions) .

Midst thunder through the mists.
The northeast wind strikes—
Madly I dart away!
Faster fly the birds!
Faster sings the song!
Faster fly the birds!
Birds in the clouds! Birds in the mists!
Song of clouds, song of mists!
My fledgling flies to Fatu'uku,
Flies straight into my famous song,
Wings spread!

## *RARI* FOR THE AMERICANS[17]

We waited long for our white-skinned American husbands,
To sail hither in their square-rigged ships of two masts,
Afterwards to fade into the rain.
For their brows our wreaths and songs, for their brows our wreaths
  and songs . . .

## *RARI*

Strong fires disturb the girl, she is mad with love.
My thoughts are sad, they are in the cruel mists and mountains.
I weep as I make my clothes and sing my song.
Why has he gone?
### *Refrain*
I wear a garland and grasp the hand of my beloved sweetheart,
  Little-ku'a.
Dewdrops are in my song, dewdrops.
A gift of a wreath, a wreath of peace.

I wrap my body
In the mists of a night cooled by the west wind.
Gentle is the path of the northeast wind.
We go to the flowers of the plumeria-tree,
By the spring we wreathe our garlands,
For he and I are together.

17 By Eina'a, Tahuata.

I wear a garland of seven-petalled flowers.
The mountains are our love,
And the sky our clothing,
And wreaths our destruction.


## *M U* [18]

Hiva'oa balances like a dancing flower-leaf,
As our canoe turns back,
Sailing like a bird in flight!
Swiftly the sun has fled, behold, it is night!
Shadows lengthen on the channel
Like wind-tossed flowers.
Ti'i gives a garland and a feast and a dance,
Singing and dancing until dawn whitens the heavens.
I sigh for my wreath of sweet flowers!
My wreath is perhaps torn,
My wreath of sweet flowers!
Pretty as a fruit-plucking-pole harvesting perfume as food
Torn to shreds!
Torn to shreds, my garland of sweet flowers!
Beauty is torn to shreds!

[18] By Ma'u, Tahuata.

# Hawaii

## THE FALL OF KUMUHONUA
## AND HIS WIFE

O Kane-Laa-uli, uli, uli,
Dead by the feast, feast, feast,
Dead by the oath, by the law, law, law,
Truly, thus indeed dead, dead, dead.

O vanish the stars!
O vanish the light!
In company
With the moon, moon, moon,
And cursed be my hand,
Cut off be my course!

O Kane-Laa-uli, uli, uli,
O Kane-Laa-huli, huli, huli,
O Kane-Laa-make, make, make,
Dead are you, you, you,
By Kane thy god, god, god,
Dead by the law, law, law,
Truly, thus indeed dead, dead, dead,
O Kane-Laa-uli, uli, uli,
O Kane disbelieving the gods, gods, gods,
O Kane returned to the muddy waters.

## THE WATER OF KANE

A query, a question,
I put to you:
Where is the water of Kane?
At the Eastern Gate

Where the Sun comes in at Haehae;
There is the water of Kane.

A question I ask of you:
Where is the water of Kane?
Out there with the floating Sun,
Where cloud-forms rest on Ocean's breast,
Uplifting their forms at Nihoa,
This side the base of Lehua;
There is the water of Kane.

One question I put to you:
Where is the water of Kane?
Yonder on mountain peak
On the ridges steep,
In the valleys deep,
Where the rivers sweep;
There is the water of Kane.

This question I ask of you:
Where, pray, is the water of Kane?
Yonder, at sea, on the ocean,
In the driving rain,
In the heavenly bow,
In the piled-up mist-wraith,
In the blood-red rainfall,
In the ghost-pale cloud-form;
There is the water of Kane.

One question I put to you:
Where, where is the water of Kane?
Up on high is the water of Kane,
In the heavenly blue,
In the black piled cloud,
In the black-black cloud,
In the black-mottled sacred cloud of the gods;
There is the water of Kane.

One question I ask of you:
Where flows the water of Kane?

Deep in the ground, in the gushing spring,
In the ducts of Kane and Loa,
A well-spring of water, to quaff,
A water of magic power—
The water of life!
Life! O give us this life!

## HOUSE DEDICATION PRAYER

Cut the umbilical cord of the house
A house that resists the rains and stormy elements.
A house for man to dwell in.
O Lono, behold the house,
A house in the presence of the giver of life.
Grant life to those who dwell therein,
Grant life to the visitors that come,
Grant life to the land-lord,
Grant life to the chiefs,
Let that be the life from the life-giver,
Life until one creeps and is weak-eyed with age,
Until one sprawls like a withered hala-leaf,
Until one reaches the very extremity of life.
Let this be the life granted to us by the gods.

O Ku, O Kane, O Lono,
Let down the gift of life,
And all the blessings with it,
Till the heavens and earth be heaped,
Let them be raised up by Kane of the living waters.
May there be life from one boundary to the other
From above to below
From roof to foundation.
May there be life—everlasting life.

## THE SONG OF KUALII[19]

. . . A chief ascending, forcing his way upwards,
To the very highest ranks, established for kings.
Such art thou, O Kualii!

[19] Extracts. Composed in honor of King Kualii by Kumahukia and He'ea.

And at that high place dost thou stand.
　　O Ku, thou axe with celestial edge.
For Ku, marches the train of clouds along the horizon,
And the edge of the sea is drawn down by Ku,
The sea of Makalii, the sea of Kaelo,
The sea that comes up in Kaulua.
The month in which grows the food—Makalii,
The worm that eats as it crawls, leaving the ribs,
The sea-crab that eats to the bone the bodies of the shipwrecked—
He is the father—all are asking many things. . . .
Through whom are we safe?
Through Ku indeed,
Through whom victorious? For him is the rain,
For him is the rain, for him is the sun,
There for him the star, the kingly star looking down,
Kaula, Haikala, Kau, and where rises the sun.
Puna, the rainy, Hana, Lanakila,
The winter rainy and muddy, and the wind.
For whom is the wind? for Ku.
Blown is the wind by Laamaomao,
The soft breeze Koolauwahine, the wind from below.
Kauai I have seen it,
The north wind of Wawaenohu,
The north wind of Niihua,
The kona is the strong wind,
The aoa the tempestuous wind.
Scattering kukui blossoms on the flood,
Carried by Lonomuka,
Beaten down to Hana,
So is the Koolauwahine of Kauai,
Coming in at Wailua.
The rain, whose is the rain?
　　For Ku.
Above is the rain of Puanalua,
Reaching the three stars of Orion, which pierce the clouds as they
　　drift along.
For whom is this rain?
　　For Ku.
Drifts along the rain of Kunaloa,
Drops of rain beating down on the skin,

Pelting comes the rain of Kananaola,
Mahike is slippery and the traveller falls.
The rain sprinkled down to make him fall,
He falls heavily at Maheleana,
The mist of the rain is at Kahalahala,
The children of the rain cling to the woods of lehua.
  The sun, whose is the sun?
For Ku indeed.
The sun comes forth at Kauwiki,
Burning is the sun at Kaupilioloula,
The children are making challenge,
Holding their breath at the sunset;
The sun in the flower-nets of Hilo.
The back of the sun is turned above,
The face of the sun is turned below,
The shade from the sun is within,
The light from the sun is without,
The heat of the sun o'er-spreads
Over the land and
Stretches forth to Lehua.
The sea, whose is the sea?
For Ku.
The vastness of the sea is from Kahiki,
Calm is the sea by the land,
Taken up is the sea in the hand,
Dressed is the hair with the sea,
White is the hair with very salt sea,
Brown becomes the hair in the sea,
Red becomes the hair in the foaming sea. . . .
A sea for surf-riding is at Kahaloa,
A sea for casting the net at Kalia,
A sea for going naked is at Mamala,
A sea for swimming to the sand-hills,
A sea for surf-riding sideways at Makaiwa,
A sea for scooping anae at Keehi,
A sea for crabs at Leleiwi,
A labyrinth harbor the sea of Puuloa. . . .
But Ku is the chief, Ku the calm sea,
The rising tide of the nights of Ku.
This is the sea that breaks on the hala trees

Breaking on the hala of Keaau,
The calabash of kneaded earth,
The deep-cut road is like a hokeo,
This is the company of travellers.
The travelled road,
Where the earth of Mahiki is made soft,
Trodden down by the foot.
Papaiakea the wave of wrath,
Kaihihii his wife.
The canoe koa is brought forth in rich soil.
A vessel carved out for the sea with its waves,
Carved out the paddle,
Then was seen the bending of the back,
The sitting still in the stern, the rushing up of the waves like the game
　　cock of Lono.
The wave that topples, the waves that break, the god that looks around,
The floating of the breasts
The dark sea, the broad sea,
The broad ocean, the cold-stiffened
Mariners, shivering, quivering with cold,
Then the sea grows still,
The sea where you put on the malo of Ku,
Ku puts on his malo for war, and you tremble,
Scattered on the ground, like an oven, like the rushing of a watercourse.
This is the plucker of feathers,
The bird-catcher of Haili, the child watching the flowers.
The people beneath like flowers.
This is the woman gathering flowers
Wreathing flowers, wearing garlands of Paiahaa,
The ghosts came chasing after,
It is past—all is deserted like Apua.
The wind of the sleep of death has passed over—they sleep. . . .


## SONG FOR THE HULA
### ALA'A-PAPA

'Twas in Koolau I met with the rain:
It comes with lifting and tossing of dust,
Advancing in columns, dashing along.

The rain, it sighs in the forest;
The rain, it beats and whelms, like the surf;
It smites, it smites now the land.
Pasty the earth from the stamping rain;
Full run the streams, a rushing flood;
The mountain walls leap with the rain.
See the water chafing its bounds like a dog,
A raging dog, gnawing its way to pass out.


## PHASES OF THE SEA

The high sea, the clouded sea,
The curling sea that came on the month
Of the summer, the month of Hinaakukele,
The loose sea, a wave of Kane,
The boisterous sea, the boisterous tide,
The ebb-tide, the rapid current, the strong-sucking current,
The transparent sea, the sea which reveals the bottom.


## STORM SCENE

When the canoe is pushed ahead,
The cause of the storm is come.
Like a slanting cliff, dark and black
Is the top of the Aluli mountain, because of the storm.
Like black raiment that is worn
Is the face of the cliffs of Kawaikapu.
Running as though seeking every crevice
Is the water that comes.
The mountains appear to be filled,
The sound is heard in the heavens,
The voice is echoed back,
The voice of the weeping sea,
Urging onward the rising sea.
Like the clouds at Kikiopua
Is the flying and swimming outrigger of Malelewaa.
The burden is swung to the back,
Kaula looks as though climbing from behind.

The cliffs of Wailau are joined and plated one on top of another,
They are joined and plated,
On the top of Pueohulunui,
The cliffs where the owls fly.


# CHANT OF WELCOME TO A KINSMAN
## OR FRIEND

Come!
You are welcome, O lehua blossom of mine from the upland forest,
A blossom around whom the birds gather;
My lehua that bloomed in the Ha'ao rain,
Light comes to our house, for you are here.
Come! Come, we are here.


# DIRGE[20]

This is a dirge, an expression of affection,
For you, O Miss Mary Binning.
My daughter in the dust-scattering wind of Na'alehu,
In the home we shared together,
Oh—my daughter.
My daughter at the cliff of Lau-hu;
Love for you makes my tears flow unchecked,
Oh my daughter at the cold spring of Ka-puna,
A beloved place to which we went,
My daughter in the rain that passes the hill of Ha'ao,
A place we were fond of going together,
We used to go up the long trail,
A little known trail, unattended by a friend.
Oh my darling—how sad I am at losing you.
You have gone on a road on which there is no returning.
Oh my darling—my pet,
My constant companion in the homeland,
Here I remain
With this great load, a yearning for you,

[20] Composed by Mrs. Pukui's mother (see Sources and Permissions) after the death of her first child in infancy.

Oh my darling, precious as a necklace of pearls,
My daughter in the warm sun of Waikapuna,
Beloved is that place where we used to go.
My daughter among the fragrant flowers,
Oh my necklace, my golden chain, farewell—oh—!

## LOVE SONG FROM A LEGEND

It is the flowers at Halemano that I long for,
Partly pecked by the birds,
As their fragrance is brought along,
Its beauty is there at Malama.
For within me I am enlightened, as I sit
The secrets within me are seen through love.
I am the lover, be compassionate.
Alas, O my love!
My lover from the cliffs of Koolau,
Where the cliffs are above and below the pathway,
And love is made a pathway for the tears,
O my love, come back!

## DAWN SONG[21]

I call to you, answer me!
Awake Makia, Makia son of Hano!
Portentous is the shadow, the shadow of him who calls,
Shadow rising from the east.
Morning climbs the heavens.
The piled up clouds, the gloomy clouds, down pours the rain,
A rush of waters, a flood;
Lightning darts and flashes in the dark heavens;
Bound with a strong covenant to that one.
The curtains of night are lifted, the stars flee away,
The king's honor is dashed, all is visible in the light of day.
Awake! Lo, the day is come!

[21] "Because of [King Makia's] desire to commit adultery with his daughter . . . he set apart certain nights as tabu, and during those nights he slept with [her]. On [his] oversleeping himself, his priest, seeing it was already daylight, called to [him] with the following words of prayer to awake him" (D. Malo, as cited. See Sources and Permissions) .

# TAUNT SONG: A WARRIOR REPLIES TO HIS DAUGHTER WHO HAS ASKED HIM TO TEACH HER HUSBAND A CERTAIN STROKE WITH THE WAR-CLUB

Our stroke with the war-club is not for your husband!
Your husband is a sandpiper running along the beach;—
When a big wave comes, down he goes!
A banana tree trunk is your husband, with standing-strength only,
When the strong south wind blows, down he falls!
Our stroke is fit for your father who is large from his head to his feet:—
He falls not when the south wind blows!
He falls not when the north wind blows!
When this trunk falls it lifts the sod with it!

# New Zealand and Chatham Islands

**Maori**    NEW ZEALAND

## COSMOGONY

From the conception the increase,
From the increase the swelling,
From the swelling the thought,
From the thought the remembrance,
From the remembrance the consciousness, the desire.

The word became fruitful;
It dwelt with the feeble glimmering;
It brought forth night;
The great night, the long night,
The lowest night, the loftiest night,
The thick night, to be felt,
The night to be touched, the night unseen,
The night following on,
The night ending in death.

From the nothing the begetting,
From the nothing the increase,
From the nothing the abundance,
The power of increasing, the living breath;
It dwelt with the empty space,
It produced the atmosphere which is above us.

The atmosphere which floats above the earth,
The great firmament above us, the spread out space dwelt with the
    early dawn,

Then the moon sprung forth;
The atmosphere above dwelt with the glowing sky,
Forthwith was produced the sun,
They were thrown up above as the chief eyes of Heaven:
Then the Heavens became light,
The early dawn, the early day, the mid-day. The blaze of day from the
  sky.

The sky which floats above the earth,
Dwelt with Hawaiki . . .

## THE MATING OF HINE AND TANE-MATUA[22]

Here am I, a man, a divine one, O Hine, e, i!
Here is a divine man, for thee, O Hine, e, i!
Here am I, a husband of thine, O Hine, e, i!
Here am I, a lover, a lover embracing, of thine, O Hine, e, i!
Let thy body closely adhere to this male,
Concentrate thy thoughts on this thy lordly husband, O Hine, e, i!
Firmly affixed to the very roots of thy thought.
Adhere to the decreed purpose of woman—
To this husband of thine, O Hine-one, e, i!
My and thy purpose of being was decreed of old, O Hine, e, i!
Come close; as this man adheres to this Hine-one, e, i!
The object of our union was decided of old;
It is firmly adhered to by this son, O Hine, e, i!
Adhere, in closest embrace, the woman to this man, O Hine, e, i!
Forget all thoughts of others, think not of nor incline
To the persuasion of other sons to thee, O Hine-one, e, i!
From the fruitless searching, from the unacquired
From the unpossessed have the thoughts of those sons
Been on thee, O Hine-one, e, i!
Nor rest on, nor turn thy looks;
Not a glance of the eye, or a secret thought,
In thy hidden innermost thoughts, be this son's alone, O Hine-one, e, i!
For we are the waters, the clothing; we are spouses,
Bound like a sister and a brother, O Hine e!

[22] "When Hine had been completely formed in the likeness of mankind, she was
delivered over to Tane-matua in order that procreation might take place" (S. P.
Smith, as cited, p. 140. See Sources and Permissions) .

We are spouses bound to one another in gladness,
We belong to one another, O Hine-one, e, i!
Who will first annul it, thou! who will be estranged, thou!
Who will lack affection, thou! who will show fear, thou!
Whose will be the evil thoughts and words, thine!
Whose were the searchings, the unacquired, the unpossessed?
'Twas Hine-one, towards those other sons, O Hine-one, e, i!
Be bound by thy eyes, be bound by thy mouth,
Bound by thy body, to this man of thine—
A man desired, a man most suitable,
A man embracing—of thine, is this man,
This Tane-nui-a-rangi—
This Tane-matua of thine, O Hine, e, i!


## CHARM

Whispering ghosts of the west,
Who brought you here
To our land?
Stand up and depart.
Whispering ghosts of the west,
Who brought you here
To our land?
Stand up and depart.


## THE SONG OF THE AOTEA CANOE [23]

Aotea is the Canoe,
And Turi is the Chief.
The "Roku-o-Whiti" is the Paddle.
Behold my paddle!
It is laid by the canoe-side,
Held close to the canoe-side.
Now, 'tis raised on high—the paddle!
Poised for the plunge—the paddle!
Now, we spring forward!

[23] One of the canoes in which the first Polynesian settlers of New Zealand were traditionally held to have arrived.

Now, it leaps and flashes—the paddle!
It quivers like a bird's wing,
This paddle of mine!

This paddle, whence came it?
It came from the Kahu-nunui,
From the Kahu-roroa,
It came from the Great-Sky-above-us. . . .

See! I raise on high
The Handle of my paddle,
The "Roku-o-Whiti."
Ha! the quick thrust in,
The backward sweep!
The swishing, the swirling eddies,
The boiling white wake
And the spray that flies from my paddle!
Lift up
The paddle to the sky above,
To the great expanse of Tu.
There before us lies our ocean-path,
The path of strife and tumult,
The pathway of this chief,
The danger-roadway of this crew;
'Tis the road of the Great-Sky-above-us.

Here is my paddle
"Kautu-ki-te-rangi";
To the heavens, raise it;
To the heavens, lift it;
To the sky far drawn out,
To the horizon that lies before us,
To the heavens, whence come all things
Holy and mighty,
Before us is our ocean-way,
The path of this canoe, the child
Of Tane, who severed Earth from Sky,
The path of the Kahu-nunui, the Kahu-roroa,
The pathway of this chief, this priest.
In Rehua is our trust,

Through him we'll reach the Land of Light.
O Rongo-and-Tane!
We raise our offerings!

## OLD DANCE SONG, ADAPTED TO CONTEMPORARY INCIDENTS IN 1885

Which is the post? which is the strength?

The Governor is the post; he is the strength. Grey, grey and wrinkled indeed have they grown while eating up the life, the fatness of my country New Zealand, and naught but the skeleton remains of Maui's fish.

And who destroyed it?

It was first wounded by the surveying. It was next pierced by the Court. And they pull and tug at the land, and snares are set to catch my shares as though they were not mine. They are squeezed and engulfed by the land-buying English. And so we fall, alas! alas!

And what does the Governor? what does he?

Why, he guides and controls the flood-gates of the laws, the torrents, that they may overwhelm New Zealand. O woe! alas!

And the bad laws come, they come and cease not. Then the afflicted ones, relief-seeking, flee to Wellington, but it is a den of lions with yawning mouths wide spread. O woe! alas!

## VAUNT OF THE HERO WHAKATAU ON GOING INTO BATTLE

If Tangaroa should enquire,
"Who is that young warrior
So daringly girding on my war-belt?"
I reply: Nobody at all; nothing, only me,
Whakatau!

A man of no rank,
A man of no notice,
A demon, a despised thing,
A poor young fellow, an eater of servants' scraps!
But,—concerning my war-belt, ha!
My war-belt which was dreaded,
Behold it now!
Fittingly and securely fixed.
It was carefully and fitly woven in the house,
Over which was sung while weaving
The mournful lament of sisters!
Lo! the favourable wind arises;
I hear it; I feel it.
The strong north wind blows,
I feel it encircling.
My foes are already hiding through fear!
Enclose me around, O Space!
O Space and Air encircle me!
O Sky encircle me!
Who am now here, engaged
In girding on the war-belt of the warrior.
I shall stand—as a rainbow,
Girt with the war-belt of the warrior.
Lo! the lightning flashes—it flashes!
The war-belt is rough as the sharp spines of the sea hedgehog;—
Dreadfully hated it is!
This war-belt, whose fame carries fear and hiding;
Whose great fame is everywhere known.
Do you still ask, "What is this war-belt?"
A war-belt of wrath!
A war-belt of flaming rage!
A war-belt that destroys and eats up its foes!
Now you know. Hurrah!

## TAUNT SUNG TO THE IMPALED HEAD OF AN ENEMY CHIEF (CA. 1820)[24]

Farewell, e koro,
Where are your friends?
Let them all see you
Standing over Waiwhetu.

Bare your lips, koro.
Well may you grin,
But be careful, lest your feet
Bring you back too soon.

I have no more blood
For you to drink.
I am done, I can no longer
Honour your great name.

Were this cooking-stone
Your brain—
I would eat it,
And it would taste good, koro.

Who will mourn,
Who will sing your fame
To the world?

Perhaps the mist that sits
On Tirohanga,
Perhaps the mist
Gathering on Kaihinu.
Yes. Better leave it at that, koro.

[24] By Paenga-Huru of Ngati-Tawa.

## SONG OF REVENGE

O the saltness of my mouth
In drinking the liquid brains of Nuku
Whence welled up his wrath!
His ears which heard the deliberations!
Tutepakihirangi shall go headlong
Into the stomach of Hinewai!
My teeth shall devour Kaukau!
The three hundred and forty of Te Kiri-kowhatu
Shall be huddled in a heap in my trough!
Te Hika and his multitudes shall boil in my pot!
The whole tribe of Ngaitahu shall be
My sweet morsel to finish with! E!

## A JOYOUS REVELLING SONG SUNG BY THE WOOD RATS

*First rat:*
Oh, Rat, O! let us two descend the tree.

*Second rat:*
Why should we two go down below?

*First rat:*
To gather up nice baits for us to eat.

*Second rat:*
What are those nice baits?

*First rat:*
The sweet ripe fruits of the pine trees.

*Second, or third, rat:*
Fudge! I am just come up from below, O my friends!
And down there is the fear and trembling, my friends;
The springbolt of the set snare resounds with a click!
My neck is caught and held fast;
I can only then squeak, *Torete! torete!*
Be assured that I will not go down below,
Seeking those nice baits; alas! no, no!

## CHORAL SONGS

### I

Your body is at Waitemata,
But your spirit came here
And roused me from my sleep.

### II

The sun is setting in his cave,
Touching as he descends
The land where dwells my mate—
He who is whirled away to
The southern waves.

### III

I don't like the habits of woman.
When she goes out—
She *kuikuis,*
She *koakoas,*
She chatters.
The very ground is terrified,
And the rats run away.
Just so.

## A LAMENT FOR HIS OWN LAND [25]

O ye waters of Honipaka,
From you, alas, I now depart,
But my spirit still clings
To that cloud floating
Thither from Te Motu,
Which remains there, my fate unheeding.
I now sorrowfully forsake my cherished land:
Unexpected indeed is this our parting;
A tribute now I render to my forsaken people,

[25] By Te Rauparaha. When Te Rauparaha reached Moeatoa in flight after the defeat of his people and their allies the Te Atiawa, he saw a cloudbank in the direction of the land where he had grown up, and thereupon sang this lament.

Who lie there in their last long sleep.
The tides will forever ebb and flow,
Lamenting as they flow o'er Te Kawau at Muriwhenua.
A fugitive in hasty flight am I,
Leaving there, a cherished bird forever;
Held captive within the house and in this summer weather.
Let the House of Mourning,
Let the House of Atiawa,
Lament and deluge with tears
This grave of all my sorrows.

## IHUNUI'S LAMENT FOR HER DAUGHTER RANGI[26]

Oppressed am I with omens and their signs,
Perturbing to my mind.
Who indeed are you who thus afflicts me?
Causing with warning vague and formless fear
This restlessness within me?
And was it you, indeed, O cherished one,—
Who would have thought that you would go, O Rangi!
Weariness my body bends, as I,
Here, in Puhirangi sit
Looking lornly forth on Hine-moana
Surging unrestrainedly beyond the headlands.
But you have gone, borne on the ocean stream
To distant Tawhiti-nui, to Tawhiti-pamamao,
To Te Hono-i-wairua on Irihia.
Fare safely on, and enter Hawaiki-rangi;
Seize as it passes that uplifting wind
Upon which Tane of old ascended
To Tikitiki-o-rangi.
That you too may enter Te Rauroha,
To be welcomed by spirit maids in Rangiatea;
There shall remembrance of this world cease,
O maid,—Alas!

---

[26] "Composed about four hundred years ago" (E. Best, as cited, p. 109. See Sources and Permissions).

## LAMENT FOR
## THE CHIEF
## TE KANI-A-TAKIRAU
## (DIED 1856)

My plume of heron's feathers!
My sprig of sweet-scented maurea!
Now dead and gone,
Beyond the lakes,
My cloud-like one!
It was he who broke their power,
It was he who urged on
To arise in war.

## DIRGE FOR A CHIEF

Alas, the bitter pain that gnaws within
For the wrecked canoe, for a friend who is lost.
My precious heron plume is cast on Ocean's strand,
And the lightning, flashing in the heavens,
Salutes the dead.

Where is authority in this world, since thou hast passed
By the slippery path, the sliding path to death?

Lone stands Whakaahu mountain in the distance,
For thou art gone, the shelter of thy people.
Flown has my singing bird that sang of ancient learning,
The keel of Tainui, the plug of Aotea,
Now bewailed by women's flowing tears.

Beautiful lies thy body in thy dogskin tasseled cloak,
But thy spirit has passed like a drifting cloud in the heavens.
All is well with thee who liest in state on chieftain's bier.
Ah, my precious green jade jewel, emblem of departed warriors!
The dragon emerged from his rocky fastness
And sleeps in the house of death.

*Tainui, Aotea:* legendary canoes.

## SONG OF A WIDOW FOR HER DEAD HUSBAND

After the evening hours
I recline upon my bed.
Your own spirit-like form
Comes towards me,
Creeping stealthily along.
Alas! I mistake,
Thinking you are here with me,
Enjoying the light of day.
Then the affectionate remembrances
Of the many days of old
Keep on rising within my heart.
This, however, loved one—
This you must do,
Recite the potent call to Rakahua,
And the strong cry to Rikiriki
That you may return.
For you were ever more than an ordinary husband;
You were my best beloved, my chosen,
My treasured possession. Alas!

## LAMENT

I silent sit as throbs my heart
    For my children;
And those who look on me
As now I bow my head
May deem me but a forest tree
    From distant land.
I bow my head
As droops the tree-fern,
And weep for my children.
O my child! so often called,
"Come O my child!"
Gone! Yes with the mighty flood,
I lonely sit midst noise and crowd,
My life ebbs fast.

## SONG BY AN UNNAMED POETESS

Love does not torment for ever.

It came on me like the fire which rages sometimes at Hukanui. If this beloved one is near me, do not suppose, O Kiri, that my sleep is sweet. I lie awake the live-long night, for love to prey on me in secret.

It shall never be confessed, lest it be heard of by all. The only evidence shall be seen on my cheeks.

The plain which extends to Tauwhare: that path I trod that I might enter the house of Rawhirawhi. Do not be angry with me, O madam; I am only a stranger. For you there is the body of your husband. For me there remains only the shadow of desire.

## A SONG FOR TE MOANA-PAPAKU [27]

Always the spirit of the loved one of Karanga,
Visits me ere I fall asleep;
And I arise in haste thinking the vision was in this world.
Me thought, O Moa', one could forget;
'Twas you who brought gifts of mountain food
From Pirongia afar. From there clearly
I would see the waves curl and break
At the headlands of Honipaka by the sea,
Where once there stood the ranks of Ati-Toa; thoughts these which
    comfort me.

## SONG OF A GIRL
## ABANDONED BY HER
## LOVER

Look where the mist
Hangs over Pukehina,
There is the path
By which went my love.

*Rawhirawhi:* her lover.    *Do not be angry,* etc.: addressed to Rawhirawhi's wife.

[27] By the poetess Topeora.

*Karanga:* another name of Topeora.

Turn back again hither
That may be poured out
Tears from

My eyes. It was not I
Who first spoke of love.
You it was who made advances
To me when but a little thing.

Therefore was my heart made wild.

This is my farewell of love to thee.


## THE SOLILOQUY OF AN INVALID [28]

### 1

Ebb then, oh tide,
Withdrawing swiftly outwards,
While here above I gaze down
On the open porches at Mihimarino;
Which place I was wont to ascend
In days that are gone by.

### 2

Sing your song, oh cicada;
You are in like case with me.
For I am as the bittern in the swamp,
Or the parrot, making its choking sound.

### 3

I look and see the star Tawera
Swimming towards the shore.
Hasten to keep vigil
With me, who am distraught,
Reeling about as one demented
Or drunken with liquor;
Like pollen carried on the wind
Or the perehia wafted afar.

[28] By Harata Tangikuku.

4

I look down and regard myself,
See how twisted are the sinews;
For food does not sustain me,
But seems to pass outside my skin.
So let me remain empty,
Like the porous seaweed on the shore.

*Moriori*    CHATHAM ISLANDS

## INCANTATION USED BY RANGITOKONA TO CREATE MAN

Stem heaped up, heaped, heaped up;
stem gathered together, gathered, gathered together;
heap it in the stem of the tree,
heap it in the foundation of the tree,
heap it in the fibrous roots of the tree,
heap it in the butt of the tree,
heap it in the root of the tree;
heap it, it grows;
heap it, it lives;
the heaven lives, e!
Stem heaped up, stem heaped up;
let the heaven stand which lives.
Heap it in the flower of the tree,
heap it in the leaf of the tree,
heap it in the swaying of the tree,
heap it in the waving of the tree,
heap it in the pattern of the tree,
heap it in the finishing of the tree;
heap it, it grows;
heap it, it lives;
the heaven lives, e!
Stem heaped up, stem heaped up, let the heaven stand which lives.

# ASIA

# Northern Siberia

## *Eskimo*

### SONGS

#### I

My heart longs only for that place, for that aunt of mine, who is always singing.

#### II

At the cape of Unisak, at the pretty one, O girls! I learned a song, good for singing, a pretty one. The steamboats were already coming.

At the cape of Unisak, at the pretty one, O boys! I learned a song, good for singing, a pretty one. O boys! You are my assistants in singing, you never refuse. My heart yearns for King Island, for the woman Acaka.

#### III

I found here for myself a woman. She walks much in an overcoat of calico. She is a ruddy one, she is a pretty one.

## *Chukchee*

### SONGS

#### I

From what country is that traveller, who is being drawn by dogs? On his way returning he came to be without a whip. Then I will make haste and walk onwards. Then I will make haste and walk to the song. Truly, let us be joyful!

II

By whom was I born? I was born by the little mother. But for what was I born?

## INCANTATION USED BY A JEALOUS WOMAN AGAINST HER RIVAL

Then you are this woman! You have so much of my husband's love that he begins to lose all liking for me. But you are not a human being! I make you into carrion lying on the pebbly shore,—old carrion inflated with rottenness. I make my husband into a big bear. The bear comes from a distant land. He is very hungry; he has been starving for a long time. He sees the carrion; seeing it, he eats of it. After a while he vomits it out. I make you into the stuff vomited. My husband sees you, and says, "I do not want it!" My husband takes to despising you.

I, who was till now neglected, I turn myself back towards him; I make myself into a deadly pain for him. Let him be attracted by the smell from here, and have desire for me. If I reject him, let him be still more insistent!

### *Reindeer Koryak*

### PRAYER TO THE SEA
[At the sacrifice of a reindeer]

To the sea I offer a reindeer; yet thou art our mother. If thou wilt not look, how shall we live?

### PRAYER TO THE CREATOR
[Sung while beating a drum]

You said to us, "Make a drum." Now let us live well, keep alive also the reindeer, and after our death grant good living to our children.

**Yukagir**

## SHAMAN'S ADDRESS TO HIS SPIRITS

You, owners of the green and trees, help me,
Sea mother, who has as cover seven snow mounds,
As bed, eight ice layers,
As collar, black foxes,
As foam, arctic foxes,
As waves, cub foxes.
Help me, sea-mother-owner.

## SONGS

### I   *Girl's Song*

When our camps separated
I looked after him
He is tall like a mountain ash
His hair covered his shoulders
Like black squirrels' tails.
When he disappeared
I lay down in the tent.
Oh, how long is a spring day?
But the evening came
And through a hole in the tent cover
I saw my love coming
When he came in
And looked at me
My heart melted
Like snow in the sun.

### II   *Love Song*

There stood a handsome fir
Vasya felled it there,
Meadow green was their bed,

Moving clouds their coverlet
Soft bush of a willow
Served them as a pillow
And the firmament
Was their upper tent.

## *Yakut*

## CEREMONIAL CHANT OF A SHAMAN

Mighty bull of the earth . . . Horse of the steppes!
I, the mighty bull . . . bellow!
I, the horse of the steppes . . . neigh!
I, the man set above all other beings!
I, the man most gifted of all!
I, the man created by the master all-powerful!
Horse of the steppes, appear! teach me!
Enchanted bull of the earth, appear! speak to me!
Powerful master, command me!
All of you, who will go with me, give heed with your ears! Those whom
    I command not, follow me not!
Approach not nearer than is permitted! Look intently! Give heed!
    Have a care!
Look heedfully! Do this, all of you . . . all together . . . all, however
    many you may be!
Thou of the left side, O lady with thy staff, if anything be done amiss,
    if I take not the right way, I entreat you—correct me! Command! . . .
My errors and my path show to me! O mother mine! Wing thy free
    flight! Pave my wide roadway!
Souls of the sun, mothers of the sun, living in the south, in the nine
    wooded hills, ye who shall be jealous . . . I adjure you all . . . let
    them stay . . . let your three shadows stand high!
In the east, on your mountain, lord, grandsire of mine, great of power
    and thick of neck—be thou with me!
And thou, grey-bearded wizard fire, I ask thee: with all my dreams,
    with all comply! To all my desires consent . . . Heed all! Fulfil all! . . .
    All heed . . . All fulfil!

*Vasya:* name of the composer of the song.

**Vogul**

## DANCE SONG[1]

Three sheldrake hunters
betrothed us to each other,
three sheldrake hunters
brought us together.
Why should I not have worked so hard in my father's house?
Now I dress in my best,
sit down in the boat.
You go around the point, I will come across it!
When we meet
we will trample down
three fields of dry grass,
three fields of green grass.

[1] Danced at a bear festival; the speaker, played by a man, is a girl about to run away with her lover.

# Central Asia

**Altaian**   ALTAI REGION, SIBERIA

## CEREMONIAL CHANTS OF
## A SHAMAN

### 1

Accept this, O Kaira Khan!
Master of the tambourine with six horns,
Draw near with the sound of the bell!
When I cry 'Chokk'! make obeisance!
When I cry 'Mé'! accept this!

### 2

Gifts that no horse can carry—
  Alás! Alás! Alás!
Gifts that no man can lift—
  Alás! Alás! Alás!
Garments with triple collar—
Turn them thrice before thine eyes,
Let them be a cover for the steed,
  Alás! Alás! Alás!
Prince Yulgen full of gladness!
  Alás! Alás! Alás!

### 3

Birds of Heaven, the five Merkyuts!
Ye with mighty talons of brass,
Of copper is the moon's claw,
And of ice its beak;

Mightily flap the spreading wings,
Like to a fan is the long tail;
The left wing veils the moon
And the right obscures the sun.
Thou, mother of nine eagles,
Turning not aside, thou fliest over Yaik,
Over Edil thou weariest not!
Draw nigh with song!
Lightly draw nigh to my right eye,
Of my right shoulder make thou thy resting-place!

4

Lord, to whom three stairways lead,
Bai-Yulgen, possessor of three flocks,
The blue vault which has appeared,
The blue sky that shows itself,
The blue cloud that whirls along,
The blue sky so hard to reach,
Land a year's journey distant from water,
Father Yulgen thrice exalted,
Shunned by the edge of the moon's axe,
Thou who usest the hoof of the horse;
O Yulgen, thou hast created all men
Who are stirring round about us.
Thou, Yulgen, hast bestowed all cattle upon us,
Let us not fall into sorrow!
Grant that we may withstand the evil one!
Let us not behold Kermes,
Deliver us not into his hands!
Thou who a thousand thousand times
The starry sky hast turned,
Condemn me not for sin!

*Kermes:* the evil spirit that attends man.

## *Altaian and Teleut*    ALTAI REGION, SIBERIA

### IMPROVISED SONGS

#### I

Strewing leaves like gold,
Is it the white birch? Yes, it is.
Hair hanging down her back,
Is it my wife? Yes, it is.

Strewing leaves like silver,
Is it the blue birch? Yes, it is.
Hair hanging down her neck,
Is it my bride? Yes, it is.

#### II

This coat of mine, made of new cloth,
What good will it do on rainy days?
This herd that I have labored to get together,
What good will it do on the day that must come?

This coat of mine, made of old cloth,
What good will it do in dewy weather?
This herd that I have worked to get together,
What good will it do on the day when I must pass over?

#### III

My seven-year-old bay horse
Felt homesick and whinnied,
The old man of seventy
Thought of earlier joys and grieved.

My six-year-old white horse
Thought of the Altai and neighed,
The old man of sixty
Thought of earlier joys and grieved.

**Teleut**    ALTAI REGION, SIBERIA

## PRAISE SONG OF
## THE WIND

Trees with weak roots
I will strike, I the wind.
I will roar, I will whistle.

Haycocks built today
I will scatter, I the wind.
I will roar, I will whistle.

Badly made haycocks
I will carry off, I the wind.
I will roar, I will whistle.

Uncovered stacks of sheaves
I will soak through, I the wind.
I will roar, I will whistle.

Houses not tightly roofed
I will destroy, I the wind.
I will roar, I will whistle.

Hay piled in sheds
I will tear apart, I the wind.
I will roar, I will whistle.

Fire kindled in the road
I will set flickering, I the wind.
I will roar, I will whistle.

Houses with bad smoke-holes
I will shake, I the wind.
I will roar, I will whistle.

The farmer who does not think
I will make to think, I the wind.
I will roar, I will whistle.

The worthless slug-a-bed
I will wake, I the wind.
I will roar, I will whistle.


**Kysyl**   SOUTHERN SIBERIA


## SONGS

### I

If the ram's horns did not fall off,
They would grow till they reached the sky,
If men did not die,
The earth would not hold them.

If the elk's horns did not fall off,
They would grow till they reached the clouds,
If people did not die,
The earth would not hold them.

### II   *Wedding Song*

The cloudy sky darkens,
My father's country is full of delights,
My beautiful body is small,
You girl whom God has given me, bare your bosom.

The clear sky is bright,
My father's country is full of delights,
My white body is small,
You girl whom the Creator has given me, bare your bosom.

**Kirgiz**     KIRGIZSTAN

## THE KALMYK MOURNS FOR HIS COUNTRY

Dear, dear mountains,
Mountains that brought me good,
Mountains where my three ancestors lived,
Mountains where three thousand head of cattle grew up,
Kazylyk, where Bajan Aul is,
Your road is scored deep
Where we wandered in summer,
There you are still, black road,
Trodden to the bone.
When we overwintered in winter
You became smooth again . . .
You lid to my kettle!
You mallet to hammer in a colt's tether,
You my noose to catch horses,
You stake to support my house,
Dear, dear mountains!
Mountains that brought me good,
Mountains that were a son-in-law to my father,
Mountains that were a daughter-in-law to my mother,
I never thought to leave this place.
Mountains that lie crowded all about,
Flat salt-steppe,
There the many-colored herds of horses lay,
You great, great stones,
Tears run from my eyes,
My one-year-old she-goats have borne no kids,
The young lambs did not remain unfruitful,
Where the big yelping dogs
Barked in the yard, my mountains,
Now we go away.
We go to find misfortune,
We know nothing of farming,
We shall die of hunger.

**Buryat**   RUSSIAN MONGOLIA

## SONG FOR THE ARRIVAL OF THE GUESTS AND THE BRIDE AT THE BRIDEGROOM'S DOOR

The swallow's young are pleased with the grass of the marsh; the sons of the Buryat father are pleased with this happy people!

A captured kite would be content with herbs from the mountains; the handsome bridegroom is content with his bride!

Our well-fed spotted dog will not bark; our respected guests will not be angry over jesting.

Our bay colt will not run far from its trotting mother; our foolish little son will not run away from the mother of his bride!


**Mongol**   MONGOLIA

## SHAMAN'S CHANT AT A WEDDING

Mother Ut,
Queen of Fire,
Thou who wert created from the elm-tree that grows on the peaks of
    Changgai-shan and Burchatu-shan,
Thou who didst appear when heaven and earth were separated, who
    camest forth from the footsteps of Mother Earth and wast formed by
    kings or gods.
Mother Ut, whose father is hard steel, whose mother is flint, whose
    ancestors were the elm-tree, whose brightness reaches the sky and
    fills the earth.
Goddess Ut, to whom we bring yellow oil as a sacrifice and a white
    ram with a yellow head,
Thou who hast a sturdy son, a beautiful daughter-in-law, and a shining
    daughter.
To thee, Mother Ut, who always lookest upward, we bring spirits in
    cups and fat in both hands.
Grant well-being to this prince and princess and to all this people.

*Prince and princess:* the bridegroom and the bride.

**Mongol**    WESTERN MONGOLIA

## SONGS

### I

I have the shade of dense firs
At the foot of high forests.
Summer of the distant plains,
Come back to us one day!

I have the shade of scented pines
At the foot of silent peaks.
Sun of the distant plains,
Come back to us one day!

I have the shade of silver aspens
Beside clear streams.
Moss and grass of the distant plains,
Come back to us one day!

### II  *Lullaby: Complaint of the Wild Goose*

We were nine to leave the lake in the north;
Of the nine travelers, I am the last.
Noble hunting falcon, have pity on me.

My country is far; the winds are contrary;
My wings grown heavy, I followed behind, alone.
Noble hunting falcon, have pity on me.

The leaders are at the nest, the stragglers are passing the halting-place;
Winter is coming, the sky is clouded.
Noble hunting falcon, have pity on me.

The sky is clouded, the snows are coming;
I hear my brothers calling me in the fog.
Noble hunting falcon, have pity on me.

The sky is gray, the winds rise;
I hear my brothers flying on through the fog.
Noble hunting falcon, have pity on me.

# Afghanistan
# Pakistan
# Kashmir

**Afghan**　AFGHANISTAN

## COUPLETS

### I

If you would see me, come quickly;
The shroud of separation is wrapped about me.

### II

I had never known sorrow;
Now it is a field I have inherited, and I till it.

**Baloch**　PAKISTAN

## *DASTANGHS*[2]

### I

The storm-clouds have thundered,
The whole camp moves away

---

[2] "The *dastangh* is a short poem of a few lines, only intended to be sung to the accompaniment of the flute" (M. L. Dames, as cited, Vol. I, p. 184. See Sources and Permissions).

And halts at Zangi's well.
Come and let our hearts meet.
They have chosen a new camping-ground,
And made their abode on Gendhari.

II

My riding is on swift mares,
My love is by the green water-springs;
For a short moment I will sit there,
I will look upon her wandering face,
I will put an end to the black delay.

## Pathan     PAKISTAN

## *DA-KUDRAT SANDRE* (SONGS OF NATURE)

I

How gracious is Allah on the black mountains;
Snow he showers on their heads and makes the flowers blossom all
  around them.

II

O my heart is like a mountain-spring.
Parrots of all lands come and delight in its water.

III

O my body is a river with my heart as its shell,
O like a pearl do I bring up the thoughts of my beloved.

---

*Gendhari:* a mountain in the Mazari country.

## *Ladakhi*    KASHMIR

### SONGS

#### I

The high ones live in high places.
Into all the heights of the sky
Besides the king of birds none flies.
During the three summer months, whatever can bloom, blooms.
Except in the three summer months, oh, there are no flowers.
I, the girl, do not belong to my mother.
In this one life-time, whatever can be happy, is happy.
Enjoy this one life-time as ever you can enjoy it.

#### II

On the meadow, on the upper meadow,
On the upper meadow there is a flower in bloom.
Halla, my boy!
A flower of very fine shape is in bloom there, my boy!
Gather the flower, my boy!
Gather the well-shaped flower!
If you gather it with your hand, it will fade.
Gather it with your soul and keep it in your mind!
Gather it with your soul and keep it in your mind!

#### III    *Song at the Kesar Festival*

On the height of the Sarican Pass
Black clouds are gathering
On the height of the Sarican Pass
Torn clouds are gathering.
In the middle of the black clouds
Lightning flashes from our good Lord's sword.
In the middle of the black clouds
Lightning flashes from the godly King Kesar's sword.

# India

**Bhil**  CENTRAL INDIA; MAIWAR

## SONG FOR A FEAST OF KRISHNA

At my pen gate stands a fig-tree.
A bird is fluting from one of its branches,
*Zire, zire.*
Flee, flee, O bird,
Mahadeo is coming from the sky today.
Today the flute sounds *zire, zire.*
If I knew that the Great God were coming
I would make ready two, four water-pipes.
The flute sounds *zire, zire.*
If I knew that the Great God were coming
I would light two, four lamps.
The flute sounds *zire, zire.*
If I knew that the Great God were coming
I would pound rice, two, four measures.
The flute sounds *zire, zire.*

## BRIDE'S SONG ON THE WAY TO HER HUSBAND'S HOUSE

The she-starling calls from the tree: Whither are you going so
  inopportunely?
Tarry, o my sister, tarry but a few days.
I will not tarry, o my brother, for my sister-in-law would torment me.
O sister with children in your arms, to what house are you going?
My father has sold me and eaten up the money.

I go to his house between the hills, where the bamboo rustles.
Where the panther roars among the bamboo canes and the bears call
    from the foot of the mountains.

## SONG OF A WOMAN TO HER LOVER

Go, O man, to Abu.
Going up Abu, my limbs tremble.
In bathing in the Naki Lake, I forgot my hair ribbon and comb, oh
    friend!
I have forgotten my ribbon and comb, my friend.
Oh friend, God has made us a perfect pair.
We will go to a far-off place, oh friend.
Oh man, let us leave my vile husband.
Come, go to another land, come, oh man.
Give my husband poison, oh man, and come away.
Come to a distant land, come oh man.

**Gond**    CENTRAL INDIA; MAIKAL HILLS; CHHATTISGARH

## DANCE SONGS

### I

O come, my love, come home with me and sleep.
How can we spend the night of God in empty dance and song?
Whose is that bed, whose is that spacious bed?
Come, rest, my love, the time for sleep draws near.
O come, my love, come home with me and sleep.

*His house:* the bridegroom's house.

II

He is cutting bamboo in the forest,
He has an order for it.
My life is alone in the forest,
And he is not afraid.

III

In the secret place of the forest,
I am going to capture you,
For your body is wonderful to me.

IV

Your body might have come from the loins of a prince.
Lovely are you as the milky heart of a coconut.
Your body captures the mind with its beauty,
And my life lives within your life.
In the dark clouds there are nine lacs of stars:
The sun and the moon have begun to sink,
And you have come instead as moon of the earth.

V

The bed says to the carpenter, Do not make me,
For if you do, to-morrow or the day after, they will carry you upon me
  to your grave.
And there will be no one to help you.

The pick says to its proud maker,
Do not make me, for to-morrow or the day after, they will use me to
  dig your grave,
And there will be no one to help you.

The cloth says to the weaver,
Do not weave me, for to-morrow or the day after, I will be your shroud.
And there will be no one to help you.

## MEN'S STICK-DANCE SONGS

### I

Every bullet falls tapak tapak,
Like a stone in water.
The arrows shoot into the sky.
Guns, nine yard long, are roaring,
The swords rise and fall.

### II

The panther roars on the mountain,
The tiger roars in the forest,
The king roars on his throne,
With sword and shield in hand.

## SONGS SUNG BY WOODCUTTERS OR WORKERS IN THE FIELDS

### I

On every side I see nothing but the trees of the forest,
And you are alone, standing by the well.

### II

You are like a cloud
That wanders in the sky.
If you really loved me
You would sleep close beside my heart.

### III

Under the leaf of a tendu tree
I found a fruit.
In your fair body
Is all my hope.

IV

Through a broken basket you can see the sun:
Through the window of the house you can see his whore.

V

Wash off the kazal from your eyes
And weep, remembering us.


## WOMEN'S DANCE SONG

*Ri rina wo rina ri ri nawo rina*
Life of my mind, where have you gone to fight?
I change my rings from toe to toe
*Khelo khelo khelo*
But my bed is lonely
*Jhelo jhelo jhelo*
Life of my mind, where have you gone?
I said, Don't go, but you would go
*Khelo khelo khelo*
I change my anklets from foot to foot
*Jhelo jhelo jhelo*
And change them back again
But my bed is lonely
*Khelo khelo khelo*
*Jhelo jhelo jhelo*


## SONGS AND DANCE SONGS

I

Blossoms the rose
Its music fills the world
And in your face there's a flower
While in the garden of your bed
Blossoms the rose.

II

Only with a rope can you draw water from a well
I told you "Don't don't." But now I am pregnant.

### III

In the Urai jungle the rain comes in torrents
If you would enjoy yourself it must be before you're married.

### IV

She was but a cubit tall
Today the sugar-cane is high as a man
With his hands above his head
She was my friend from childhood
And I have made her wise in love.

### V

There is white water on the hill
How suddenly
As I was drawing water
He made me his bed.

### VI   *Song of an Old Man*

How young I was
When I planted the mango
And the tamarind
And still their leaves are full of life
But there is none in my old body.


## FERTILITY

O Mother, do not again give me a woman's birth
From the beginning there is great suffering for women
O Mother, in the shadow of the twelfth year
My head was found defiled and soon I was pregnant
The first month is over, Mother
The blood gathers drop by drop
The second month is over, Mother
In the shadow of the third month
My body is yellow as haldi
And I long for buttermilk
My hands and feet are heavy as earth

I cannot bear the sun
O Mother, do not again give me a woman's birth
The fourth month is over, Mother
In the fifth month the life comes *phud phud*
My body feels lighter than before
In the shadow of the sixth month
My body begins to look big
My mind thinks, what shall I eat
And what shall I avoid?
But to no one can I tell my desire
The seventh month is over, Mother
The child born in the seventh month
Can hardly live
The child born in the eighth month
Is sure to die
Under the shadow of the ninth month
The children of all the world are born.


## SONG

The moon rises
Stealing the sun's light
Between her thighs
The man steals the nectar
Between her thighs.


**Pardhan**    CENTRAL INDIA; UPPER NARBODA VALLEY;
HYDERABAD


## DANCE SONGS

### I

I am looking out of my house;
The sun is but a bamboo's length above the hills.
Where can you go now it is grown so late?

Leaf of the plaintain, lover in whom my heart is wound,
Like a dry leaf in the wind,
You are ever blown to and fro away from me.
Where can you go now it has grown so late?

II

As I was going along the road, a thorn ran into my foot.
But since it was for love of you that I came,
I cared not for the thorn.

III

It is growing lighter: we can see the fields.
The hour of parting has come.
My heart is full of anger against the dawn.
For in this field we must part from one another.
Now home will be no longer home to me,
The forest is no more a forest.
I will be restless in the village where I found rest till now.
But part we must, for our enemy the dawn has come.

DIRGE

My son, while you lived I was a queen
For you lay between my breasts
As on a royal throne.
But now you are dead
I must lay you
In the hard ground.

SONGS

I

My singer,
From that earthen drum
What sweet music you bring.
From the earthen drum of my body

Who can bring such music
As you, my singer?
Take, take me in your arms,
Sling me about your neck,
Play on me, on my body
Till I give the drum's sweet note.


II

Buy a beautiful sari
For the beautiful body you love,
I will wear it
And my body will be more beautiful
In your eyes.
I will wear it
While my body lasts;
Tomorrow when my body is cold
It will wear the earth
On which you tread.
Buy a sari while you can
For the body you love.


III

O lover wake!
Your bed sparkles with diamonds.
In their light look at me.
Let your eyes shine when you see me.
You must climb the steep hills,
Beyond which lie the joys of life.
Come climb them quickly,
And as you descend exhausted,
Lie beside me, and with my soft hands
That you adore
I will soothe your tired limbs,
With my soft hands.
I have sung Karma songs
As the line of dancers swayed under the moon.
I have sung Dadaria songs
As the girls picked mangoes in the forest.
With many a lovely girl

I have conversed in song,
But I have not known love
Till I met you today.

### IV

Why will she not
Join her dark eyes to mine?
I go round and round her
With my drum hungrily.
I gaze at her
As the line circles round.
Why will she not
Join her dark eyes to mine?
As she comes towards me dancing
I press my foot on hers.
I squat with my drum,
My eyes on her fair face.
But she avoids my eyes,
She has eyes for everyone but me.
I press my drum against her,
I press my free hands against her breasts,
I swing and leap and press my hands
Against her breasts.
Why will she not
Join her dark eyes to mine?
Unless she looks at me,
The thunder of the drums, the song
Is like the croak of frogs,
The altercation of a flight of crows.
Why will she not
Join her dark eyes to mine?


## THE BIRTH OF THE GODDESS JANGU BAI[3]

. . . On the isle Kaiabhandar dwelt the god Sardur,
His son was the god Kosejartar: what did he say?

---

*Karma songs:* dance songs.     *Dadaria songs:* songs for one singer.
[3] Part of a long poem on the mythical origin of the Gonds.

"Worms and ants have their mates, I am without.
To ask for the reason I'll go to god Shembu."
He made himself ready, saddled his winged steed.
A Thursday it was; he mounted the flying horse,
Rode on the wings of a raging storm,
Hills were upturned, and trees were derooted,
The stones on the ground flew into the air.
From Mount Dhauragiri, god Shembu saw him
Saw Kosejartar cross sphere after sphere,
Ere he reached the mount Dhauragiri.
So great was his force that it shook the mount Dhauragiri
Where fifty-six crores of gods were seated in council;
When the mount shook, they pressed round god Shembu:
"Who is this powerful god, who is coming to see us?"
Abruptly in mid-air halted the horse, Kosejartar dismounted,
Bowed to the gods and greeted them "Ram, Ram."
Bhagawan blessed him; "Ram, Ram" bade the assembly,
Then Bhagawan turned to the god Kosejartar:
"Leaving your throne on the isle Kaiabhandar, why have you come?"
"In search of a mate I have come.
Sparrows and larks are in pairs,
Worms and ants are in pairs,
Why should I live alone? Without a mate
How shall I further my line?" Thus he questioned.
Bhagawan called the four Brahmadevas, told them to bring
The book seven yards long and as broad as the sky,
The book of men about to be born, the silvery book.
"Look in your book and tell Kosejartar where is his mate."
The Brahmadevas opened the book and started to search.
From morning twelve hours passed, but nothing they found;
Dusk was coming; lighting their lamps they continued to search,
But still found nothing; midnight passed, yet in vain was the search,
Again next day they went on searching from morning till noon,
Another day passed, three days and four days passed in searching,
At last, on the fifth day they found the word and announced:
"Where the sky meets the water, there on the water's surface
Is Jara Dip with fourteen palm trees, there water rises;
A girl, twelve years old, dances and plays on the spouting water,
In her winnowing fan she tosses pearls and golden mohurs,
Seraj Mahi her father, her mother the goddess Kankani,

Their daughter's name Surebhangral Jaramoti."

"Thus in the book is it written," so said Brahmadev to the god
  Kosejartar.

"If you will go, then depart; if not, then return to the isle Kaiabhandar.

That is your mate." — "Is this truth or a falsehood?" asked Kosejartar.

"My book does not lie." — "Well, then I will go,"

So said Kosejartar; he bade "Ram, Ram" and prostrated himself,

God Shembu gave him his blessing and told him to go.

He mounted the horse, it rose and took the way of the stars,

A rising cloud, a threatening storm,

Hidden he was from the girl,

His hands did not touch her, only his shadow fell on her,

Above her the horse stormed past,

Kosejartar rode on to the sea to bathe,

Washed away his desire, then took the road to Kaiabhandar.

Fire seized Surebhangral Jaramoti,

Fire burnt in her loins, fire ran through her body.

"Why does my body burn? Twelve years have I played

Yet never before has such a thing seized me.

Could I but see it, I would grasp it and throw it away.

Is it a god or a demon, a ghost or a ghostlike being?"

As she spoke, she gave birth to a girl. . . .


**Agaria**    CENTRAL PROVINCES


### SONG[4]


Hai Re! The train whistles, it is leaving Bilaspur.
In front is the train, behind is the signal.
The villagers leave their work and run to see it.
At every station the engine takes coal and water.
In front runs the wire to give the news.

[4] "The Agaria [iron-smelters and blacksmiths] are specially fascinated by trains
and no wonder, for here are iron and fire and coal combined in a gigantic moving
furnace. An Agaria who had actually travelled in a train—I only know one who has—
composed the following Karma song which was sung in the wilds of the Motinala
forest" (V. Elwin, as cited. See Sources and Permissions) .

Behind, we sit clutching our tickets in our hands.
In front goes the motor,
Behind goes the cycle.
Leaving their food, the children run to see.


**Baiga**    CENTRAL PROVINCES


## WOMEN'S DANCE SONG

Among the trees I'm playing on my flute.
But who careth for this poor forest-dweller?
No mother have I, nor brother, nor friend in all the world,
All day I'm making music on my flute.

Among the trees I'm playing on my flute.
A mother have I, and brother, and friends to eat with me,
But none of them can help this poor forest-dweller,
So all day long I play upon my flute.

In the shade of a creeper sits a man;
The scorpion bites him and he weeps—
Who careth for the dweller in the forest?
Among the trees I'm playing on my flute.


## DIALOGUE

*Girl*: Come, take your axe and we'll go to the jungle.
    Listen to my songs with your left ear.
*Boy*: I've come to the jungle for jamun-berries,
    O girl, they all say that you are a teacher of songs.
*Girl*: I've come to the jungle to find kerela.
    Tell me why you are sad, O friend.
*Boy*: I've come to the jungle for khamer-fruit.
    How I long for you! Come and sit with me.
*Girl*: I've come to the jungle to gather thorns.
    I weep with desire for a faithful lover.

*Boy*: I've come to the jungle to kill a wood-pigeon.
My love, I will leave everything for you.
*Girl*: Look, on that dry tree the monkeys are sitting.
O little brother, they all suspect us.
*Boy*: I've come to the jungle to dig for roots.
Don't be frightened, I'll pay a bullock for you.
*Girl*: O the mango in the valley and the creeper on the hill!
O love, come to me and I will hide you in my dress.
*Boy*: I've come to the jungle to gather leaves.
It is in our youth we must take delight.
*Girl*: O my love, come drink some water and enjoy me.
As much as anyone could enjoy in all their life-time.
*Boy*: I've come to the jungle to kill a porcupine.
We'll sleep together by the mango-tree.
Hold me so close that no air can pass between us.


SONGS AND DANCE SONGS

I

Her long hair is all scattered on the ground.
I am going to pick the flowers.
At sunset her hair is all scattered on the ground,
And I am going to pick the flowers.
At bed-time her hair is all scattered on the ground.
I have picked a lovely flower.


II

Long, long are the pumpkins!
They are milky and long.
He sleeps all night with me,
But in the day he calls me sister.
Often, often he plays with my firm breasts.
They are his playthings.


III

Honour to thee who made the moon.
There was none to help thee make it,
But only black clouds girt about with swords.

IV

In the morning my beautiful girl asks for her dress of the night before.
Time is passing, she says. Dress me in my flowered sari.

V

O love, come silent as a thief.
The door is shut, come silently.
I open it, come silently.
O love, you take me as a thief.

VI

Take me to some country that I have never seen
Where, O my love, the thunder roars,
Where, O my love, the lightning flickers,
And the rain pours down.

VII

In every lamp the wick longs for oil;
My eyes long for your bed.
My youthful heats desire the play of love.

VIII

In my garden is a well;
All round it hang the mangoes.
How deep and cool my well is.
But you are deeper far in love.
The sun beats down and you are thirsty,
But you care not for my water.
You know the deep love of the heart.

**Halba**    CHHATTISGARH

A REAPING SONG

I am going to reap the grain
But on the bank sits the wanton boy

While I am reaping
His eye catches mine
How can I go on reaping
If our eyes rob one another?
My husband beat me
He beat me at midnight
So I must be very careful
My handsome wanton takes my arm
He speaks sweetly to me
When the reaping is over
He will go away for ever
And in the world
There will be nothing more for me.

**Kamar**    CHHATTISGARH

## SONG

I caught the fish in the pool,
Tell me if you will eat it or not?
In a day or two I shall leave this kingdom,
Tell me, will you go with me or not?

## DANCE SONG

Tastefully did I cook the rice,
And came to you at midnight.
Alas! nowhere did I find you, my love!
For the rest of my life I will weep for you.

*Adibasis (Ho)*   KOLHAN, BIHAR

## FESTIVAL SONGS

### I

We have come to a lonely place,
Sweet breeze is blowing over us;
Will you come to my side,
Or shall I go to yours?
We have reached the midst of forest,
And the storm has come;
Will you go back to your village,
Or shall we search for a new one?

### II

When you are coming from the river,
When you are coming over the fields;
You are swinging like an ear of corn.

*Ahir*   BIHAR

## LAMENT

I fix my mind on God
Because he has made my cage
In the cage he has placed a *maina*
Ten doors has the cage
Bolted are nine and one is open
No one can say from where the cat will come
When God will let the *maina* fly
The mother will weep and beat her breast
The father will cry and strike his head
The wife will weep and tangle her hair
The neighbors will come and console her

And tell her "nothing is gained by crying
Who owned the *maina* has let it fly."
I shall never have a husband as handsome as you
In a moment God made the cage
In a moment he has made it desolate.


## DIALOGUE BETWEEN A NEWLY MARRIED COUPLE

"My father gave me my dress
And my father dyed it
Lie away from me, you fatherless boy
Or you will crumple it."
"My father gave me my turban
And my father dyed it
Lie away from me, you wanton girl
Or you will stain it with your scarlet."
"Had I known my husband was coming
I would have planted him a garden
Then you would have had shade to come in
And shade to go in
And your heart would have been calm
I would have tied my breasts in a black slip
And added bells to the ribbons
I would have washed my face with white earth
And piled my hair
I would have given a scarlet streak to the parting
With a whisker of barley."

*Maina:* a bird. The *maina* and the cage symbolize the relation of the body and the personality.

**Kayesth**   SHAHABAD DISTRICT, BIHAR

## SONG

Darling I am giving myself to you
Let go of the sari on my breasts
I will let it go
On the road where the motors pass
I will let it go
On the railway line
I will let it go
At the well where the women gather
I will let it go
In the garden where the flowers are planted
I will let it go
On the bed of your darling where lovers have their sport.

**Santal**   BIHAR

## FESTIVAL SONGS

### I

Elder sister, elder sister
Go out, O elder sister
The festival like an elephant has come
How shall we welcome it
How shall we receive it
Sister, O elder sister
How shall we bring it in?
With a glad heart
And a sound of joy
We shall open our hearts' door
And take it to our hearts.

## II

Sit down, stand up
O friends, we have no food or drink
But in the eyes' meeting there is pleasure.

## JUNGLE SONGS

### I

Yesterday we said
We will go out when the moon is up
The moon had gone half way
But O my love, I could not see you
It was the love of the milk tree
O my love
It was the love of the flowering tree
But still I was to come
When the moon had gone half way.

### II

On the mountain a crab
Rustles in the leaves
On the hill a crab
Slowly drags along
If I had seen my friend
I would have killed myself with running
I would have died from striking my brow
If I had seen my girl
How the lily would have burst into bud.

### III

In our court-yard is a white blossom
In my lover's court-yard is an akar-plant.
How shall I get to his court-yard?
I will pretend I went for flowers
But I will see my lover.

IV

O my love, your body is fullgrown
And I am still too young
You will damage my young body
O my love, do not catch at me
O my love, do not force me
If you force me, I shall weep
With your young body, O my love
You may cry and mourn
But I've seen your breasts
Poking from your dress
And I've caught them in my hands.

## MARRIAGE SONGS

I

O two white doves of the white mountain
What was your sorrow that you flew away?
It was the heat of the day
It was the dew in the night
It was the dew that made you fly away.

II

At the end of the street
The sound of violin and flute
To the spring I had gone for drawing water
Hearing and hearing,
Listening, listening at the spring
O friend, I left behind my pot of water.

III

In what a lovely way you flaunted
O you true one, how I loved and fondled you
My heart is a glass and I look at you in it
But how dimly I see you now.

## JUNGLE SONGS

### I

Under the bushes
Which two are struggling?
The girl has caught his chest
The boy is holding her breasts
Boy and girl, they rock together

### II

The first time
And she sobbed and sobbed
But in three days
She smiled and smiled.

### III

Under a tree by the rock
We spread a cloth and loved each other
Boy, it may only be for now
It may only be to-day.

### IV

Like a creeper falling
And water
Swilling from a cup
My friend went quickly away.

### V

Friend, we have left going
To the rice field in the jungle
They have given you a wife
They have found for me a husband
O my friend when we meet now
We must never flutter our eyebrows
Or show the teeth in our mouths.

# SONGS

### I

"O my love
My mind has broken
For the spring has ceased its flow"
In the gully by the plantain
Drink cups of medicine
Swallow down some pills
Like a black cow
That has never had a calf
You will again be neat and trim.

### II

In a lucky month
The child was born
And so my love
It did not live.

### III

Like a bone
Was the first child born
And the white ants have eaten it
O *juri,* do not weep
Oh do not mourn
We two are here
And the white ants have eaten it.

### IV

In the unploughed field beneath the palm tree
Uncle, what birds are hovering?
The kites and vultures hover
The child of an unmarried girl
They are tearing into shreds.

*Juri:* girl friend or boy friend.

**Birhor**     CHOTA NAGPUR

## DANCE SONG

Up above the sal-tree the children of the Moon!
Their silver nagera and mandal of gold
Played on with copper sticks how sweet at mid-day sound!

**Uraon**     CHOTA NAGPUR

## MARRIAGE POEMS

### I

Green is the paddy, mother, green is the paddy
Green is the paddy, mother, and the parrots cannot leave it
Whose house has a ripe daughter, mother
On to that house, mother, the mind fastens
Inside that house, mother, the mind revels.

### I I

Under the hills
From the clear springs the water flows
Water that the doves sip and the pigeons drink
In pairs they have come the wild geese
In pairs they have come
No. It is not the wild geese. It is not the doves
It is the girl the elder brother chose.

### I I I

Mother, for whom is the marriage bower?
Mother, for whom is this weeping?
For the son, mother, is the marriage bower
For the daughter, mother, is the weeping.

*The children of the Moon:* the stars.     *Nagera, mandal:* two varieties of drum.

IV

Wood, you are cutting wood, mother
But the shoots will not spring again
Will never spring again
My mind is dying in the rocky uplands
Never will the shoots spring again.

V

In the jungle the peacock cries
By the spring the parrot calls
Parrot, do not call; hawk, do not cry
As yours is my sorrow
As yours is my fortune.

## DANCE SONGS

I

*Juri,* leave me
My clothes are coming down
Are coming down
Let them come down, *juri*
Let them come down
We will dance the *bheja* naked
We will dance the *bheja* naked.

II

Come and visit us, brother
With your diamond girl
In the morning, brother
With your diamond girl.

III

From where are the black clouds rising?
Noise of the rain falling
Where is the rain falling?
In the east the clouds are massing
Noise of the rain falling

In the west the rain is falling
Whose is the red turban which the rain is wetting?
Noise of the rain falling
Whose is the long hair which the rain is wetting?
It is the red turban of the flirting boy which the rain is wetting
Noise of the rain falling
It is the long hair of the pale-skinned woman that the rain is wetting
Where shall I dry the red turban?
Noise of the rain falling
Where shall I dry the long hair?
I shall dry the red turban on the dead bushes
Noise of the rain falling
I shall dry the long hair in the body's core
Choose the cloth and tie the red turban
Noise of the rain falling
Comb and tie the long hair.

### IV

June and the human sacrificers stop me
July August and the rivers check me
Under the hills you married me, mother
From full eyes the tears drop.

### V

Come girl I say
It is muddy she answers
Come later, *juri,* she says
Come later
Lying we will lie
Sleeping we will sleep
Then we shall be happy.

### VI

Come closer, girl, in your dress with the coloured border
Without you there is no pleasure
Come closer, girl, come closer
The shining girl is coming.

### VII

I went to pick flowers, mother
But I am coming with an empty basket

When they will ask for flowers
What shall I offer them and
What shall I not?

### VIII

In the scattered clouds the stars show
In the grove the moon is drowned with stars
From the east a golden girl is coming
In the grove the stars have drowned the moon.

### IX

Girl, throw down your wood
My thirst is killing me
On the slope of the hill
I am dying from thirst.

### X

Bats, bats
Are you awake or asleep?
The bats hang in the trees
The cock has crowed
The dawn has broken
And the bats
Hang in the trees.

## *Bhattra*    BASTAR STATE

## SONGS

### I

White flower
There is none like you
From a great crowd
I choose you.

*Juri:* girl friend or boy friend.    *Bheja:* a dance in which the men and women form a mixed line.

II

O lovely girl
The flowers grow quickly
And we who once were small
Are ready now for love.

III

O girl with swaying hips
The plough goes straight across the field
And I will come for you
Who have hidden many days.


**Muria**    BASTAR STATE


### SONGS AT A WEDDING

I    *The Bride to the Head of the Ghotul*

O sirdar, when you came to the ghotul and found it dirty
With ashes and dust and no one had swept it,
You called for me and asked me whose fault it was.
The Kotwar and Kandki defended me,
But you said, We are not Maria that we should sleep in dirt,
And so you fined us.
Now I am going away and whom will you have to fine?
Daily I cleaned the ghotul,
But now who will clean it?
With you I used to play and dance,
But now my feet are bound, and I shall not meet you even in my
    dreams.
Who knows whether I shall find joy or sorrow in this stranger's house.
Sometimes I combed your hair and laughing rubbed your arms.
But sometimes I was tired and slept.
Then you all said, Why don't you comb our hair,
And massage our limbs today?
You must have been to someone, why don't you come to us today?
For this you punished us, turning us out, and saying,
Never come more to the ghotul.
But I brought you liquor and with folded hands

Begged you to let us in again.

Now even in my dreams I may not massage you,

And who will there be to comfort you?

## 11  *The Chelik Replies*

Only yesterday you came to our ghotul to press our hands and arms.

But now who will comfort us?

Only yesterday you made us happy with your talk and laughter,

But now who will comfort us?

We used to trouble you in every way,

Yet you always gave us comfort.

If you didn't come to the ghotul for two days, we used to ask in the
village where you were.

Sometimes they said you had gone away or had fallen ill.

Then when you came at last and we asked you what you had been
doing,

You replied "I went to such and such a village" or "I was ill and so I
couldn't come."

But when we knew that you had not gone anywhere,

When we heard that you were not ill, but had been to sleep in some
rascal's house,

When we knew that you had deserted us for that worthless fellow,

We had to punish you.

But now you will never be punished again,

For you are going away to a husband's house.

Never in your life will you be punished again like that.

Only yesterday we told you to fill our leaf-pipes, to fetch us leaves, to
sweep the ghotul rooms,

But now you will never do that again.

We shall look at you from far away and whisper, There goes Belosabai.

No more can you go with us or sit with us.

But live happily there as you lived with us.

Love your husband and comfort him as you loved and comforted us.

Roll his leaf-pipe for him, fetch him leaves and water,

Clean his house, comb his hair, massage his arms and back.

But leave your games and loves and laughter.

Your games and loves and laughter now are for your husband.

*Ghotul:* boys' and girls' dormitory.     *Sirdar, Kotwar, Kandki:* officers of the
ghotul.     *Maria:* a tribe.

## SONG

Here's a twig of the tendu-tree,
Here's the twig you were telling me of.
No one can use it at either end.
I have offered water in a brass pot,
I have offered gruel in a leaf-cup,
I have served him rice in a dish,
I have given him curry in a leaf-cup,
But he does not speak to me.
He doesn't know what to do.
I cannot live just looking at his house,
I cannot live just to fill my belly.
I can only live if my heart is filled.
I will go away to my father's house.
How can I live so long without my proper work?

**Bondo**    ORISSA

## SONGS

### I

O girl, let us live in sport and laughter, for you are my starling.
O girl, we will live to see many buffaloes killed,
We will see many a forest grow again, my starling.
O girl, you will go to catch crabs and fish while I lie on the sindibor
at ease, for you are my starling.
O girl, let us lie together on the great rocks Tumlaida, Tirada and
Usame, for you are my starling.
Let us go to the meeting-place of the Sunadak and Bunadak and drink
its water from a single cup, for you are my starling.
Let us go to Budingber, Pesangber, Pasangre, Talang and Marangre,
where the rocks make music as of drums.
Let us offer leaves on the runnukbor-sindibor, for you are my starling.
Let us walk together on the paths Gugusing and Ogiksing, for you
are my starling.
O girl of Andra, Sisa and Sampe, you are my starling.

11

Come, let me give you some rice-beer and tobacco
And we will pass our time alone in the forest.
Holding your shoulders, twisting your breasts,
I will have you on my knees.
I will have you in the forest where I can embrace you shamelessly.


**Juang**    ORISSA


### DANCE SONGS

I  *For the Vulture Dance*

Golden vulture
Silver vulture
With ungainly hop
She devours the corpse
Golden vulture
Silver vulture
With exploring bill
She pulls out the offal
Golden vulture
Silver vulture
Flapping her wings
She pecks the eyes
Golden vulture
Silver vulture
She breaks the rai-tree
And drinks the sweet juice
Golden vulture
Silver vulture.

II  *For the Peacock Dance*

Red and green
Are the peacock's
Feathers

*Sindibor:* megalithic platform.    *Runnukbor:* sacred wall.

As the long-tailed peacock dances
He watches his own shadow
Which is the dance, girl
That wearies your loins?

### III  *For the Deer Dance*

O phantom deer
As the deer are grazing they suddenly leap away
First goes the roe
Then goes the buck
The phantom deer are grazing
With lowered horns they graze
There is a hunter by the way
He fits and shoots his arrow
The deer falls
O phantom deer.

## SONG

The clitoris is the vagina's ornament
The penis gets its beauty from the testes.
If you cut off these two
Man and woman will not live a day longer.

## *Kharia*    ORISSA AND CHOTA NAGPUR

## SONGS

### I

The water lily blossoms in small white flowers!
Those small white flowers, ah, my girl!
O wind! do not wring them!
O water! do not break them!
Those small white flowers, ah, my girl!
In daytime they blossom, at night they wither!
Those small white flowers, ah, my girl!

II

The herons, my boy, like kings are holding court,
Like kings are holding court!
On buffaloes' backs, like kings, they sit in state,
Like kings they sit in state!

III

To Barway and Biru, O Brother, thou didst go,
With flutes all around thy waist, O Brother!
A maiden black as ripe durib didst thou choose,
With flutes all around thy waist, O Brother!
A maiden black as ripe durib by thy flute was charmed,
With flutes all around thy waist, O Brother!
The girl black as ripe durib did come as wife with thee,
Flutes all around thy waist, O Brother!

**Dafla (Nisi)**    SUBANSIRI DIVISION, NORTH-EAST FRONTIER
AGENCY

LOVE SONGS

I

Both of us are in the prime of our youth
Let us be friends
Let us cling to each other
As two young leaves of a banana
If we are to climb a hill
We will climb together
If we are to cross a river
We will cross together.

II

Let us cultivate the fields together
And grow old
Our hair will grow grey
And our teeth will fall
But we shall live.

**Assamese**     ASSAM

### SPRING FESTIVAL SONGS

I

Again and again do we sport,
we sport as long as we live,
do we in death?

II

First God created the world,
He also created the creatures,
the same God made love,
why not we?

III

On the other bank of the Luit the kahua has blossomed,
Miri girls are sporting there,
this month of Phagun your breasts have blossomed,
my mind is sporting there.

IV

Yours three and three mine
altogether six cloths made our fold,
pick up your three,
listen, the cock crows.

V

O you cock, the outcast cock,
I would give you a blow,
it is hardly dawn and you crow out,
my darling has to leave me now.

VI

The bell-metal pot sounded of a sudden,
unwittingly did I ask: Who's that?
I told you to come just at evening,
far gone is the moon now.

VII

I could scale the hills,
the creeper I could not climb,
I could tame the wild elephant,
you I could not tame.

VIII

One herdsman reached the sand-bar with his buffaloes,
he picked bananas on the way and ate them,
but the herdsman that followed glanced around
and now my spindle stops turning.

IX

The cock crows *Keo,*
like a twig that snaps did our minds part,
no god was there to bring them together.

X

The maina is caught in the cage,
the elephant is caught in the trap,
my darling is caught in a Government job,
all night I do not have sleep.

XI

Thinking of you my body thins,
I forget all work,
if I remember you while taking my meal
the morsel in my mouth comes out.

XII

The chrysanthemum blossoms in your garden,
its shadow falls on mine,
all day I think of you,
at night my body burns.

XIII

I dreamt of you yesternight,
you were having your meal,
I dreamt of you this night,
my hand was on your breasts.

XIV

It thundered up in the hills,
it rained in the plains:
like water from a breached dam
my mind was breached,
there was none to console me.

**Miri**    ASSAM

## SAD SONGS

I

Would that, some way or other, even once, I saw you on the soil of this dale. The cry of the cicadas of this day submerges the cry of old, and my mind too forsakes its hope of ever getting you.

II

God put us together, at the time of creating the world, only for an hour.

III

Perching on a branch the fish-eagle looks about and cries wildly; my heart too becomes restless at some unaccountable feeling.

**Ao Naga**    NAGA HILLS, ASSAM

## LOVE SONG

*Man:*
From far Lungkungchang
All the long road to Chongliyimti
Have I come to where my beloved sleeps.
I am handsome as a flower, and when I am with my beloved
May dawn linger long below the world's edge.

*Girl:*

Countless suitors come to the house where I sleep,
But in this lover only, handsome as a flower,
Do mine eyes behold the ideal of my heart.
Many came to the house where I sleep,
But the joy of my eyes was not among them.
My lover is like the finest bead on the necks of all the men of all
   the world.
When my lover comes not to where I sleep
Ugly and hateful to my eyes is my chamber.


SONG CONTEST


*The Chantongia man sings:*
When men were going to their fields
A hunting dog, looking for trouble,
With ears erect wandered through the village.
You were foolish enough to rouse the dog sleeping by the house.
It chased you and bit your throat.
Oh how you put your tail between your legs!
How you scurried away, looking back as you went!
It is not with the whole Yimsungr clan,
But with the seed of Molunglamba
That I contend in song.
I will stop for no one.
You are like a bellyful of mustard leaves:
When they are cooked they go to nothing.
Come, try your skill with me.
O Ningsangnungba, taker of ne'er a head,
Not a word do you say worth hearing,
You chatter and jibber, and call it a speech.
As light as dry leaves, that is the weight of your words.

*The Yongyimsen man replies:*
Glory to brave Alumungba and Ashuba
Born of old at Lungterok.
Their foes from Lishi they sent flying in wild rout.
They drove back on every side the warriors of Kabza who dared to
   challenge them.

Like a huge branching rubber tree were the two brothers,
And under its shade the village dwelt in peace.
From the ripe berries that fell from the tree
Sprang a race splendid as cock hornbills.
On the Langbangkong and Asukong ranges they dwell,
The Yimsungr clan, priests of the Ao tribe.
With heads and mithan they perform due rites.
You who dare to contend with me in song
Your mother gave birth to you on the village path.
No one holds you worth aught.
Look at him, you fellows.
By the tradition of the Yimsungr clan I am priest,
Mine the race that built iron steps at Chongliyimti.
From the spreading roots of the great tree
I sprang up mighty in my village,
A priest of the tribe.
What man can fight with the mighty Kibulung rock?

**Konyak Naga**    ASSAM

# SONG

Yinglong and Liwang
They loved each other
Loving, they lay together,
Red as the leaf of the oubou-tree
Flamed love and desire.
On paths to the village,
The two lit fires,
Sky-wards, upwards curling,
The smoke of the fires united,
And mingled, never to part.

**Lhota Naga**    NAGA HILLS, ASSAM

## LULLABY SUNG BY A WIDOW

*Ole iyi le he-e*
*O iyi e he-e,*
My little one, why are you crying so much?
Is it because you want a drink of madhu that you are crying?
I will give you well-kept madhu to drink.
Do not cry so much.
O my little one,
O my child,
Why are you crying so much?
Even if you cry like this
Your father, who has become a young brave among the dead,
Cannot come back and call you and take you in his arms.
O do not cry so much.
*O iyi e he-e.*

# Ceylon

*Vedda*

## LULLABY

Ro-ro-ro
Child, why are you crying?
Child, is it for the fat of the monitor lizard?
Give the whole of it.
Child, why are you crying?
Child, is it for the gonala-yams you are crying?
Give all of them.
Child, why are you crying?
Child, is it for the head of the wandura-monkey?
Give the whole of it.
Child, why are you crying?
Child, is it for the head of the rilawa-monkey?
Give the whole of it.
Ro-ro-ro
Child, creeping child;
are you crying for sleep?
Sleep child,
are you crying for sleep?
Ro-ro-ro
Darling, Ro-ro-ro.
Darling, for what are you crying?
Darling, is it for bathing you are crying?
Child, what are you crying for?
Child, is it for sleep?
Darling, Ro-ro-ro.

## SONG

For want of gruel or food, the life will not depart;
owing to cold or wind, the life will not depart;
owing to rain or dew, the life will not depart.
If there be no wife, the life will depart.

# Andaman Islands

**Andamanese**

## TWO SONGS COMPOSED ON
## STEAMER VOYAGES

### I

*Solo*

Master Nyunga-la sang with me on the steamer, and he learnt my song.

*Chorus*

Nyunga-la learnt my song.

### II

*Solo*

From the country of the Yerewas the moon rose, it came near. It was very cold, I sat down.

*Chorus*

It was very cold, I sat down.

## SONG ON CUTTING A BOW

*Solo*

You did not make this, I made it, I, I, I, made it.

*Chorus*

I, I, I, made it.

## PIG-HUNTING SONG

*Solo*

Bow    its lower part    pulled back,
Bow    its lower part

*Refrain*

On tiptoe    I crept silently.

## SONG FOR A DEAD MOTHER

*Solo*

I am now an orphan;
When you were alive, and I was cold, you used to hush me to sleep,
   saying:

*Refrain*

"You will soon get my breast,
You will soon get my breast,
Sleep well, sleep well,
Ara-la-lo, Ara-la-lo,
My breast is there."

# China

**Na-Khi (Mo-So)**     TIBETAN-CHINESE BORDER

IMPROVISED SONGS BETWEEN A
BOY AND A GIRL ON THEIR WAY
TO COMMIT SUICIDE FOR LOVE

*The boy:*
We are going, going along;
We have gone a long way our feet are aching;
To the alpine meadow of Yu-ch'ou on the snow range;
There at that meadow we have arrived;
We two,
Pile up the wood and light a big fire;
Let us sit by the fire;
The yellow bamboo k'a-kwuo-kwuo;
Let us strike it once more;
I myself;
Who was born in that home;
The golden threshold of my home;
Over it I stepped when I came out;
I myself;
My white small hand;
I put upon my heart;
And once more I pondered;
My father who brought me up;
His heart is hard and stern;
My mother who brought me up;
Her heart is soft and kind;
I myself;
The wooden threshold of my home;
When I stepped over and came out;

My feet stepped swiftly along;
At first three steps forward;
Then three steps backward;
Golden tears I shed;
And they dropped on the ground;
The ground alone saw them;
My mother who gave me birth;
She did not see them;
I indeed am he
Whose heart was filled with sadness;
We two;
This time indeed;
The measuring worm contracts;
We cannot retract our steps;
Our tears made a road;
And led us up on high;
Now, at this time;
I love you dearly girl;
In your golden heart;
What thinkest thou?
Whatever you wish to say;
You must tell me now for certain.

*The girl:*
I love you my dear boy;
Why,
You were born in that home;
The golden threshold of your home;
When you stepped over it outside;
Your mother who gave you birth;
You said her heart was kind;
You thought of your mother;
And your heart was it not sad?
Why were you so sad?
All your older relatives:
The mushrooms at the foot of the pine;
They also will grow old;
Like the wua-ndshi-shi-mushroom at the foot of the pine;
They will once die, that is the law;
Die all must, there is no escape;

All your older relatives;
You must not think of them;
So in your heart you must not be sad;
We two;
To-morrow or after to-morrow;
We will always walk together;
Holding our hands;
The boy's foot raised;
The girl's foot put down;
This we can do;
There is still else;
In death in life one road we travel;
Once har-la-llü they will perform;
We two;
The a-ndshi-mint dies on the rocks;
If we quickly die;
We will be earlier reborn;
If we are early reborn
We will the earlier die;
*La-ler-gyi-zaw man,*
You are not the only man;
I am not the only girl;
Under all the heavens
Such rule there is;
You my passionate boy;
You must not be sad at heart;
This golden evening indeed;
This evening it is;
My boy you were born in that small village;
Those people who do not like us;
Will search for us like a needle lost;
They will search for you my boy;
As they will search for me;
This golden evening;
This night indeed;
On the nine mountains at the foot of the pine they rise;
The stone pheasants call;
The Amherst pheasants call;
I love you my boy;
Do not show remorse;

Think neither left nor right;
Do not be worried;
The yellow poison, the poison oil;
Come let us drink a little;
The ndi-li-fern is the bedding of the pig;
To sleep, come let us sleep.
My boy why do you ponder?
Please do tell me.

*The boy:*
I indeed;
Think left and right?
Of such I am not thinking;
In winter the owl is calling;
It is not the custom,
But let us call it custom to commit yu-vu;
There would still be lots to say;
Of words there is no end;
In my heart I would still become sadder;
So I will say no more.
Of the yellow poison, of the poison oil;
We now must drink.
Together come let us drink,
We two;
Let us pass through the land of death!
To go we must!
Let us be gone.

## Ch'uan Miao    WESTERN CHINA

### NATURE SONGS

I  *The Insects and Birds Report That Spring Has Arrived to Cause People to Plow and Sow*

The weather is cold in the winter. The earth is cold during two months in the winter. Today it is the new spring in the first lunar

*K'a-kwuo-kwuo:* the mouth harp, to which the songs are sung in a whisper.
*Har-la-llü:* a ceremony performed to enable the souls of suicides to go to the realm of the ancestors.    *Yu-vu:* suicide for love.

month. The New Year meal has been eaten. In the winter the insects and birds are all sleeping with hands and feet folded. When the spring has arrived and the weather is mild and the earth is warm, the insects clap their wings and come early. When they clap their wings the daylight is about to come. Then the birds get up and sing, calling to Ba Na's industrious son to get up early and go to the edge of the land and do his early farming. The insects get up and call to Je Ji's industrious son, and he goes to the wilderness to sow the soil. Then the birds sing industriously and urge the industrious son's planted corn and rice to flower. The insects quickly cause the corn and grain to grow seeds. The rice in the mother's field yields until the flat is all yellow. The father's corn covered the mountain with yellow. After the birds got their rice to eat, they sat quietly. When the insects got corn to eat, they also went under the ground and slept peacefully until next spring.

### 11   *A Nature Song*

In the night the dew comes out on the leaves and the grass.
Then the insects come forth and drink the dew.
When they have drunk their fill,
They begin to sing.
Then the buddhas and the gods enjoy their sweet music.

## Lolo   SOUTHERN CHINA

### SONG OF A YOUNG MAN ABOUT TO BE MARRIED

You, daughter of your mother,
You smell sweet, like an only daughter.
Sesame from Yun-nan smells sweet, they say,
But I would rather smell the sweat of the girl I love.

Yesterday, last night,
I slept three times,
I dreamed of this and that,
I thought I was close to her.

Today at work I rest three times,
Three times I think of her.

Today,
I think it will be a good day for me.
Even as the shuttle meets the thread,
Today I think I shall meet her.

You daughter of your mother,
You are not a peach blossom,
Yet you are like a peach blossom,
You are not an apricot flower,
Yet you are like an apricot flower.

Stone does not change,
It always remains what it is.
It is not for a day that I would be with you,
It is a hundred years that I would be with you.

I, an only son, I go to the mountain to cut kindling,
Cutting kindling, I think of her.
If I go to the mountain to cut wood,
Cutting wood, I see many insects,
Seeing each one, I think of her.

I, an only son, when I go to fetch water,
Fetching water, I think of her.
An only son, I go to work,
Working, I think of her.

Eating my morning rice,
I hold my bowl in the palm of my hand,
I do not eat, I think of her.
I hold my chopsticks ready,
But instead of picking up vegetables, I think of her.

It is not for a day that I think of her,
I think of her for ten days.
It is not a day that I would be with her,
It is a hundred years that I would be with her.

At noon, when I go to light my pipe,
I take my lighter from Ma-chang,
I strike it once, for her,
I strike it again, for me.

Smoking my pipe at noon,
I smoke one pipeful, for her,
I smoke another pipeful, for me.

The folds of the turban fit each to each.
Please come with me!
I will say "I am happy with her."
You will say "I am happy with him."

## COMPLAINT OF A
## NEW WIFE

Mother, your daughter is sad,
You have been gone for three days;
Mother, come back, come back,
Mother, I think of you.

Mother, your daughter is sad;
The tree dies, the root lives.
The root dies, the leaf withers:
Mother, your daughter is sad.

The wind stirs the leaf,
Mother, your daughter is sad;
The leaf still lives,
Your daughter has no life.

My father, marrying his daughter,
Obtained a jar of wine
Of which I shall not taste;
Your daughter is always sad.

My mother, marrying her daughter,
Obtained a basket of rice

Of which I shall not eat;
Your daughter is always sad.

They go to bed, I stay awake
Like a thief;
They get up, I do not get up
Like one sick with the plague.

Every day I gather vegetables,
Three bunches a day,
In three days nine bunches:
Still their words are harsh.

Mother, your daughter is sad;
Sad I go to the woods.
What is in the woods?
The cricket sings in the woods.

Mother, your daughter is sad;
Sad, I go to the fields.
In the fields there is grass;
Grass has grass for company.

Mother your daughter is sad,
Your daughter has no friend;
Always thinking,
Her heart is sad.

# Southeast Asia

***Karen***   BURMA

## SONG OF A WAR-BAND
## SETTING OUT

I go to war. I am sent.
I go to fight. I am sent.
Clothe me with an iron breastplate.
Give to me the iron shield.
I am not strong. May I take on strength.
I am weak. May I attain vigor.

I go with a host of men.
We will reach the steps of the house
And fire muskets and shout aloud.
The men will come with wives and children.
Raise the spear and draw the sword.
Smite the neck and pierce the side.
The blood is gushing purple.

The great hawk flies above the house.
It pounces on the chief's red cock.
It grasps its prey near the lowest step.
It seizes then the chief's white cock,
And the great hawk flies away,
Leaving the chief behind in tears.

***Thai***    THAILAND

## FUNERAL POEM

On the other side of the great river
The apes call loudly to each other and cry.
They cry, 'tis said, because death comes so readily:
Men vanish like water rolling from the caladium leaf;
They enter life suddenly and die quickly.
One by one they tread in the steps of God's sons.
They return whence they came as attendants of God;
They spread his mat and roll his cigars.

The Lord of death does his work swiftly.
The servants of Death are prompt in their task.
By the light of dawn they sharpen their spears.
In the evening glow they whet them again.
They ponder where they will go to fight.
They choose whom they will overcome.
They steal through the vales and over the hills.
They vanquish the sons and daughters of men.
Into the huts of the poor, among the fowls,
Into the great houses and into the guest-rooms,
Where the oblations of brass and silver are seen
And the fowls are killed and offered, they come.

Go, kill a black chicken.
Prepare it and offer it.
Go forth, and offer it on the main road,
At the intersection of the main roads.
If the curious person should eat it,
We would say that our grief has gone to him;
That he has carried it a great distance.
Let not evil's combings fall on us.
Let them fall 'midst the trees of the woods
Or elsewhere: the country is spacious.

## *Kha*　LAOS

### DIALOGUE

*Young man:*
I want to live under your roof,
Be with you from dawn to dark,
Help you work in the fields,
Dig the ground, pull up weeds,
Fetch brush, light the fire,
Cut down the wood which, at the end of the day,
We will carry together.

*Girl:*
Alas! I hear you, but I cannot take courage,
For my poor hut is not clean,
My station is lower than yours.
Are you not a son of the morning star?
But I am the daughter of the black crow.
How could you love me?

*Young man:*
My sister, why do you say and think such things?
Like you, I live in the mountains.
In what is my hut finer than yours?

*Girl:*
What you say to me comes from your lips,
In your heart, I know, there is no love.


## *White Meo*　LAOS

### NIGHT SONG

the night darkens
what to do now?
the woman is there
no one hears crying
crying in the dark night
no one hears sobs

the woman is there
she kisses the child
the sleeping child
kisses it in the dark night
her child in its bed
the woman is there
do not startle her awake
(in the sky it is midnight)
wake her in the dark night
do not startle her awake
startle her in the dark night
the woman is there
she goes to look
to look at the pillar
she goes through the door
but to see what
there is nothing
something
there is nothing to see
except her husband
lifeless there
the flame gives light
a great flame
gives light all around
the woman is there
she goes to look
at the man, her husband
cold, lifeless
like a stone
grown cold
like a tree-trunk
the woman is there
she goes to look
at the man, her husband
eat a mouthful
eat what?
powdered bamboo
powdered wood.

---

*The pillar:* at the foot of which the dead are laid before burial.     *Powdered bamboo:* powdered internodes of bamboo, a deadly poison.

*Cambodian*    CAMBODIA

## SONG

Sadness at sundown!
Now along the streams
Flights of kingfishers perch.
Sadness at sunset
While the air of royal
Angkor is played to put the King to sleep.
Sadness at sundown!
Now flights of blackbirds
Have settled high in the sdok-trees.
But I and my sweetheart
Never look into each other's faces:
We see only how far apart are
Her country and mine.
At sunset I take off my turban
And I walk along the edge of the forest.
I walk, I walk, and my eyes look for her,
I walk along the edge of the forest,
And there she is, drawing water!
Yes, I see her and look at her!
But it is the morning star,
Come to draw water
There in the misty sky.

*Vietnamese*    VIETNAM

## LULLABY

That high mountain, who built it so high?
That deep river, who dug it so deep?

## LOVE SONG

First, I admire you for your hair dressed like a rooster's tail.
Second, I love you because you speak so charmingly.
Third, I love you for your features, which are sweet to look at.
Fourth, I love you for your clothes, which are all the same color.
Fifth, I love you because you have pins in your hair and a Chinese
   fan in your hand.
Sixth, I love you because your hair is green.
Seventh, I love you because your parents brought you into the world.
Eighth, I love you because your phoenix eyes look at me most lovingly.
Ninth, I love you because we are going to be married and live together.
Tenth, I love you because you will not marry anyone but me.

**Mnong Gar**    VIETNAM

### SONG OF COUGHING

Coughing: *khuk! khuk!*,
     cough by the moon.
Cough in broad daylight,
     cough by the genii.
Cough at the edge of day,
     cough of a lover.
Cough at the edge of a forest,
     the lover is there cutting wood.

### SONG OF A GIRL WHOSE LOVER
### HAS MARRIED ANOTHER
### WOMAN

May your wife be ill
     and you ask me to visit her:
     I will refuse to visit her.
May your wife fall ill
     and you ask me to go to see her:
     I will refuse to go to see her.

I want to see a coffin of boards, with long horns;
I want to see a decorated coffin, with long horns.
In it I will look at an unshrouded human head;
In it I will look at a rotting creature, at nightfall;
Coffin of boards, coffin of wicker, in them I will see
The left leg crammed into a tube of giant-bamboo,
The right leg bound to the bars of justice,
The ear-lobe stretched enough to hold a drum,
O my love . . .

**Radhe**    INDO-CHINA

## SONG

Hola, pretty girl!
Your silver ring is beautiful,
You have beautiful arms and beautiful feet,
You are pretty,
And how I would like to idle with you in the field,
At the spring, or anywhere!
How I would enjoy it if I could catch you and hold you
By your skirt or your tunic,
So that I could talk with you!
For you are pretty.
Why are your breasts prettier than the breasts of other girls?
Your chest and your legs are as clear as ivory,
Your whole body is as white as if it had been scraped with a knife,
Your back is flexible, your eyes are bright,
How beautiful you are!
May I meet you at a festival, so that I can sleep with you!

## PRAYER AT THE SACRIFICE BEFORE THE COFFIN

Oh! Genius of this dead man's spirit, you are decayed like the paddy-stalk, dead like the grass, the demons and fiends take you and carry you off.

Now the posts are prepared, the coffin is made; tomorrow, day after tomorrow, you will be in the ground that is red below and black above, you are in the coffin, you will be in the grave. Your fingers will be doves and your nails eagles; you will be a genius, you will be a mountain, you will be a vulture, you will be a stream.

Tomorrow, day after tomorrow, you will be in the ground, do not move, you will be in the mountain, do not stir, you will be in the Back-of-the-Ancestors, be still.

You want to eat rice—ask the Genius of the stars; you want to eat chicken—ask the Genius of the moon; your belly is hungry—ask the Master of the sky; another Master watches over you, another Master keeps you.

Tomorrow, day after tomorrow, do not come, do not come near, do not love your wife, do not love your children; henceforth you are apart as the m'naeh-leaf falls from the tree, as the banana-leaf leans away; from now on, it is over.

Now three jars and a buffalo are offered at your feet. . . . Tomorrow, day after tomorrow, when we carry an axe, do not try to make us cut ourselves, to wound a foot or a hand, genius, do not try to confuse our minds.

Tomorrow, day after tomorrow, someone will want to sing on the road to the fields, someone will want to sing on the road to the forest, do not confuse his mind, genius, the m'naeh-leaves have fallen, the banana-leaves diverge, from now on it is over, from now on it is done,

Genius of this dead man's spirit!

*The Back-of-the-Ancestors:* the earth.

# Malay Peninsula

## *Jakun: Besisi*

### THE COCONUT-MONKEY

*Kok, kok* is the cry of the gantang-monkey,
The gantang-monkey and the rangka-monkey
And the buku-monkey that peers-peers.
The monkey's muzzle is dimpled-dimpled,
The monkey's fingers are crooked-crooked,
The monkey's haunches are bowed-bowed,
The monkey's tail is a waving tree.
He is eating fruit, fruit of the durian. . . .
Ho brother! Mamat the Firstborn,
Ho brother, take your blowpipe,
Stalk it craftily, look very carefully.
Whiz! it sticks, the dart has hit him,
The monkey has run off helter-skelter.
Now he vomits, falls,
Thud-thud the monkey falls.
Pick him up, Mamat the Firstborn,
Carry him home on your bent back,
Carry him home and throw him down.
Aunt Eldest-born, scorch the monkey,
Mamat the Firstborn, quarter the monkey,
Give each one a little to eat;
When your belly is gorged
Stand up, Mamat the Firstborn,
Stand up and drink in the common house,
The long house, the broad house.
Tomorrow and after shall be a year of plenty.
Tell of the monkey and fruit shall be plenty.
Fruit . . . fruit, fruit, fruit, fruit.

# THE TIGER

The tiger roars at the end of the point.
What does he want? He wants to eat,
Eat wildfowl, eat wild pig,
Eat sambur-deer, eat chevrotin,
The striped tiger that crosses the sea—
Do not forget this in the telling.
The headlands are the land of the tiger.
The tiger has sworn an oath against someone,
The tiger jumps five fathoms,
Dodge the tiger, jump to the right.
The tiger walks the length of a tree-trunk,
The tiger sees a high hill,
The tiger sleeps at noonday.
Get up, O tiger, and walk the forest.
The tiger looks for live beasts,
The tiger walks to Mount Ophir,
That is the tiger's place of origin,
There is his second-chief, there is his grandfather.
There is his second-chief, there is his high-chief,
There lives the great-chief-of-tigers.
The tiger dies at the house of his great chief.

# THE PULAI-TREE

*Kik kik kik* creaks the pulai,
Its base rocks with the blowing wind,
Spreading and thick and dangling
Are the leaves of the pulai, the roots of the pulai,
Roots that go down, roots on the surface,
Its roots on the surface are like dragons fighting,
Its buds are like a virgin's nipples, the pulai,
Its leaves have sap like milk, the pulai,
Its stem is gray and mottled, the pulai,
Its shoots are like the peak of a headcloth, the pulai,
Its shoots are like scrollwork, the pulai,
Its buttresses are high, the pulai,

Its blossom falls like scattered rice-ends,
Its blossom falls like rain drizzling,
That is called the custom of the pulai.
Take your hatchet and fell the pulai,
Make a canoe and paddle to Malacca,
Sell coconuts, barter goods,
Bring home your canoe of pulai-wood,
Pull it up on the shore, do not let it get old,
Sell it to the Chinese for one hundred dollars.

## Semang

### FRUIT SONG

The fruit-cluster turns in the wind
The fruit-cluster at the end of the spray
The fruit-cluster turns in the wind
The fruit-cluster we climb for
The fruit-cluster at the end of the spray
The fruit-cluster turns in the wind
The fruit-cluster waves to and fro
The fruit-cluster whose fruit is acid
The fruit-cluster sways to and fro
The fruit-cluster turns in the wind
The fruit-cluster spins round and round.

### SONG OF THE WILD GINGER

The stem bends as the leaves shoot up
The leaf-stems sway to and fro
To and fro they sway in many ways
We rub them and they lose their stiffness
On Mount Inas they are blown about
On Mount Inas which is our home
Blown about by the light breeze
Blown about is the fog. Blown about is the haze
Blown about are the young shoots

Blown about is the haze of the hills
Blown about by the light breeze
It multiplies upon the hills
It multiplies upon the Hills of Inas
Hills of Beching, Hills of Siong
Hills of Malau, Hills of Kuwi
Hills of Mantan, Hills of Lumu
Upon every mountain is our home.


## Semang: *Kenta*


### SONG OF THE CHINOI AS THEY COME OUT OF FLOWERS

A o wah! we glide down the cliff
music, flutes, with flute music we glide down the cliff
we girls of Ple, we glide down the cliff
with flute music we glide down the cliff
we girl-Chinoi, we glide down the cliff
let us glide down the cliff, we glide down the cliff
let us strike our weapons together, we glide down the cliff
let us strike the lightnings together, we glide down the cliff
let us grasp our weapons, we glide down the cliff.


## Semang: *Kintak Bong*


### SONG OF A SUNRISE CHINOI

Father, I shake up and down where the sunrise is seen all fiery.


*The Chinoi* (Ćenoi) : spirits who live in the sky, singing and playing; their favorite resort is the mountain Batu' rib'm, whose cliffs they climb to pick the fruits on which they live; the seeds and skins that they drop become fruit trees on earth. *Ple:* another name for Ta Ped'n, the High God of the Semang.   *Weapons:* the Chinoi's weapons are mats with lightning-flash decorations.

## Semang: Telad'n Jahay

### IMPROVISED SONG OF THE BABY COCONUT-MONKEY

He runs to and fro, he jumps from branch to branch

> *Refrain (after every verse)*: Oi! his mother looks on in wonder!

He runs to and fro on the branch of the anag-tree,
he peers, he stuffs a manow-fruit
into his cheek-pouch.
>    All look on, his mother,
>        his brothers and sisters, his father.
He runs to and fro, looks every way
and spies bateg'n-fruits.
"Give them to your father, you!"
>        Quiet! Do they hear the voice of the mawa-monkey,
>        the berual wind, his brothers and sisters?
>        Quiet! they listen, they crane forward.
The hunter shoulders his blowpipe
of suor-bamboo, and loads it
with rabo-cotton, with a gase-arrow,
straight it flies, the bertam-arrow.
O, mother of the child!

## Senoi: Orang-Bukit

### PRAYER TO THE GODDESS JA PUDEU

>    Take one, throw him away,
>    Take two, throw them away,
>    Let one die, or even two,
>    Of those who live by one stream,
>    Have pity, do not kill twenty or even ten.

# Malay

## PANTUNS

### I

This dress is a dress of silk,
When you go to the pool, do not beat it on the stones.
This game is a game between us two,
When your death day comes, do not be sorry that we played it.

### II

The pigeons fly in thousands,
Only one perches on my fence.
I wish I could die at the end of your fingernail,
Be buried in the hollow of your hand.

### III

Cotton is changed into thread.
Thread is changed into dresses.
You let me go. Forget me.
I am already someone else.

### IV

Many people have bracelets on their arms,
Only I have bracelets on my ankles.
Many people say: "It is forbidden."
Only I obey my heart.

### V

If the tide rises
Shall we two bathe together?
If death and its hour come
Shall we die together, we two?

### VI

Day after day I sit and brush,
Brush my flower-patterned dress.
Day after day I sit and think
But what I think of has not yet happened.

### VII

What is the sign that night is coming?
The fledgling magpies peep.
What is the sign that I will come?
The blood beats faster.

## LINKED PANTUNS

*He:*

Jasmine flowers and blue champak flowers,
Flowers together in the betel-nut box.
Seven nights are like one night of longing.
You have not come to me yet.

*She:*

Flowers together in the betel-nut box,
With cloves from Peringit.
You have not come to me yet.
My longing is not little.

## INVOCATION TO THE RICE SOUL
## AT HARVEST TIME

Soul of my child, Princess Splendid!
I sent you to your mother for six months, to receive you growing tall
  in the seventh month.
The time is fulfilled, and I receive you.
I told you to sail to the sea that is black, the sea that is green, the sea
  that is blue, and the sea that is purple,
To the land of Rome, to India, China, and Siam.
Now I would welcome you up into a palace hall,
To a broidered mat and carpet.
I would summon nurses and followers,
Subjects and soldiers and court dignitaries for your service;
I would assemble horses and elephants, ducks and geese, buffaloes and
  goats and sheep with all their din.
Come, for all is ready!
I would call you hither,
Soul of my child, Princess Splendid!

Come, my crown and my garland, flower of my delight!
I welcome you up to a palace hall,
To a broidered mat and carpet.
Soul of my child, Princess Splendid!
Come! I would welcome you!
Forget your mother and wet-nurse.
White and black and green and blue and purple! get ye aside!
Brightness of genie and devil begone!
The real brightness is the brightness of my child.

## CHARM FOR STRIKING FEAR INTO A TIGER AND HARDENING ONE'S OWN HEART

O Earth-Shaker, rumble and quake!
Let iron needles be my body-hairs,
Let copper needles be my body-hairs!
Let poisonous snakes be my beard,
A crocodile my tongue,
And a roaring tiger in the dimple of my chin.
Be my voice the trumpet of an elephant,
Yes, like the roar of the thunderbolt.
May your lips be fast closed and your teeth clenched;
And not till the heavens and the earth are moved
May your heart be moved
To be angry with me or to seek to destroy me. . . .
Let splendor reside in my person.
Whoever talks of encountering me,
A cunning lion shall be his opponent.
O all things that have life,
Endure not to confront my gaze!
It is I who shall confront the gaze of you,
By the virtue of "There is no god but God."

## LOVE CHARM

If Muhammad can be sundered from Allah
And a corpse move in the grave,
Only then shall my lover's desire move to another.

The desire of his heart shall be only for me;
Straying nowhither he shall be my mate unto death,
Safe near me like a corpse in the grave.


## CHARM AGAINST THE DEMON WHO UNLOOSES THE SNARES OF HUNTERS

Peace be with you, grandson of the Spectre Huntsman,
Whose dwelling place is a solitary patch of primeval forest,
Whose chair is the nook between the buttresses of trees,
Whose leaning-post is the wild areca-palm,
Whose roof the leaves of the tukas,
Whose body-hairs are leaves of the resam,
Whose mattress leaves of the lerek,
Whose swing the tree medang jelawei,
And whose swing-ropes are malacca-cane-plants
The gift of His Highness Sultan Berumbongan,
Who lived at Pagar Ruyong,
In the house whose posts were heart of the tree-nettle,
Whose threshold a stem of spinach,
Strewn over with stems of the purut-purut,
Whose body-hairs were inverted,
And whose breasts numbered four,
To whom belonged the casting-net for flies,
And whose drum was headed with the skins of lice.
Break not faith with me,
Or you shall be killed by the impact of the sanctity of the four corners
   of the world,
Killed by the impact of the forty-four angels,
Killed by the impact of the Pillar of the Ka'bah,
Killed by the thrust of the sacred lump of iron,
Killed by the shaft of the thunderbolt,
Killed by the pounce of twilight lightning,
Killed by the impact of the thirty sections of the Koran,
Killed by the impact of the saying, "There is no god but God."

*Malay*   SELANGOR

## CHARM OF THE RICE-REAPERS WHEN THEY START THE DAY'S WORK

A swallow has fallen, striking the ground,
Striking the ground in the middle of our house-yard;
But you, O Shadows and Spectral Reapers,
See that you mingle not with us.

*Malay*   KELANTAN

## ON THE KELANTAN OBOE

Let it sound once,
the world is peopled;
let it sound twice,
knowledge comes into the world;
let it sound three times,
there is life or death.

## BEFORE A MAGIC DANCE, CHARM FOR THE *REBAB*

O miraculous instrument, Lord Naga Ulih, this is your origin:
your head is made of royal wood which had its origin in Dewa Daru,
your neck is made of the male bamboo of languishment;
it is fixed to the sounding box—a noble box, it murmurs the truth—
which rests with but one foot on the ground,
covered with a skin which once long ago had four feet,
and over which are stretched the white untwisted strings.
You travel over seven mountains
you travel over seven plains

so that your voice may sound twelve tunes,
twelve melodies of twelve kinds.
All you lords, great and small,
listen to the voice of the instrument with anxious desire,
day and night. . . .
whoever hears it is not drunk,
whoever hears it is not mad.
O young women and old men,
you came here yesterday,
some of you two by two,
to hear the voice of the instrument.
Such is its origin, whence it comes and how. . . .
By the grace of the blessing!

## BEFORE A MAGIC DANCE: CHARM FOR THE OIL

Soul and breath, desire beyond desire, ecstasy beyond ecstasy,
soul and breath, joy of love!
Let my voice be heard like the voice of the Prophet Daud,
let my looks charm like the looks of the Prophet Yusup!
Desire beyond desire . . .
Let the sudden storm stop when it hears my voice, as at the voice of
    the Prophet Daud,
the flying bird stop when it hears my voice, as at the voice of the
    Prophet Daud.
Desire beyond desire . . .
Let the running stream stop when it hears my voice, as at the voice of
    the Prophet Daud,
let it go back to its source to listen to my voice.
Oh! let the peoples of the Prophet Muhammad in all the world
listen to my voice as the voice of the Prophet Daud,
and let me charm them with my looks like the Prophet Yusup. . . .
If you do not listen to my voice
you will be rebels to Allah!
*Insha' Allah!*

# MAGICAL CHANT: SUNG BY THE CHIEF MUSICIAN WHILE THE SORCERER IS GOING INTO TRANCE

He who is at the beginning is about to open
the seven locks, to draw aside the nine screens,
the seven locks, legacy of the father,
the nine screens, legacy of the mother.
Now they are open,
the seven gates, the nine roads.
He who is at the beginning will set in motion the vital wind, Sakapit
    Si Jaya Lenga,
the vital wind Sakati Na'li;
the vital winds come out from the gates of the body;
they are born from the shadows of the body.
He who is at the beginning will open the gate of the unacknowledged,
the gate of will, the gate of feeling,
the gate of sensation, the gate of desires, the gate of the appetites.
Watch! wind of the observance,
watch over the pores and the skin;
watch, wind of truth,
watch over the blood and the flesh;
watch, wind of knowledge,
watch over the sinews and the bones;
watch, wind of intuition,
watch over the soul and the seed.
He who is at the beginning will set in motion the slumbering prince
on the little raised couch,
jewel of ivory and precious stones,
set in great pearls,
on the cushions and the carpets,
under the skies of the awning,
on the spurge of gold and the spurge of silver.
The rain does not come, the wind does not blow,
the wind is not laden with desires
in the country of the maharajah of the vital winds,
His Gloriousness, Tiong Bunga Kembait Muda.
At the famous gate of the palace, the slumbering prince wakes,
he takes the water jar and washes his face;

when he has washed his face, he turns to Lih,
murmuring the testimony;
when he has murmured it ten times he still repeats it.
He takes the betel and the implements;
when he has chewed two or three portions he pushes it aside;
the prince takes the mother-of-pearl box;
when he has opened it he takes out a checked cloth with a flower
    border,
he unfolds it, its shape is like the spread tail of a peacock,
he takes the yellow coat, the magic coat for the service of the gods,
the coat that clings softly to his skin.
The large body burrows to rise up,
the small body follows to enter. . . .
The prince clothes himself in the magical cloth woven with gold,
the winged scarf, he winds it about his waist in a threefold twist like
    the coiled naga;
the little kriss, he thrusts it into his girdle
like the young male tiger.
On his little finger the prince puts the ring with seven stones
bright as the light
of the star of the East leading the procession of day;
he puts on the crown
and strikes against the mountain like the moon in its full.
The prince stands before the censer, in which smokes
the incense of the three brothers;
the eldest sets princes in motion,
the next-born the officers,
the youngest the gods of the beginning,
with them will watch Sulong Nading, the pilot of princes,
Sulong Sayang, the pilot of gods,
Sulong Genta Sari, the pilot of officers,
Sulong Tamau Sari, the pilot of Jin.
The prince leaves the gulf of ivory,
he vanishes from the cape and appears at the palace,
vanishes from the palace and appears at the sultan's palace:
the heart where the prince is without sorrow,
the heart where the prince is without grief,
the heart where the prince is without sadness.
Alas, alas! the prince has left the advanced posts of his dwelling place,
he has left the palace. . . .

He has come out by the gate of the palace,
swaying supplely
like the pheasant waiting to fight,
like the mast bending in the wind,
like the owl desiring the moon.
All the people of the land are excited, men of rank,
the Chancellor, Treasurer, First Minister, Grand Admiral, Wazir.
Then the fringed parasol of the Kingdom is opened.
The prince turns to the left, turns to the right,
he goes to the five bridges,
he goes to the seven gates of the enclosure,
straight to the plain, the vast, endless plain.
The plain is without grass, the mountain without woods. . . .
The prince comes to the threefold meeting place of the four roads.
Farewell to you,
Farewell, lords,
Farewell, little brothers!
Until the time comes and the moment of the day,
the propitious moment of the favorable day.

*The slumbering prince:* the prince is here desire in man's heart. *The country of the maharajah of the vital winds:* the human body, and at the same time the audience, for the maharajah is now the sorcerer and the prince is also the sorcerer. *The prince stands before the censer,* . . . *the pilot of Jin:* the power of the sorcerer is establishing equilibrium between the outer world and the inner world, i.e., his patient. *The gulf of ivory:* symbolically, the mouth. The prince is now the power of the sorcerer manifested in speech and breath. *The plain:* the face. *The mountain:* the head. *The threefold meeting place of the four roads:* the eyes and the ears, *four roads* by which the outer world enters the inner world; the nostrils and the mouth—the *threefold meeting place*—converging into one road of communication between the outer and inner worlds.

# NORTH AMERICA

# The Northwest

## *Tlingit*

### SONG ON THE DEATH OF AN UNCLE

I always think within myself that there is no place where people do
not die.
I do not know where my uncle is. Probably the spirits threw down
my uncle into the spirits' cave around this world.

### WOMAN'S LOVE SONG

Why have I come to you to Dyea from far inland only to find that you
have gone away to another town? Here I am, crying for you.

### SONG OF A MAN WHOSE SWEETHEART
### HAD ABANDONED HIM

If one had control of death, it would be very easy to die with a Wolf
woman. It would be very pleasant.

## *Haida*

### MOURNING SONGS

#### I

Are you going down?
The sun there is going down, dear.

II

It becomes too much, it becomes too much, dear.
It becomes too much, it becomes too much, dear.


III

If I could see the trail [of the dead], I would enter upon it.
Elder brother, I want to see your whole body.


IV

For what am I, unfortunate one, looking?
Alas! my niece.


v    *Sung by the wife of a man lost at sea*

If you had seen land, beloved, you would have saved yourself, dear.


## *Kwakiutl*


## SONG FOR THE THUNDER BIRD DANCE

You are swooping down from heaven, pouncing upon a whole tribe.
You are swooping down from heaven, burning villages, killing every-
    thing before you, and the remains of the tribe are like the rest
    of your food, great thunder bird; great thunderer of our world.
You are swooping down from heaven, going from one tribe to the other.
    You seize with your talons the chiefs of the tribes.


## SONG OF A SUPERNATURAL BEING

I was a little too late to witness the blood of his victims, to see the
    putrid heap of those whom he had killed, to see the remains of the
    food of the warrior of the world.
He was made great; he was made wild by his father. He will not take
    pity. He will kill. He comes to make poor the tribes.

## HEALING SONG

Do not cry, you will come back safely.

## MOURNING SONG FOR MODA'NA, WHO WAS DROWNED

*Ye he he ya!* It deprived me of my mind, when the moon went down at
the edge of the waters. *Ye he he ya!*
*Ye he he ya!* It deprived me of my breath, when the mouse-dancer
began to gnaw on the water. *Ye he he ya!*
*Ye he he ya!* It deprived me of my mind when Moda'na began to utter
the cannibal-cry on the water. *Ye he he ya!*

## PARTING SONG

You are strong-minded to leave your lover here, your lover here, my
dear!
You are true-minded to leave your pain here, your pain, my dear!
Where is he going, the one of surpassing strength of mind, my dear?
Oh, he is going far away. He will be taken to the pretty place named
New York, my dear!
I shall ask all of you who walk the ground with me, my dear.
Is New York far away, where he will be taken, my love?
Oh, could I fly like a poor little raven by his side, my love!
Oh, could I, like a poor little raven, carry home news from him, my
dear!
Oh, could I fly down by the side of my dear, my love!
Oh, could I lie down by the side of my dear, my pain!
The love for my dear kills my body, my master!
The words of him who keeps me alive kill my body, my dear!
For he said that he will not turn his face this way for two years, my
love!
O my lord! O my dear! My master! My dear!
Oh, could I be the featherbed for you to lie down on it, my dear!
Oh, could I be the pillow, for your head to rest on, my dear!
Good bye! Now I am downcast! Now I weep for my love.

## SONG OF A WARRIOR FOR HIS
## FIRST-BORN SON

You were given by good fortune to your slave, you were given by good
fortune to your slave, to come and take the place of your slave,
*wa ya ha ha!*
O tribes! hide yourselves. I have come to be a man, and my name is
Hellebore, *wa ya ha ha!*
Already are twisted the cedar-withes which I shall pass through the
mouths of the heads that I obtain in war, for I am true Hellebore.
For I shall take in war the heads of the princes of the tribes, when I
come to be a man,
That I may have your names, as was done by my father, who has your
names for his names, *wa ya ha ha!*

## A BOY'S SONG (SUNG WHILE THE CHILD IS
## BEING ROCKED ON THE KNEE)

Baby, baby all the children call me baby when I am playing mischief
among them.
Baby, baby all the children tease me and call me baby.
Who is teasing the girls?
Who puts his finger into their vaginas?
Who throws stones at the children?
It is baby.

## WAR SONG OF THE KWAKIUTL

I am the thunder of my tribe.
I am the sea monster of my tribe.
I am the earthquake of my tribe.
When I start to fly the thunder resounds through the world.
When I am maddened, the voice of the seabear resounds through the
world.

*Seabear:* a fabulous sea monster.

## LOVE SONGS

### I

*Yiyawa,* wish I could go and make my true love happy, *haigia hayia.*

*Yiyawa,* wish I could arise from under ground right next to my true
   love, *haigia hayia.*

*Yiyawa,* wish I could alight from the heights of the air right next to
   my true love, *haigia hayia.*

*Yiyawa,* wish I could sit among the clouds and fly with them to my true
   love.

*Yiyawa,* I am downcast on account of my true love.

*Yiyawa,* I cry for pain on account of my true love, my dear.

### II

Like pain of fire runs down my body my love to you, my dear!

Like pain runs down my body my love to you, my dear!

Just as sickness is my love to you, my dear.

Just as a boil pains me my love to you, my dear.

Just as fire burns me my love to you, my dear.

I am thinking of what you said to me.

I am thinking of the love you bear me.

I am afraid of your love, my dear.

O pain! O pain!

Oh, where is my true love going, my dear?

Oh, they say she will be taken away far from here. She will leave me,
   my true love, my dear.

My body feels numb on account of what I said, my true love, my dear.

Good bye, my true love, my dear.

## LOVE SONG OF THE DEAD

You are hard-hearted against me, you are hard-hearted against me, my
   dear, *ha ha ye ye ha ha!*

You are cruel against me, you are cruel against me, my dear, *ha ha
   ye ye ha ha!*

For I am tired waiting for you to come here, my dear, *ha ha ye ye ha ha!*

Now I shall cry differently on your account, my dear, *ha ha ye ye ha ha!*

Ah, I shall go down to the lower world, there I shall cry for you, my
   dear, *ha ha ye ye ha ha!*

## *Clayoquot*

### GIRL'S SONG

I will not, I will not have him because he is too old.
His head and shoulders are good looking but
I will not have him anyway because he is too old.

## *Snuqualmi*

### LOVE SONG[1]

It rises    the    sun    I think of    my love
it rises    the    sun    I think of    my love    *ade*
my love    *ade.*

## *British Columbia**

### RESPONSIVE SONG FOR THE DEAD CHILD OF A CHIEF

*Chief.*—Don't mourn any more, don't mourn.
*Chorus.*—We do not mourn any more.
*Chief.*—He went up to play with his brethren the stars. Don't mourn any more.
*Chorus.*—We do not mourn any more.
*Chief.*—There he is hunting with the hunters the nimble deer. Don't mourn any more.
*Chorus.*—We do not mourn any more.
*Chief.*—We will see his beloved face in the new moon. Don't mourn any more.
*Chorus.*—We do not mourn any more.

*Hunters . . . deer:* constellations.

[1] Literal translation.
* People not specified.

# The East and the Great Lakes

*Passamaquoddy*

## THE SONG OF THE STARS

We are the stars which sing.
We sing with our light.
We are the birds of fire
We fly across the heaven,
Our light is a star.
We make a road for Spirits,
A road for the Great Spirit.
Among us are three hunters
Who chase a bear:
There never was a time
When they were not hunting;
We look down on the mountains.
This is the Song of the Mountains.

## GIRL'S SONG FROM A LEGEND

Now I am left on this lonely island to die—
No one to hear the sound of my voice.
Who will bury me when I die?
Who will sing my death-song for me?
My false friends leave me here to die alone;
Like a wild beast, I am left on this island to die.

I wish the wind spirit would carry my cry to my love!

My love is as swift as the deer; he would speed through the forest to find me;

Now I am left on this lonely island to die.

I wish the spirit of air would carry my breath to my love.

My love's canoe, like the sunlight, would shoot through the water to my side;

But I am left on this lonely island to die, with no one to pity me but the little birds.

My love is brave and strong; but, when he hears my fate, his stout heart will break;

And I am on this lonely island to die.

Now the night comes on, and all is silent but the owl. He sings a mournful song to his mate, in pity for me.

I will try to sleep. I wish the night spirit to hear my song; he will tell my love of my fate; and when I awake, I shall see the one I love.

I am on this lonely island to die.


## LOVE SONG

Come, my love, let us go up that shining mountain, and sit together on that shining mountain; there we will watch the beautiful sun go down from the shining mountain.

There we will sit, till the beautiful night traveller arises above the shining mountain; we will watch him, as he climbs to the beautiful skies.

We will also watch the little stars following their chief.

We will also watch the northern lights playing their game of ball in their cold, shiny country.

There we will sit, on the beautiful mountain, and listen to the thunder beating his drum.

We will see the lightning when she lights her pipe.

We will see the great whirlwind running a race with squall.

There we will sit, 'till every living creature feels like sleeping.

There we will hear the great owl sing his usual song, *teeg-lee-goo-wul-tique* ["Go to sleep all"], and watch the little stars in their sleepless flight. They do not mind the song, "Go to sleep all"; neither will we mind it, but sit more closely together and think of nothing but ourselves, on the beautiful mountain.

Again, the "Go to sleep all" will be heard, and the night traveller will
come closer to warn us that all are dreaming, except ourselves and
the little stars. They and their chief are coursing along, and our
minds go with them. Then the owl sleeps; no more is heard "Go to
sleep all"; the lightning ceases smoking; the thunder ceases beating
his drum; and though we feel inclined to sleep, yet will we sit on the
beautiful, shining mountain.

## Chippewa

### LOVE SONG

I will walk into someone's dwelling.

I will walk into somebody's home.

My sweetheart, into thy home
I will walk, in the night.

My sweetheart, in the winter
I shall walk into your abode.

This night I will walk into your lodge.

### HUNTING SONG

My war club
Resounds through the sky
To summon the animals to my call

### LOVE-CHARM
### SONGS

I

What are you saying to me?
I am arrayed like the roses
And beautiful as they

*Night traveller:* the evening star.

II

In the center of the earth
Wherever he may be
Or under the earth

## MĬDÉ SONG

Toward calm and shady places
I am walking
On the earth

## DREAM SONGS

### I  *Thunder*

All over
The world
My voice resounds

### II  *Storm*

From the half
Of the sky
That which lives there
Is coming, and makes a noise

### III  *Crow*

The first to come
I am called
Among the birds
I bring the rain
Crow is my name

*Mĭdé:* the religion of the Chippewa.

## LOVE SONGS

### I

A loon
I thought it was
But it was
My love's
Splashing oar

### II

Do not weep
I am not going to die

### III

Although he said it
Still
I am filled with longing
When I think of him

### IV

Come
I am going away
I pray you
Let me go
I will soon return
Do not
Weep for me

Behold
We will be very glad
To meet each other
When I return
Do not
Weep for me

## WOMAN'S-DANCE
## SONG

My sweetheart
A long time
I have been waiting for you
To come over
Where I am

## DEATH SONG OF
## A WARRIOR

the odor of death
I discern the odor of death
in the front of my body

## SONG AFTER A BATTLE
## WITH THE SIOUX

the Sioux women
pass to and fro wailing
as they gather up
their wounded men
the voice of their weeping comes back to us

## SONG AFTER
## A VICTORY

it shall be
that I rejoice
O, my son
your elder brother
you have brought back
O, my son
it shall be
that I rejoice
O, my son

## WAR SONG ON A
## BRAVE WOMAN

greatly
she
defending her children
the old woman
fought for us all


## SONG OF A MAN URGED
## TO JOIN THE WARRIORS

they are talking about me
saying "come with us"

is there anyone who
would weep for me?
my wife
would weep for me


## LOVE SONG

you desire vainly
that I seek you
the reason is
I come
to see your younger sister


## SONG OF ONE
## WHOSE LOVER IS DEAD

I might grieve
I am sad
that he is gone
my lover

## DREAM SONG: SPRING

as my eyes
search
the prairie
I feel the summer in the spring


**Ojibwa**


## DAWN SONG

Let us go home before daybreak or people will find out what we have
been doing.


## SONG OF A WOMAN WHEN HER
## LOVER WENT ON A JOURNEY

Now I start to weep.
My lover went away.
Without him how will I cross
When I come to the Path-leading-to-the-river?

He told me, my lover,
"Don't cry, don't,
When I depart for the Path-leading-to-the-river.
Do not worry, do not mind."

Indeed, I will follow him.
To the Path-leading-to-the-river he went.
But indeed, how will I cross
When I come to the Path-leading-to-the-river?

Ah-h-h, then I will see my lover.

## Onondaga

### ON THE IROQUOIS LEAGUE

Woe! Woe!
Hearken ye!
We are diminished!
Woe! Woe!
The cleared land has become a thicket.
Woe! Woe!
The clear places are deserted.
Woe!
They are in their graves—
They who established it—
Woe!
The great League.
Yet they declared
It should endure—
The great League.
Woe!
Their work has grown old.
Woe!
Thus we are become miserable.

## Seneca

### FROM THE NEW YEAR'S CEREMONY
### (FEBRUARY)

. . . Oh you who were born of Earth, you who live in the sky!
In the beginning you thought that you would lay this sacred tobacco
  by man's side
That man should have an incense with which to send his words up to
  the sky,
With which to lift his words when the year ended.

Truly we have fulfilled your desires and here we have that basket of
    sacred tobacco,
Oh you who were born of Earth, you who dwell in the sky!
So now the smoke arises!
Oh inhale the incense as you listen!
For now do we commence to speak of what you have created.
In the beginning you thought that there should be a world
Upon which men beings should travel
That you might say, "They are my descendants."
Now there is a shaft that reaches up to you, Ganeowi, the sacred song
    of the morning it is.
Now of your descendants as many as remain are gathered here. . . .

Now you thought that there should be a world
Upon which grasses of different kinds should grow
And that some should be medicinal,
And that some should yield fruits for a help to the men beings who
    dwell upon the earth.
Thus did you think, oh you who dwell in the sky!
Now it was ordered to be so when the warm season warmed the earth
And that it should be fulfilled then and that your descendants should
    see the return of things.
Now again the smoke arises
And the people speak through it to you,
Oh you who dwell in the sky!
Now we implore you that it may so occur again when the earth warms,
That your desires may be fulfilled and that your descendants may again
    see your creations. . . .

So now another.
Now you did think that there should be forests upon the earth
And that they might be a help to the people.
So now moreover you did think that there should be a certain tree
That should yield sweet water from its trunk.
Now that tree is the Maple and it is faithful to its design.
May this continue to be,
Oh you who dwell in the sky!

Now again the smoke arises,
And the people pray that this may still continue when the earth
    becomes warm again!

So now this thing is done.
Our words are as straight as we could make them.
Only this can we do for we are all young,
Oh you who were born of Earth,
Oh you who dwell in the sky!
So now this one thing ends. . . .

## FROM THE MEDICINE LODGE INITIATION CEREMONY

### I  *Darkness Song*

*Ha go wa nah u na*
*Ha go way nah u na . . .*
We wait in the darkness!
Come, all ye who listen,
Help in our night journey:
Now no sun is shining;
Now no star is glowing;
Come show us the pathway:
The night is not friendly;
She closes her eyelids;
The moon has forgot us,
We wait in the darkness!

### II  *Invitation Song*

*Ha wa ga na hoe*
*Ha wa gah nae*
*Na ho oh ha na*
*Ga na ho hi-e-e-e-eh!*

So says the whip-poor-will
Follow me, follow me!
So says the chief to him,
Yes I will follow thee!

See the night darkening;
The shadows are hiding,
No light to follow for,
So says the waterfall,
So sings the river voice!

Someone is nearing me,
Soft he comes creeping here,
Two eyes glare close to me,
Lighting the forest path —
Hear how his breath blows by!

Follow me, follow me, —
So sings the whip-poor-will!
Yes, I am following, —
So the chief answers him.

## *Cherokee*

## LOVE INCANTATIONS

### I

Now! I am as beautiful as the very blossoms themselves!

I am a man, you lovely ones, you women of the Seven Clans!

Now! You women who reside among the Seven Peoples, I have just come to intrude myself among you.

All of you have just come to gaze upon me, the most beautiful.

Now! You lovely women, already I just took your souls!

I am a man!
You women will live in the very middle of my soul.

Forever I will be as beautiful as the bright red blossoms!

### II

Now! Ha! Very quickly I have just come to take away your heart.
Ha! Very quickly I have just come to take away your thought.
Ha! Very quickly I have just come to take away your breath.
Ha! Very quickly I have just come to take away your saliva.

## *Seminole*

### SONG CONCERNING THE REMOVAL OF THE SEMINOLE TO OKLAHOMA (1836–1840)

They are taking us beyond Miami,
They are taking us beyond the Caloosa River,
They are taking us to the end of our tribe.
They are taking us to Palm Beach, coming back beside Okeechobee
   Lake,
They are taking us to an old town in the west.

# The Plains

*Mandan*

### DANCING SONG
### OF THE SKUNK

my tail rattles
my ears rattle
each end rattles
my whole body rattles
my face is striped
my back is striped

### SONG OF A SCOUT
### REMEMBERING HOME

a certain maiden
to the garden
goes
lonely
she walks

### BLACK MOUTH
### SOCIETY SONG

earth
always
endures

## Dakota

### SONG OF THE PASQUE FLOWER

I wish to encourage the children of the nations of flowers
Which are now appearing about the countryside;
While they wake from sleep,
While they rise above their Mother the Earth,
I stand beside them, an old man with gray hair.


## Teton Sioux

### SONG OF THE FINAL VISIT TO THE VAPOR LODGE BEFORE THE SUN DANCE

a voice
I will send
hear me
the land
all over
a voice
I am sending
hear me
I will live

### SONG COMMEMORATING A DEAD SIOUX WARRIOR

Sitting Crow
that is the way he wished to lie
he is lying as he desired

*Pasque flower:* The pasque (*Pulsatilla patens*) is the first flower to bloom in spring on the northern prairies. By the time the other spring flowers bloom, the pasque has gone to seed and, with its hairy stem and head of plume-tipped achenes, it suggests a gray-haired old man.

## SONG OF A
## MEDICINE MAN

my heart
is different
behold me
my heart
is different
I have shown it
from the north
a wind
comes to get me


## SONG OF THE
## HORSE SOCIETY

daybreak
appears
when
a horse
neighs


## WAR SONGS

I

friends
I have said
in common life
the customs
are many
friend
those
are not [do not interest me]
I have said

II

well
when I was courting
"horses you have none"
to me was said
therefore
over all the land
I roam


## SONG SUNG DURING
## OR AFTER A FIGHT

the old men
say
the earth
only
endures
you spoke
truly
you are right


## SONGS OF A MOTHER
## MOURNING HER SONS
## KILLED IN BATTLE

I

that Fox leader
now
did not return
you said
White Butterfly
is whom you mean
but then
he went looking for this and it has come to pass

II

boys of the Hunkpapa band
whenever you pursue anything
Long Buffalo
is foremost
you said
he lies over there

## SONG IN HONOR OF A PROMINENT WARRIOR

Onihan
that warrior
now
is no more

## OLD LOVE SONGS CONNECTED WITH WAR

I

you may
go on the warpath
when
your name
I hear [announced among the victors]
then
I will marry you

II

as the young men go by
I was looking for him
it surprises me anew
that he is gone
[it is] something
to which I can not be reconciled

III

the one
I was going to marry
is
again
gone [on the warpath]
it was I whom she meant by saying this


PRAISE SONG

 friends
 Sitting Crow
 friends
 returned not


SONG OF THE
MAIDEN'S LEAP

 he is gone to war
 you said
 I love him
 I am sad


SONG OF A GHOST

finally
I weep
weeping
I roam
[among] young men
courting
[I was] most enthusiastic of all
weeping
I roam

## MODERN LOVE SONG

if you are truthful, come
Walks Visibly [woman's name]
has said this

## SONG CONCERNING A
## MESSAGE FROM
## WASHINGTON

The great grandfather [the President]
has said
so they report
"Dakotas
be citizens,"
he said
so they report
but
it will be impossible for me
the Dakota [ways]
them
I love
I said
therefore
I have helped [to keep up the old ways]

*Crow*

## WAR SONGS

I

Whenever there is any trouble, I shall come through it. Though
arrows be many, I shall arrive. My heart is manly.

II

Eternal are the heavens and the earth; old people are poorly off;
do not be afraid.

## *Arapaho*

### GHOST-DANCE SONGS

I

My children, when at first I liked the whites,
My children, when at first I liked the whites,
I gave them fruits,
I gave them fruits.

II

Father, now I am singing it—*Hinini!*
Father, now I am singing it—*Hinini!*
That loudest song of all,
That loudest song of all—
That resounding song—*Hinini!*
That resounding song—*Hinini!*

## *Cheyenne*

### OLD WAR SONG

The stones are all that last long.

*Pawnee*

## SONG OF THE WOLF SOCIETY

Yonder it comes.
The expanse of earth is wide,
My brother the fox spoke and said,
"Behold and see the wideness of the earth,
The white foxes know the earth is wide."

## SONG OF A WOMAN WELCOMING VICTORIOUS WARRIORS

Ah, now I have seen you.

*Omaha*

## LITANY TO THE HIGH GODS

Sun there on high, you are a god,
You show yourself on your seat
So I pray of you
Whatever I do only good I desire.

Moon, there on high, have pity upon me.
A good road, give to me.
Pity and help me
Whatever I do only good I desire.

Sky, Father above
You are seated there.
I pray to you.
Whatever I do only good I desire.

Earth, there
I pray to you Mother.
Pity and help me.
Whatever I do only good I desire.

Winds of Four Quarters
A good road give to me.
I pray to you
Whatever I do only good I desire.

Rock, O Grandfather,
Seated there,
Like you to be I desire
Firmly seated to remain I beg of you.


## SONG OF
## TWO GHOSTS

My friend
This is a wide world
We're traveling over
Walking on the moonlight.


## DEATH-DANCE SONG

While you are here I cry
When you come there I'll end my crying.


## LOVE-MAGIC
## SONG

At daybreak I walk
Going home at daybreak.

## VICTORY SONG

You emulated me, and now you are crying,
Among surrounding tribes I only am the brave,
You tried to be like me—behold, you weep your dead.

## WOMAN SONG[2]

*Dadun na*—I have made myself known, *the!*
*Dadun na*—I have made myself known, *the!*
Last night when you sang I uttered your name, *the!*
*Dadun na*—I have made myself known, *the! hi.*
"Who is it that sings?" *the!* they said, and I sitting there, *the!*
"Waguntha is passing," I said, *the!*
It was your name I uttered, *the! hi.*

## Osage

## RITUAL RECITATION: THE SYMBOLIC PAINTING

With what shall the little ones adorn their bodies, as they tread the
  path of life? it has been said, in this house.
The crimson color of the God of Day who sitteth in the heavens,
They shall make to be their sacred color, as they go forth upon life's
  journey.
Verily, the God who reddens the heavens as he approaches,
They shall make to be their sacred color, as they go forth upon life's
  journey.
When they adorn their bodies with the crimson hue shed by that God
  of Day,

---

[2] "Another class of songs . . . were called *wau'waan*, 'woman songs.' They were
composed by men yet they always represent the woman as speaking, betraying her
fondness for . . . a young man" (A. C. Fletcher and F. La Flesche, as cited. See
Sources and Permissions) .

Then shall the little ones make themselves to be free from all causes
of death, as they go forth upon life's journey.

What shall the people use for a symbolic plume? they said to one
another, it has been said, in this house.
Verily, the God who always comes out at the beginning of day,
Has at his right side
A beam of light that stands upright like a plume.
That beam of light shall the people make to be their sacred plume.
When they make of that beam of light their sacred plume,
Then their sacred plume shall never droop for want of strength as they
go forth upon life's journey.

What shall they place as a pendant upon his breast? they said to one
another.
The shell of the mussel who sitteth upon the earth,
They shall place as a pendant upon his breast.
It is as the God of Day who sitteth in the heavens,
Close to his breast they shall verily press this god,
As a pendant upon his breast they shall place this god,
Then shall the little ones become free from all causes of death, as they
go forth upon life's journey.

Verily, at that time and place, it has been said, in this house,
They said to one another: What shall the people place upon his
wrists?
It is a bond spoken of as the captive's bond,
That they shall place upon his wrists.
Verily, it is not a captive's bond,
That is spoken of,
But, it is a soul,
That they shall place upon his wrists.

Verily, at that time and place, it has been said, in this house,
They said to one another: What is he upon whom a girdle is to be
placed?
It is a captive, they said,
Upon whom a girdle is to be placed.
Verily, it is not a captive that is spoken of,
It is a spirit upon whom they will place a girdle, they said, it has been
said, in this house.

Verily, at that time and place, it has been said, in this house,
They said to one another: What is he upon whose feet these moccasins
  are to be placed?
It is a captive,
Upon whose feet these moccasins are to be placed.
Verily, it is not a captive that is spoken of,
It is a spirit,
Upon whose feet these moccasins are to be placed, they said, it has
  been said, in this house.

## LITTLE SONG OF THE SUN

Lo, it has come to pass,
Behold, the hawk that lies outstretched,
Is now born they proclaim. Is now born they proclaim.
Welcome! be it said. Lo, it has come to pass!

Lo, it has come to pass,
Behold, it is of the One who is of the Day,
He is born they proclaim. He is born they proclaim.
Welcome! be it said. Lo, it has come to pass.

Lo, it has come to pass,
Behold, the blackbird that lies outstretched,
Is now born they proclaim. Is now born they proclaim.
Welcome! be it said. Lo, it has come to pass.

Lo, it has come to pass,
Behold it is of the One who is of the Night,
He is born they proclaim. He is born they proclaim.
Welcome! be it said. Lo, it has come to pass.

## HUNTING SONG

One I have wounded, yonder he moves,
Yonder he moves, bleeding at the mouth.

One I have wounded, yonder he moves,
Yonder he moves, with staggering steps.

One I have wounded, yonder he moves,
Yonder he falls, yonder he falls.


## WAR SONG

Grandfather, O, grandfather,
When I find the enemy,
I fall upon him unawares.

Grandfather, O, grandfather,
When I find the enemy,
I make him fall to the earth in death.

Grandfather, O, grandfather,
When I find the enemy,
I reduce his house to white smoke.

Grandfather, O, grandfather,
When I find the enemy,
I reduce his house to gray ashes.

Grandfather, O, grandfather,
When I find the enemy,
His bones lie whitened and scattered.


## WOMAN'S SONG OF CORN GROWING

Footprints I make! I go to the field with eager haste.
Footprints I make! Amid rustling leaves I stand.
Footprints I make! Amid yellow blossoms I stand.
Footprints I make! I stand with exultant pride.
Footprints I make! I hasten homeward with a burden of gladness.
Footprints I make! There's joy and gladness in my home.
Footprints I make! I stand amidst a day of contentment!

# California and the Southwest

*Wintu*

## SONG OF THE SPIRIT OF THE POLE STAR

The circuit of earth which you see,
The scattering of stars in the sky which you see,
All that is the place for my hair.

## DREAM SONGS

### I

It is above that you and I shall go;
Along the Milky Way you and I shall go;
Along the flower trail you and I shall go;
Picking flowers on our way you and I shall go.

### II

From the old camping place
Comes a flash of flowers.
I love flowers.
Give me flowers.
Flowers flutter
As the wind raises them above.
I love flowers.
Give me flowers.

### III

Daybreak people have been chirping.
Above on the roof
Alighting they chirp.

## *Yokuts*

## RATTLESNAKE CEREMONY
## SONG

The king snake said to the rattlesnake:
Do not touch me!
You can do nothing with me.
Lying with your belly full,
Rattlesnake of the rock pile,
Do not touch me!
There is nothing you can do,
You rattlesnake with your belly full,
Lying where the ground-squirrel holes are thick.
Do not touch me!
What can you do to me?
Rattlesnake in the tree clump,
Stretched in the shade,
You can do nothing;
Do not touch me!
Rattlesnake of the plains,
You whose white eye
The sun shines on,
Do not touch me!

*Daybreak people:* sparrows.

*Maidu*

## SONG OF THE RED CLOUD

I am the Red Cloud.
My father formed me out of the sky.
I sing [among] the mountain flowers.
I sing [among] the flowering chamize of the mountains.
I sing in the mountains [like] the *wek-wek*.
I sing [among] the rocks like the *wek-wek*.
In the morning I cry in the mountains.
In the morning I walk the path.
I cry [to] the morning stars.

*Navaho*

## PRAYER TO
## DSILYI NEYANI

Reared Within the Mountains!
Lord of the Mountains!
Young Man!
Chieftain!
I have made your sacrifice.
I have prepared a smoke for you.
My feet restore thou for me.
My legs restore thou for me.
My body restore thou for me.
My mind restore thou for me.
My voice restore thou for me.
Restore all for me in beauty.
Make beautiful all that is before me.
Make beautiful all that is behind me.
Make beautiful my words.

*Wek-wek:* (not explained).

It is done in beauty.
It is done in beauty.
It is done in beauty.
It is done in beauty.

## SONG OF THE PROPHET
## TO THE SAN JUAN RIVER

That flowing water! That flowing water!
My mind wanders across it.
That broad water! That flowing water!
My mind wanders across it.
That old age water! That flowing water!
My mind wanders across it.

## SONG OF THE THUNDER

The voice that beautifies the land!
The voice above,
The voice of the thunder
Within the dark cloud
Again and again it sounds,
The voice that beautifies the land.

The voice that beautifies the land!
The voice below;
The voice of the grasshopper
Among the plants
Again and again it sounds,
The voice that beautifies the land.

## PROCESSIONAL SONG FROM
## THE NIGHT CHANT

This I walk with, this I walk with.
Now Hastseyalti, I walk with.
These are his feet I walk with.
These are his limbs I walk with.
This is his body I walk with.

This is his mind I walk with.
This is his voice I walk with.
These are his twelve white plumes I walk with.
Beauty before me, I walk with.
Beauty behind me, I walk with.
Beauty above me, I walk with.
Beauty below me, I walk with.
Beauty all around me, I walk with.
In old age, the beautiful trail, I walk with.
It is I, I walk with.

## SONG OF A BEAR

There is danger where I move my feet.
I am whirlwind. There is danger when I move my feet.
I am a gray bear.
When I walk, where I step lightning flies from me.
Where I walk, one to be feared.
Where I walk long life.
One to be feared I am.
There is danger where I walk.

## GAMBLING SONGS

### I  *Magpie Song*

The magpie! The magpie! Here underneath
In the white of his wings are the footsteps of morning.
It dawns! It dawns!

### II  *Antelope Song*

The dun one, lo! The dun one, lo!
Truly in distant glade below
Wanders the antelope.

### III  *Ground-Squirrel Song*

The squirrel in his shirt stands up there,
The squirrel in his shirt stands up there;
Slender, he stands up there; striped, he stands up there.

*Hastseyalti:* God of dawn and eastern sky, of animals and the chase.

## TRADING SONG[3]

The beautiful thing is starting toward me
I being son of the sun
The white shell bead horse is starting toward me
From the center of the sun's home it is starting toward me
It eats out of the white shell basket
The dark clouds' dew streams from it as it starts toward me
The pollen from the beautiful flowers streams from its mouth
As it starts toward me
With its beautiful neigh it calls as it starts toward me
Soft goods of all sorts are attached to it as it starts toward me
Hard goods of all sorts are attached to it as it starts toward me
It shall continue to increase without fail as it starts toward me
It shall be beautiful in front as it starts toward me
It shall be beautiful behind as it starts toward me
Good and everlasting one am I as it starts toward me. . . .

They eat
I being the son of the moon
The turquoise bead horses they eat
From the center of the moon's home they eat
They eat out of the turquoise basket they eat
The dew of the dark fog streams from them as they eat
The pollen from the beautiful flowers streams from their mouths
As they eat
With their beautiful neighs they call as they eat
Soft goods of all sorts are attached to them as they eat
Hard goods of all sorts are attached to them as they eat
They shall continue to increase without fail as they eat
Behind them shall be beautiful as they eat
In front of them shall be beautiful as they eat
Good and everlasting one am I as they eat.

[3] First and last of seven stanzas. The intervening stanzas are variations based on the material of the beads and the actions and number of the horses.

**Zuni**

## FROM A SEASONAL PRAYER

When our earth mother is replete with living waters,
When spring comes,
The source of our flesh,
All the different kinds of corn,
We shall lay to rest in the ground.
With their earth mother's living waters,
They will be made into new beings.
Coming out standing into the daylight
Of their sun father,
Calling for rain,
To all sides they will stretch out their hands.
Then from wherever the rain makers stay quietly
They will send forth their misty breath;
Their massed clouds filled with water will come out to sit down with us;
Far from their homes,
With outstretched hands of water they will embrace the corn,
Stepping down to caress them with their fresh waters,
With their fine rain caressing the earth,
With their heavy rain caressing the earth.
And yonder, wherever the roads of the rain makers come forth,
Torrents will rush forth,
Silt will rush forth,
Mountains will be washed out,
Logs will be washed down,
Yonder all the mossy mountains
Will drip with water.
The clay-lined hollows of our earth mother
Will overflow with water,
From all the lakes
Will rise the cries of the children of the rain makers,
In all the lakes
There will be joyous dancing—
Desiring that it should be thus,
I send forth my prayers.

## PRAYER AT AN OFFERING OF FOOD TO THE ANCESTORS

This day my children,
For their fathers,
Their ancestors,
For you who have attained the far-off place of waters,
This day
My children
Have prepared food for your rite.
Now our sun father
Has gone in to sit down at his sacred place.
Taking the food my children have prepared at their fireplaces
[I have come out.]
Those who hold our roads,
The night priests,
Coming out rising to their sacred place
Will pass us on our roads.
This night
I add to your hearts.
With your supernatural wisdom
You will add to your hearts.
Let none of you be missing
But all add to your hearts.
Thus on all sides you will talk together.
From where you stay quietly
Your little wind-blown clouds,
Your fine wisps of cloud,
Your massed clouds you will send forth to sit down with us;
With your fine rain caressing the earth,
With all your waters
You will pass to us on our roads.
With your great pile of waters,
With your fine rain caressing the earth,
With your heavy rain caressing the earth,
You will pass to us on our roads.
My fathers,
Add to your hearts.
Your waters,

Your seeds,
Your long life,
Your old age
You will grant to us.
Therefore I have added to your hearts.
To the end, my fathers,
My children:
You will protect us.
All my ladder descending children
Will finish their roads;
They will grow old.
You will bless us with life.

## *Tewa*

### SONG OF THE SKY LOOM

Oh our Mother the Earth, oh our Father the Sky,
Your children are we, and with tired backs
We bring you the gifts that you love.
Then weave for us a garment of brightness;
May the warp be the white light of morning,
May the weft be the red light of evening,
May the fringes be the falling rain,
May the border be the standing rainbow.
Thus weave for us a garment of brightness
That we may walk fittingly where birds sing,
That we may walk fittingly where grass is green,
Oh our Mother the Earth, oh our Father the Sky!

### PRAYER FOR LONG
### LIFE

Our old women gods, we ask you!
Our old women gods, we ask you!

*You who have attained:* the dead.    *Those who hold our roads:* any super-
naturals who influence human affairs.    *The night priests:* the night itself.
*Ladder descending children:* the inhabitants of Zuni.

Then give us long life together,
May we live until our frosted hair
Is white; may we live till then
This life that now we know!

## AT THE GRAVE OF A WARRIOR

This very day, a little while ago, you lived
But now you are neither man nor woman,
Breathless you are, for the Navahos killed you!
Then remember us not, for here and now
We bring you your food. Then take and keep
Your earth-walled place; once! twice!
Three times! four times! Then leave us now!

## LOVE SONG

My little breath, under the willows by the water side we used to sit
And there the yellow cottonwood bird came and sang.
That I remember and therefore I weep.
Under the growing corn we used to sit,
And there the leaf bird came and sang.
That I remember and therefore I weep.
There on the meadow of yellow flowers we used to walk
Oh, my little breath! Oh, my little heart!
There on the meadow of blue flowers we used to walk.
Alas! how long ago that we two walked in that pleasant way.
Then everything was happy, but, alas! how long ago.
There on the meadow of crimson flowers we used to walk.
Oh, my little breath, now I go there alone in sorrow.

## *Isleta*

## CORN-GRINDING SONGS

### I

Early this morning the coming of the sun,
For what purpose is it coming?

Perhaps for the cornmeal it is coming.
Yonder in the west at Shiawibat
All Isleta maidens, what do you think?
What do you say? Shall we sit and sing?

Early this morning the coming of the sun,
For what purpose is it coming?
Perhaps for the yellow dust from the corntassels [pollen] it is coming,
Yonder in the west at Shiawibat,
People of Shiawibat, what do you think?
What do you say? Shall we sit and sing?

Early this morning the coming of the sun,
For what purpose is it coming?
Perhaps for sons and daughters of the people it is coming.
Yonder in the west,
People, what do you think?
What do you say? Shall we sit and sing?

### II

Flower-fly, how pretty you sound.
I am very lonely but you sound too far away.

## Acoma

## HUNTING SONG

Deer-youth, the one who is four times ahead,
That is the one of whom I am thinking,
It is the kind of robe and the kind of face, the whole body and the
   kind of health he has,
That is the one I am thinking about.
Antelope-youth, the one who is four times ahead,
That is the one of whom I am thinking,

---

   *Shiawibat:* native name of Isleta Pueblo.    *For sons and daughters of the peo-ple:* "The sun brings human lives to earth and also takes them away" (F. Densmore, as cited, p. 50. See Sources and Permissions) .

   *Flower-fly:* bee.

It is the kind of robe and the kind of face, the whole body and the kind
   of health he has,
That is the one I am thinking about.
Somewhere along the edge, under a pine tree,
There you are looking for me, you are waiting for me,
Now I shall follow where you have gone.
Somewhere out on the plain, somewhere among the sages,
There you are looking for me, you are waiting for me,
Now I shall follow where you have gone.

## WINTER DANCE SONG

Nicely, nicely, nicely, nicely, there away in the east,
The rain clouds are caring for the little corn plants as a mother takes
   care of her baby.

## FLOWER DANCE SONG

Butterfly, butterfly, butterfly, butterfly,
Oh look, see it hovering among the flowers,
It is like a baby trying to walk and not knowing how to go.
The clouds sprinkle down the rain.

## Cochiti

## OUWE DANCE SONG FOR GOOD CROPS

They go on, on, on, on,
In the early morning, speaking, singing,
There they come by the sacred spring with the rain-boy, while the
   rain-spirits sing.
We hear this while we listen and it makes our hearts happy,
And out in the great open the people and crops rejoice, for it is for our
   sakes they have come, and it makes us sing.

Early this morning the happy rain-boy came forth to meet the chief of
   the warriors, to beckon him to this happy gathering,

While the young maidens join them, happily dancing as other members
   look on.
Then the rain-spirits also come and form themselves above, and the
   earth-sign appears in the skies and comes down to alight.

They descend and then go onward.

## Santo Domingo Pueblo

### SONG OF A DEPARTED SPIRIT

(*The spirit speaks:*) I am on the way, traveling the road to where the
   spirits live, at *shipap,*
I look at the road, far ahead, down that way.
Nothing happens to me, as I am a spirit.
I am a spirit, of course I am, as I go on the nice clean road to *shipap,*
It is true that my spirit meets the others who come toward me.
I am glad to see them and be with them,
I have a right to be there.

I cannot help it; I must leave because the spirit has called me back.
I must go, I must obey.
So I am going direct to my spirit,
There are places down there where all the people live whom you have
   seen; [they have gone] when the time has come.

Now I cannot say what they will make of me.
I may take the form of a cloud;
I wish I could be a cloud.
I take the chance of whatever is offered to me.
When a cloud comes this way, you will say, "That is he!"
When I get to the place of spirits, I will hear everything you ask.
You must always remember me.
You have talked about me, and in *shipap* I can hear everything you say.

I am a spirit, and I bless you.
I thank you for all you have done for me in past years.
I shall repay you in spirit ways.

We hope to see you some day.
We send you many good wishes, many good things.

Thank you.

## CLOSING SONG OF A CEREMONY TO PROCURE ABUNDANCE

The dance is finished; they crowd around the ladder.
All who take part say, one man speaking after another:
"We hope we have good crops."
"We hope we shall have watermelons."
"All over the world is spreading [spirit]."
"When we go to rest tonight, we hope to feel better in the morning."
"May there be an increase of wild animals all over the country."
"May we have plenty of parched corn."
Someone hearing these things says, "Most valuable words and best
    things are being said."
People say: "How can he say such good things. He must have them
    from his fathers. He learned them well—most intelligent things."
When we get to our homes, the next evening we shall talk about it.
"What a good dance that was, everybody feels better.
"We wish we could have it oftener, but it is only once a year."

## SONG CONCERNING THE CORN HARVEST

(*The corn speaks:*) Look at the field, how our corn is coming up.
In that place the corn will get some drink,
Also from the black cloud and white cloud.
Clean, pure water coming from the clouds they give us.
My! How lovely! Coming from the sky, from our Mother Cloud.
Heavy clouds, we are so happy to see them.
We carry so many ears, the corn has such rich flavors of milk.
Why? It is because the rain comes to us.
Mother Earth drinks.     —
We all share together, Mother Earth and us people.

As we grow older, maybe it is only once we get the drink the cloud
    gives us.

Now we are getting old, we are ready to leave this field.
Cacique, *hochan nawai* are preparing, we feel in our heart.
He tells his own people to get the corn,
Everybody gets ready to get us out.

Here they come now on the road with cornmeal and prayerstick.
They step in our house,
They talk nicely to us, then his parents and people order him, so he
    tells us all.

Of course, then we explain to the rest of the corn, touching one another
    and rustling,
We say, "Now is the time to go."
We agree in the kindest thoughts.
We are preparing.
Here come the brothers, uncles, and others.

How lovingly he takes me and puts me down where I shall rest a while.
They take off our clothes and pile us up.
Then we are frightened. Why?
Somebody comes near us—the bear, the quail, and the birds and rabbits
    come around.
We want to be safe and go to the reservation to our fathers and mothers.
I wish they would hurry and put us in the wagons and take us home
    now.

Well, here they come with the wagons to take us home.

In the first wagonload, one ear says, "I wish I could be on top, so that
    I could look around."
Another says: "I want to be down at the bottom, so that the father and
    mother will look for me and not find me right off. They will say:
    'We looked for you everywhere. Here you are. Now you must come
    in. You are welcome. The house is open for you all.'"
Red, blue, white, and yellow corn, we go and rest on the porch or
    upstairs.
We are glad; we know we will stay outside a couple of days, because
    we are home.

*Our house:* the cornfield.    *Puts me down:* the man puts the ears of corn in a
container fastened to his waist, then piles them up at intervals. The stalks are still
standing.    *Take off our clothes:* husk the ears.    *Our fathers and mothers:* the
remainder of last year's seed corn, stored on the reservation.    *"I wish . . . look
around":* One ear of corn sometimes sticks straight up.

**Chircahua Apache**

## SONG AT THE PAINTING OF
## CEREMONIAL DANCERS

In the middle of the Holy Mountain,
In the middle of its body, stands a hut,
Brush-built, for the Black Mountain Spirit.
White lightning flashes in these moccasins;
White lightning streaks in angular path;
I am the lightning flashing and streaking!
This headdress lives; the noise of its pendants
Sounds and is heard!
My song shall encircle these dancers!

## LOVE SONG

My sweetheart, we surely could have gone home,
But you were afraid!
When it was night we surely could have gone home,
But you were afraid!

## SONG OF
## REJECTION

Man from a distant land,
Why do you talk to me?
Why do you talk to me?
Why do you talk to me?
What have you done for me
But just talk to me?

## *Mescalero Apache*

### SONG AT SUNRISE ON THE LAST DAY OF THE GOTAL CEREMONY

The black turkey gobbler, under the east, the middle of his tail, toward
us is about to dawn.
The black turkey gobbler, the tips of his beautiful tail, above us the
dawn whitens.
The black turkey gobbler, the tips of his beautiful tail, above us the
dawn becomes yellow.
The sunbeams stream forward, dawn boys, with shimmering shoes of
yellow;
On top of the sunbeams that stream toward us they are dancing.
At the east the rainbow moves forward, dawn maidens, with
shimmering shoes and shirts of yellow, dance over us.
Beautifully over us it is dawning.
Above us among the mountains the herbs are becoming green;
Above us on the tops of the mountains the herbs are becoming yellow.
Above us among the mountains, with shoes of yellow I go around the
fruits and herbs that shimmer.
Above us among the mountains, the shimmering fruits with shoes and
shirts of yellow are bent toward him.
On the beautiful mountain above it is daylight.

## *San Carlos Apache*

### SONGS FROM THE DEER CEREMONY

I

I go after it on the earth.
Panther boy they call me,
I go after it.
With dark mouth blood lying under my soles, ˙
With dark mouth blood making a black strip between my toes,
I go after it.

With mouth blood making stripes on me,
I go after it.
With mouth blood making stripes running out from each other on my
    face,
I go after it.

II

I came to the one they brought me.

I, called Turquoise Boy, came to her.
Someone not wild, I came to her.
Someone laughing, I came to her.
Walks-on-the-water, her mind not wild, her walking not wild.

I came to the one they brought for me.

## Pima

### FESTAL SONG

Singing to the gods in supplication;
Singing to the gods in supplication,
Thus my magic power is uplifted.
My power is uplifted as I sing.

Prostitutes hither running come;
Prostitutes hither running come,
Holding blue flowers as they run.
Talking in whispers they file along.

Along the crooked trail I'm going,
Along the crooked trail going west.
To the land of rainbows I'm going,
Swinging my arms as I journey on.

The bright dawn appears in the heavens;
The bright dawn appears in the heavens,
And the paling pleiades grow dim.
The moon is lost in the rising sun.

With the women Bluebird came running;
With the women Bluebird came running;
All came carrying clouds on their heads,
And these were seen shaking as they danced.

See there the Gray Spider magician;
See there the Gray Spider magician
Who ties the Sun while the Moon rolls on.
Turn back, the green staff raising higher.


## DANCE SONG OF THE SWALLOW

Now the Swallow begins his singing;
Now the Swallow begins his singing.
And the women who are with me,
The poor women commence to sing.

The Swallows met in the standing cliffs;
The Swallows met in the standing cliffs.
And the rainbows arched above me,
There the blue rainbow arches met.

The Black Swallows running hither;
The Black Swallows running hither,
Running hither came to lead me,
Lead me there, lead me there.

Haiya! Far in the distant east
Lie the clouds hidden under the mountain.
Far in the east direction
To the hidden clouds come running.

We are beating the basket drums;
We are beating the basket drums.
I am singing, I am listening;
From my feathers clouds are shaking.

I ran into the swamp confused;
There I heard the Tadpoles singing.
I ran into the swamp confused,
Where the bark-clothed Tadpoles sang.

In the west the Dragonfly wanders,
Skimming the surfaces of the pools,
Touching only with his tail. He skims
With flapping and rustling wings.

Thence I run as the darkness gathers,
Wearing cactus flowers in my hair.
Thence I run as the darkness gathers,
In fluttering darkness to the singing place.

I am circling like the Vulture,
Staying, flying near the blue.
I am circling like the Vulture,
Breathing, flying near the blue.

Now the Reddish Bat rejoices
In the songs which we are singing;
He rejoices in the eagle down
With which we ornament our headdress.


## MEDICINE SONGS

### 1 *Hare Song*

Hare is jumping and singing;
Hare is jumping and singing,
While the wind is roaring,
While the wind is roaring.

Hare is dancing and singing;
Hare is dancing and singing,
While the clouds are roaring,
While the clouds are roaring.

With headdress of owl feathers;
With headdress of owl feathers,
He comes to my far country;
He comes bringing hence his bow.

The Gray Mouse came at nightfall;
The Gray Mouse came at nightfall,
Came running in the darkness,
Came breathing in the darkness.

I am shut in at day dawn;
I am shut in at day dawn,
All night I am free to run
But am shut in at day dawn.

### 11    *Wind Song*

Wind now commences to sing;
Wind now commences to sing.
The land stretches before me,
Before me stretches away.

Wind's house now is thundering;
Wind's house now is thundering.
I go roaring o'er the land,
The land covered with thunder.

Over the windy mountains;
Over the windy mountains,
Came the myriad-legged wind;
The wind came running hither.

The Black Snake Wind came to me;
The Black Snake Wind came to me,
Came and wrapped itself about,
Came here running with its song.

Swiftly with a cup of water
I came running to make you drink,
I make you drink the water
And turn dizzily around.

Among the white cactus leaves;
Among the white cactus leaves,
I came running to that place;
I came running to that place.

## WAR SONG

Over that black sandy land,
Over the top came running,
Over the top came running.
The Apache slave was killed
And his hide tanned for leather.

## *Papago*

## INVITATION TO DRINK CACTUS LIQUOR AT A RAIN-BRINGING CEREMONY

Am not I a messenger
Desiring a delightful thing?

Once I knew not what to do
To make the liquor.
At the foot of a tree, prone I lay.
The wind blew.
Dust it blew along the ground
And cast it in my face.
Twigs it blew along the ground
And tangled them in my hair.

Then I arose.
Of the kinsmen living around me I bethought me
And they had pity on me.
Some liquid in the bottom of a jar
They gave me.
Crouching, I sat before it,
Desiring that speedily it should ferment.
But still it did not.

Then it had pity on me
And, after two mornings,
Gloriously it fermented.

Then of those whose desires were like to mine
I bethought me,
And straight to you a shining road was stretched.
As I started upon it,
It was the wind that met me
And rainily it blew.
It was this that I desired in what I did.

As again I started upon it,
It was cloudiness that met me
And soft rain sprinkled.
It was this that I desired in what I did.

Then I came to your sacred house and saw.
All kinds of winds there lay,
All kinds of clouds there lay,
All kinds of seeds there lay.
Seated upon them was One who powerfully touched you.
He swayed to and fro and blew out his breath.

Then came I to my sacred house and saw.
All kinds of winds there lay,
All kinds of clouds there lay,
All kinds of seeds there lay.
Seated upon them was One who powerfully touched me.
He blew out his winds and his clouds.

He pressed against me
And left me moistened and healed.
Then came forth the growing things.
Therewith were delightful the evenings,
Delightful the dawns.

Then hurry and, in any way you can,
Come swallow my fermented liquor.


### DREAMING LIQUOR SONGS

The powers I had won, beneath my bed I placed.
I lay upon them and lay down to sleep.

Then, in a little time, mysteriously there came to me
Beautiful drunken songs,
Beautiful songs for the circling dance.


## LIQUOR SONG

Dizziness is following me;
Close it is following me.
Ah, but I like it.
Yonder far, far
On the flat land it is taking me.


## HUNTING SONG

(*The deer speaks:*)
Lo,, surely I shall die.
Over there, toward the west,
Here and there I went running.
Over there in the west
It thundered; it shook me.

Lo, surely I shall die.
Over there, toward the east,
Here and there I went running.
Over there, in the east,
It echoed, it threw me down.


## RAILROAD
## RAILS

Yonder far I ran,
Walked and ran.
Iron stretched out.
Then I beside it ran.
Nowhere did it end.
It stretched out.

## TELEGRAPH
## WIRES

Westward is an iron road
Above it iron stretches;
Humming, it stretches.


## DISTANT TRAIN

Teìmot Mountain!
Teìmot Mountain!
Up there, on the edge I lie,
Everywhere looking.
Far yonder, toward me,
A burning feather headdress
Upon me shines.


## SONGS OF THE LIGHT
## WOMEN

### I

The heart of the light woman
Comes out of her.
Far yonder it is running about.
All through the long night it is running,
Giving her light.

II    *Sung by a light woman*

A dizzy man seizes me
Yonder he leads me.
In my way darkness falls
I know not [what I do].

## SONGS RECEIVED IN DREAMS

### I

Close to the west the great ocean is singing.
The waves are rolling toward me, covered with many clouds.
Even here I catch the sound.
The earth is shaking beneath me and I hear a deep rumbling.

### II

A cloud on top of Evergreen Trees Mountain is singing.
A cloud on top of Evergreen Trees Mountain is standing still,
It is raining and thundering up there,
It is raining here,
Under the mountain the corn tassels are shaking,
Under the mountain the horns of the child corn are glistening.

## SONG AT A CEREMONY FOR SECURING GOOD CROPS

Now as the night is over us we are singing the songs that were given
   to us.
You see the clouds beginning to form on top of the mountains.
They look like little white feathers.
You will see them shake like feathers in a wind.
Soon the raindrops will fall and make our country beautiful.

## SONG SUNG ON AN EXPEDITION TO OBTAIN SALT

By the sandy water I breathe in the odor of the sea,
From there the wind comes and blows over the world,
By the sandy water I breathe in the odor of the sea,
From there the clouds come and rain falls over the world.

# CENTRAL AMERICA

# Central America

## Aztec   MEXICO

### HYMN TO THE MOTHER OF THE GODS

The yellow flower has opened,
she our Mother, she with the thigh-skin of the Goddess painted on
   her face,
she came from Tamoanchan.

The yellow flower has blossomed,
she our Mother, she with the thigh-skin of the Goddess painted on
   her face,
she came from Tamoanchan.

The white flower has opened,
she our Mother, she with the thigh-skin of the Goddess painted on
   her face,
she came from Tamoanchan.

The white flower has blossomed
she our Mother, she with the thigh-skin of the Goddess painted on
   her face,
she came from Tamoanchan.

O, she has become the God,
on the melon cactus, our Mother,
the Obsidian-Butterfly.

O, thou sawest the nine plains,
on the hearts of deer she feeds,
our Mother, the Ruler of the Earth.

O, fresh with chalk, fresh with down
she is smeared and daubed,
the reed-arrow was shattered at the four quarters.

Become a stag on the plain they saw thee,
Kiuhnel and Mimich.

## THIS IS THE SONG THEY SANG AT FAST EVERY EIGHT YEARS

The flower, my heart, has opened,
he, the Lord of Midnight.

Our Mother has come,
The Goddess has come, Tlacolteotl.

Born is the Corn-God
in the house of coming thence,
in the place where flowers are,
the God "One Flower."

Born is the Corn-God
in the place of the rain and the mist,
where the children of men are made,
in the place where they fish for jewel-fishes.

It will soon be day, dawn is rising,
and the various quechol-birds are sipping
in the place where the flowers are.

Here below on earth you appear in the market-place,
I the Prince, Quetzalcoatl.

Joy shall reign among the trees in flower,
the various kinds of quechol-birds
shall rejoice, the quechol-birds.
Hear the word of our God
hear the word of the quechol-bird,
thy brother, our dead, shall not be blown to destruction,
thy brother shall not be shot with the blowpipe.

I will bring my flowers,
the yellow toncaxochitl,
the white izquixochitl,
from the land where flowers are.

Ball he plays, the old Xolotl plays ball,
on the magic ball-court Xolotl plays ball,
the Lord of the Land of Jewels.
Look, see if Piltzintecutli descends
into the House of Darkness, into the House of Darkness.

O Piltinzintli, Piltinzintli
with yellow feathers thou daubest thyself,
from the ball-court thou descendest
into the House of Darkness, into the House of Darkness . . .

The merchant, the merchant,
the subject of Xochiquetzal, who reigns in Cholula,
already my heart is afraid, already my heart is afraid
that the Corn-God has not yet come.
Let us go to . . . the merchant, the man from Chacalla.
Blue ear-plugs are his wares.
Blue wrist-bands are his wares.

The sleeper, the sleeper, he sleeps,
I have rolled him up with my hand.
Here the woman,
I the sleeper.


# PRAYER

I call upon thee, Giver of life: I am unhappy!
Be thou our friend, and let us speak thy beautiful word to each other,
let us tell each other why I am sad:
I seek the delight of thy flowers, the joy of thy songs, thy riches!

It is said that the place of happiness is in the sky,
that life is there, there joy, there the drum is ready,
there the song is heard which ends
our sadness, our grief in an instant. In his house is life!

Would that your hearts had known it, O princes!

## WARRIOR'S SONG

He who gives life
made none so strong, none so precious
as the eagle which must fly, as the tiger whose heart is the mountains:
now they are my slave and my shield-bearer.

## WAR SONG

Let there be embraces among Eagles and Tiger, O Princes!
Let the shields clatter, the Band is ready,
the Band that will take prisoners!
Only by our efforts do the flowers of battle take on color,
only by our efforts do they sway.
It is time for the God to be satisfied.
Let the shields clatter, the Band is ready,
the Band that will take prisoners!
The bonfire is alight, it seethes, it coils:
it is time to gain glory, time to make the shield famous!
Amid the noise of the ankle bells
the dust spreads like smoke.
The flower of war will not fail for an instant!
It is open beside the river,
flowers of the tiger, flowers of the shield were budding
amid the noise of the ankle bells.
The dust spreads like smoke.
Eagle shields mingle with Tiger banners.
Quetzal-feather shields mingle
with standards of green and yellow feathers.
They coil, they seethe . . .
Now sounds the noise of war! Now loud war sounds!
Arrows broke, clattering,
obsidian points were smashed to fragments,
the dust of the shields spreads over us. . . .
Now loud war sounds!

## SONG: THE BIRD AND THE BUTTERFLY

In the place of trilling, what says the red bird of the god?
It tinkles like a bell in the place of trilling.
Now it sucks honey: oh, let it rejoice:
its heart opens like a flower!
Now comes, now comes the butterfly:
flying it comes, it comes spreading its wings,
it has passed over flowers.
Now it sucks honey: oh, let it rejoice:
its heart opens like a flower!

## THE POET'S MISSION

### I

We come on earth but as those who fill an office, O friends:
we must leave beautiful songs,
we must leave flowers too. Alas!

Therefore I am sad in thy song, O thou through whom we live:
we must leave beautiful songs,
we must leave flowers too.

Flowers bud, they thrive, they germinate, they open their petals:
from within you, O poet, buds the flowery song which you
pour out like rain, refreshing other men.

### II

There the flower spreads open, there the song:
I pierce emeralds, I melt gold: my song!
I set emeralds: my song!
Does not a poet polish a song like a turquoise?
Does not Totoquihuatzin vibrate his shield of quetzal-feathers?

You rival the troupial, the green-blue bird, the bird of fire:
your heart rejoices: it sucks the flower of painting, painted song.

Already you spread your quetzal wings,
you strut with iridescent feathers, you red-throated, purple-plumaged
     bird:
suck the honey here! now the scented flower has come down on earth!


## THE ORIGIN OF SONGS

I take counsel with my heart:
"Where shall I gather beautiful fragrant flowers? Whom shall I ask?
Should I ask the green, glittering hummingbird,
the emerald flycatcher? should I ask the golden butterfly?
Yes, they will know: they know where the beautiful sweet-scented
     flowers open their petals.

"If I go deep into the groves of blue-green firs,
or deep into the groves that blossom in the color of flame,
there they yield themselves to the earth, wet with dew, under the
     radiant sunshine,
there, one by one, they attain their perfection.

"There perhaps I shall see them: and when the groves have shown
     them to me,
I will put them in the hollow of my cloak,
That I may regale the noblemen with them, that I may give them as a
     joyous gift to the princes.

"Here, surely, they live: already I hear their flowery song,
as if the mountains were talking together,
here, where the spring of greenish water rises,
where the turquoise spring sings among pebbles,
and the mocking bird answers, singing, the bell-bird answers,
and there is a constant sound of bells, the sound of the various
     singing birds:
there, all adorned with rich jewels, they praise the lord of the world."

And I speak, I call out sadly: "Forgive me if I break in upon you, O
     dear ones . . ."
Instantly they were silent: then the green glittering hummingbird came
     and spoke to me:

   *Totoquihuatzin:* king of Tlacopan, *ca.* 1500.

"What are you seeking, O poet?"
And at once I answer him, saying:
"Where are the beautiful fragrant flowers
That I may offer them as a delight to those who are of your kind?"
Instantly they answered me with a great noise of voices:
"If we show you the flowers here, O poet, it will be that you may offer
   them
to rejoice the princes who are of our kind."

Into the mountains of the Land of Our Sustenance,
of the Flowering Land, they took me:
there where the dew does not vanish under the radiant sunshine.
There at last I saw flowers, precious flowers of many kinds,
flowers of precious scent, adorned with dew, under a mist of shining
   rainbows.

There they say to me: "Pick as many flowers as you will
according to your pleasure, O poet, that you may offer them
to our friends the princes,
to those who give pleasure to the lord of the world."

And I went about, putting in the hollow of my cloak
the many kinds of fragrant flowers which delight the heart,
which give pleasure, and I said:
"If only some of our band could come here,
how many, many flowers we would pick!
But now that I know this place, I will tell my friends of it,
so that at all seasons we can come here to gather
these precious fragrant flowers of many kinds,
to sing many beautiful songs
with which to delight our friends the noblemen,
the lords of the land, the Eagles and Tigers."

So I, a poet, went gathering them
to bring flowers to the noblemen,
flowers to garland them with or to put in their hands:
then I sang a beautiful song, praising
the noblemen in the presence of him who is near and at hand.

But nothing for his vassals?
Where shall they pick, where see, beautiful flowers?

Will they come with me, perhaps, to the Flowering Land, to the Land
   of Our Sustenance?

Nothing for his vassals, those who are afflicted,
for those who suffer misfortune on earth?
Yes! those who serve him on earth who is near and at hand!
My heart weeps when I remember that I went, I, the poet,
to rest my eyes upon the Flowering Land.

But I said: "Truly this earth is not a good place:
the end of the journey is in another place: truly, happiness is there.
What comfort is on earth?
The place of life is the place to which all go down.
There may I go! there may I sing with the many kinds of precious
   birds,
there may I enjoy beautiful flowers,
fragrant flowers which rejoice the heart,
flowers which delight, perfume, and intoxicate,
flowers which delight, perfume, and intoxicate!"


## ONE POET PRAISES ANOTHER

You are a red flower of popcorn:
here in Mexico you are opening your petals:
bright butterflies of the land suck honey from you;
flying birds of eagle kind suck honey from you.

Your iridescent house of sapota-wood shines like a sun,
your dwelling is of jade water-flowers:
you rule in Anahuac.

Flowers are scattered, bells sound:
it is your drum, O Prince!

You are a red flower of feathers:
here in Mexico you are opening your petals;
you give fragrance in the world; it is scattered over all men.
A jade-stone fell to earth: a flower was born: your song!
Only when you raise your flowers here in Mexico
does the sun shine.

## Cora   MEXICO

## OUR FATHER THE SUN

Now our father thinks of departing with his thoughts, with a word,
  with his words.
There he is above us, from there he comes down, thinking of his world.
Now he approaches the place beyond his world and descends.
Lingering beyond his world he thinks of coming forth.
Now he comes forth and moves upward to his other world.
He comes. Well knowing what he intends, he walks along the road
  above us.
Now he is near the zenith. He rises to the middle of the sky.

Here now, he thinks that he will celebrate the feast of awakening.
He thinks and remembers his world.
Here his words are present, which he will give to us his children that
  we may live here in them and exist in the world.
Now all his words are present here, which he has decreed and left here.
Here he left his thoughts to his children.

Now he is ready to descend, he goes down on the road to the west.
He descends close to the west. He arrives in the middle of the west.
He prepares to cross over to his other world.
There he went down to tell Nasisa: "Now you shall sing to them."
Soon he will tell her. Here he vanished with all his words.

## THE EAGLE ABOVE US

In the sky the eagle, there is his place, there far above us.
Now he appears there.
He holds his world fast in his talons.
The world has put on a gray dress, a beautiful, living, watery dress
  of clouds.
There he is, far above us in the middle of the sky.
There he waits for the words of Tetewan.

  *Nasisa:* the Corn Goddess, here identified with the Earth Goddess and the Moon
Goddess.

Shining, he looks down on his world.
He looks far into the west.
Shining, he looks upon the water of life.
His countenance is full of terrible disaster.
His eye is glorious.
His feet are already dark-red.

There he is, far above us in the middle of the sky.
There he remembers those who live here on earth.
He spreads his wings over them.
Under his spread wings the gods rain, under them the dew falls.
Beautiful dew of life appears here on earth.

Here he speaks above us.
Here below men hear it, beautiful are the words that are heard here
    below.
They are heard below, where Mother Tetewan dwells far in the
    underworld.
There the Mother hears him.
She too speaks: Tetewan's words are heard here above.
Here they meet the words of the eagle, here they both come together.
We hear them already mingled together.
The eagle's words fade away over the far water of life.
There the Mother's words blew away.
There they die away in the middle of the sky.
There very far off they die away.


## THE MORNING STAR IN THE NORTH

From the north come dancing, wearing your younger brother as a
    crown,
From the north come dancing with blue magpie feathers.
From the north come dancing, from the north with blue magpie
    feathers.
From the north come dancing with turas-flowers.
Wear cempasuchil-flowers.
Wear zacalosuchil-flowers.
Wear tsakwas-flowers.

*The eagle:* the sky by day; his *eye:* the sun.    *Tetewan:* Goddess of the Underworld.    *The water of life:* the stream that surrounds the world and reaches the
Underworld.

Clouds you wear as a crown,
Their whiteness you wear as a crown.
Life you wear as a crown.


## *Tarahumare*    CHIHUAHUA PROVINCE, MEXICO


## DANCE SONG OF A SHAMAN

In flowers is jaltomate, in flowers stands up,
In flowers stands up getting ripe, getting ripe.
On the ridge yonder, yonder
On the ridge fog, on the ridge fog.
The water is near;
Fog is resting on the mountain and on the mesa.
The bluebird sings and whirs in the trees, and
The male woodpecker is calling on the llano,
Where the fog is rising.
The large swift is making his dashes through the evening air;
The rains are close at hand.
When the swift is darting through the air he makes his whizzing,
    humming noise.
The blue squirrel ascends the tree and whistles,
The plants will be growing and the fruit will be ripening,
And when it is ripe it falls to the ground.
It falls because it is so ripe.
The flowers are standing up, waving in the wind.
The turkey is playing, and the eagle is calling;
Therefore, the time of rains will soon set in.


## *Miskito*    NICARAGUA


## LOVE SONG

My girl, I am very sad for you,
I remember the smell of your skin,

I want to lay my head on your lap,
But here I am lying under a tree.
In my ear I only hear the noise of the sea.
The surf is rising in the offing;
But I cannot hear your voice.
Alas! alas! alas!


## *Cuna*   PANAMA


## THE SONG OF THE BIRDS

The paro-bird,
The red bird,
The aitirkwa-bird,
The keli-bird,
The tete-bird,
Theirs is the katteppa-tree,
Theirs is the paila-tree.
The waki-bird,
The parakeet,
The tulu-bird,
Many other birds,
They make a noise like the parrot,
They make a noise like the waki-bird,
They make the world alive with the sound of the waki-bird.
The red bird makes the world alive with sound,
The keli-bird makes the world alive with sound,
All over the space of the world, all over the space of the world.
The paro-bird makes the world alive with sound,
All over the space of the world.
The suppisuppi makes the world alive with sound,
All over the space of the world.
The aitirkwa-bird makes the world alive with sound,
All over the space of the world.
The red bird makes the world alive with sound,
All over the space of the world.
The keli-bird makes the world alive with sound,
All over the space of the world,

Like the parakeet it makes the world alive with sound,
All over the space of the world.
Like the waki-bird it makes the world alive with sound,
All over the space of the world.
The parrot makes the world alive with sound,
All over the space of the world.
The tete-bird makes the world alive with sound,
All over the space of the world.
Many other birds make the world alive with sound,
All over the space of the world;
Like the tolo-flute they make the world alive with sound,
All over the space of the world:
Like the suppe-flute they make the world alive with sound,
All over the space of the world;
Like the kuli-flute they make the world alive with sound,
All over the space of the world;
Like the panpipes they make the world alive with sound,
All over the space of the world;
Like a watch they make the world alive with sound,
All over the space of the world;
Sounding like the rooster they make the world alive with sound,
All over the space of the world.
The katteppa-tree has grown up,
All through the space of the world,
The paila-tree has grown up,
All through the space of the world, all through the space of the world.
The clouds rise,
All through the space of the world,
The clouds rise high,
In the space of the world, in the space of the world.
The clouds rise,
All through the space of the world.
Like the ship of the white man,
Ascending as it were the white man's boat,
All over the space of the world.
The clouds are hanging,
All over the space of the world;
The rain clouds are hanging,
All over the space of the world.
The Sun goes on board of his ship,

Like the macaw he makes the world alive with sound,
Grandfather Sun calls out "hi,"
All over the space of the world;
Like the pakkakka-bird he makes the world alive with sound,
All over the space of the world.
The universe, in time of rain, makes the world alive with noise,
Like the karsese it makes the world alive with sound,
Like the cockroach it makes the world alive with sound,
Like the cricket it makes the world alive with sound,
All over the space of the world;
Like the tolo it makes the world alive with sound,
All over the space of the world.
The high trees are rising,
The wind blows,
Its garments are hanging,
As far as the ground
Its garments are hanging.
Their fruits are shining,
Down to the ground,
The rabbit is hunting among their fruits.
He sits putting on golden shoes,
The high tree trembles
As the wind rushes through space.
The clouds are rising,
In the space of the world,
The skies are clearing,
All over the space of the world;
The sky is becoming brighter,
All over the space of the world,
The sky is clearing,
All over the space of the world;
The sky is clearing,
Like the ship of the white man,
All over the space of the world.
All over the space of the world,
The clouds are becoming red,
All over the space of the world,
The clouds are becoming purple,
All over the space of the world,
The clouds are becoming yellow,

All over the space of the world,
The clouds are becoming blue,
All over the space of the world,
The clouds are becoming white.
In the bright sunshine,
Before the sun, the golden birds are soaring,
In the space of the world.


## OLOWILASOP VISITS THE MORNING STAR

The girl Olowilasop is fastening her coin ornaments,
The girl Olowilasop is fastening her nakki-flower dress,
The nakki-flower dress is hanging down, she is fastening the striped shirtwaist,
Before going to see the Morning Star she is fastening her dress, she is girding her body.
The girl Olowilasop stands fastening her net-like dress,
Her net-like dress is swishing as she stands, her dress ornaments are jingling,
All like metal, all like bells, all like cicadas her net-like dress is sounding;
As if unaffected by chicha she is moving her body.
The girl Olowilasop climbs the golden ladder,
Ascending Tutulikalu, she is climbing the golden ladder,
She goes to climb Tutulikalu's eight stories on the golden ladder.
She hurries to the dwelling of the Morning Star, the Morning Star's room is closed.
The girl Olowilasop stands looking around. She stands looking afar:
Encircling the sky, only rain clouds are floating, only rain clouds are moving,
They bring down rain, which is washing the dwelling of the Morning Star.
The girl Olowilasop stands looking around:
Near the Morning Star's gate, the Morning Star goes to sit down, aiming his bow,
The girl Olowilasop stands knocking at the Morning Star's door,
The Morning Star's door is opening, the Morning Star's door is swinging wide open, looking like gold,

The Morning Star's door is creaking, the Morning Star's door is clapping,

Like Thunder the Morning Star's door is roaring,

The Morning Star's door makes the sound of two trees meeting,

Like the Black Monkey, like the animal Kostulele the Morning Star's door is sounding.

The girl Olowilasop stands watching and listening:

The Morning Star's dwelling is turning all aflame, the Morning Star's dwelling is shining inside.

The girl Olowilasop hurries to approach the Morning Star . . .


## SONG BEFORE GATHERING MEDICINAL HERBS FOR THE TREATMENT OF SICK CHILDREN

I go to look for medicine in the cool places where the rivers start,

I see the medicine that I want; it is a vine high up in a tree,

It will be strong, like the way it clings to the tree.

The fruit is blue clusters, cool like bunches of raindrops—

Cool as the rain falling gently.

O medicine, you must make the little children cool and you must not let them be sick again,

You must cool the houses of the sick children.

You will be used to bathe their little bodies.

O medicine, your name is *nugli, nugli, nugli*

(I say it three times to make it strong).

The thunder always falls from you, the lightning falls from you.

When they are far away they come to you and burn like a fire.

The thunder rolls, the rain falls, and the rivers overflow.

Rain clouds fall from you, that is why you are always cool.

Rain clouds come to your vines and tie up to them,

Rain comes to the *nugli, nugli, nugli.*

When you come to the child's house you must be cool and make everything cool like a cool rain,

You will go into the child's body and make him cool inside so he will get well, and you will make him strong,

You will not be alone when you come into the child's house.

*Chicha:* a fermented beverage.

A strong man-spirit watches to see the medicine work, and two
  spirit-girls will bathe the child.
The girl knows the child is sick by looking at it.
She is coming down the river to see the child.
When she enters the room it grows cool, even the clothing of the
  people is cool.
The man brings a cool fan,
The girl is bathing the child, you will bathe the child's body.


## SONG AFTER A MAN DIES

*(The sick man addresses his wife:)*
The fever returns. I drink the medicine and throw it on my body.
The sickness comes more and more. I am going to die.
My breath grows harder. I am going to die.
My face grows pale, the medicine is not helping me.
I am going to leave my two children to you,
After I die you will feel sorry for them.
After I die you must always talk of me to the children.
Go to the cocoanut farm after I die,
Take the children with you and be sad for me.
If people go into the cocoanut farm and cut the trees
Track them and find out who did it.
Always think of me when you go to the cocoanut farm.
There will be plenty of property for the children.
I will leave the plantain farm.
Always think of me when you go to the plantain farm.
I leave the small fruits, the bananas, mangoes and other fruits,
When you pick them you must think of me.
Before I was sick I went fishing and caught fish for the children,
I cannot get any more fish.
Before I was sick I went hunting and got wild birds, wild turkey and
  all kinds of game,
After I am dead I cannot do this any more,
Think of me when you eat the wild game.
I always killed the wild hog, I always killed the wild turkey,
I asked everybody to the big feast, but I cannot do this any more,
I am going to die now, I cannot talk.
My breath goes, I speak faintly.

You must remember me a *little* bit.
In a little while you will forget me,
Perhaps three days after I die there will be a big party,
I believe you will paint your face, dress up and not think of me,
You will begin to love some other Indian.
There will be many Indian boys for you,
But I will learn many new things where I am going.[1]


## CONVERSATION BETWEEN A BOY AND TWO GIRLS LOOKING THROUGH A SPYGLASS[2]

*(The older girl speaks:)*
You cannot see mountains and valleys in the clouds,
I see the clouds as big as trees,
When I look far away the clouds are like cliffs of high, gray rocks.
I see a cloud that looks like a cocoanut tree.
The clouds come up and come up in different shapes.
There are clouds that look like breakers,
You do not see the colors and shapes of the clouds,
I see them like people moving and bending, they come up like people.
There are clouds like many people walking.
I see them every time I look out to sea with the glass.
Sometimes a cloud comes up like a ghost, and sometimes like a ship.
I look through the glass far away and see everything.
I see a cloud that looks like a sea horse, a wild sea horse that lives in
     the water;
I see a cloud like a deer with branching horns.

*(The boy speaks:)*
You do not see that.

*(The older girl speaks:)*
From the time I was a child I did not think I would see such things
     as these.
If I do not look through the glass I cannot see them.
Now I find out the different things that the clouds make,
Do you want to see them too?

---

   [1] The man then dies, and the remainder of the song describes the journey of his spirit.
   [2] Sung by the official musicians at an entertainment.

(*The boy speaks:*)
All right. I want to see them too. (*He looks through the glass.*)
Now I see funny things.

(*The girl speaks:*)
You see all those funny things.

(*The boy addresses the younger girl:*)
Do you want to see too?

(*The younger girl speaks:*)
No. I am too young.

(*The boy addresses the older girl:*)
Look down into the water with the glass.

(*The older girl speaks:*)
Now I see strange things under the water.
I see things moving around as though they were live animals,
I see things that look like little bugs, and many strange animals under
   the sea.


## LOVE SONG

Many pretty flowers, red, blue and yellow,
We say to the girls, "Let us go and walk among the flowers."
The wind comes and sways the flowers,
The girls are like that when they dance,
Some are wide-open, large flowers and some are tiny little flowers.
The birds love the sunshine and the starlight.
The flowers smell sweet,
The girls are sweeter than the flowers.
I go among the girls and see them all,
But I like only the one I walked with first,
My eyes are open for her but I look at the others as though I were
   dreaming,
I say to her, "When I die you must think of me all the time."
I look at the others as though I were dreaming,
The girl is dreaming too.

# SOUTH AMERICA

# South America

*Inca*

## HYMN OF AN INCA TO THE GOD
## VIRACOCHA

Viracocha, Lord of the Universe!
Whether male or female,
at any rate commander of heat and reproduction,
being one who,
even with His spittle, can work sorcery.
Where art Thou?
Would that Thou wert not hidden from this son of Thine!
He may be above;
He may be below;
or, perchance, abroad in space.
Where is His mighty judgement-seat?
Hear me!
He may be spread abroad among the upper waters;
or, among the lower waters and their sands
He may be dwelling.
Creator of the world,
Creator of man,
great among my ancestors,
before Thee
my eyes fail me,
though I long to see Thee;
for, seeing Thee,
knowing Thee,
learning from Thee,
understanding Thee,
I shall be seen by Thee,

and Thou wilt know me.
The Sun—the Moon;
the Day—the Night;
Summer—Winter;
not in vain,
in orderly succession,
do they march
to their destined place,
to their goal.
They arrive
wherever
Thy royal staff
Thou bearest.
Oh! Harken to me,
listen to me,
let it not befall
that I grow weary
and die.


## VERSES OF AN
## INCA POET AND
## ASTROLOGER[1]

Beautiful Princess.
This your brother
Is breaking
Your pitcher,
For which reason
It thunders and lightens
And bolts fall.
You, Royal Lady,
Raining, will give us
Your beautiful waters,
And sometimes
You will hail for us
And snow.
The Creator of the World,
The God who animates it,

1 Recorded about 1550.

Great Viracocha,
Long since they laid
This duty on you
And gave you being.

## TO A TRAITOR

The traitor's skull, we shall drink out of it,
His teeth we shall wear as a necklace,
From his bones we shall make flutes,
Of his skin we shall make a drum,
Then we shall dance.

## SONG OF AN IMPRISONED PRINCE

Thinking takes away from me,
Weeping takes away from me,
Just my heart.
I am going to kill myself.
Harai haraui,
Oh prison-house,
Oh fetter-house,
Pray, let me loose!

## SONG

Has your field pepper?
On the pretext of pepper I shall come.
Has your field flowers?
On the pretext of flowers I shall come.

## SONG[2]

To the song
You will sleep
At midnight
I will come.

[2] Recorded about 1550.

**Witoto**    COLOMBIA

## SONG OF THE VICTIM AT A CANNIBAL FEAST

I tell this to the many friends of the tribe of the Iane: I was caught,
dragged away, and killed in my youth.

## SONG OF THE SWEET-SMELLING LOVE CHARM

Up and down she pulled his member, for Hitoma's sweet-scented herb
had already excited her. Up and down Husikobikanyo pulled his member, for Hitoma's love-scented herb was urging her. The shining hummingbird sang.

**Jibaro**    ECUADOR AND PERU

## SONG OF THE PRIESTESS AT A VICTORY FEAST

Let us sing and dance!
May all of you come!

Arranged in a file may you come and dance!
Arranged in a file may you come without feeling shame!

Well dressed,
having adjusted your tarachi,
having arranged your ornaments,
may you sing and dance!
Grasping one another by the hands
may you dance!

Like the swallow which is moving his body to and fro,
Like the hawk, which is making his circles in the air, may you sing
    and dance!

## PLANTING SONG OF
## WOMEN TO THE
## EARTH-MOTHER

Being daughters of Nungüi, the woman,
we are going to sow.
Nungüi, come thou and help us,
come and help us!
Art not thou, art not thou our mother,
are not we thy children?
Whom should we call upon?
We only behold wood and hills.
Thou art the only one who can help us,
us that are going to plant the fruit.

## INVOCATION SUNG
## BY A HUNTER
## SETTING OUT

I am a son of Etza
my blowpipe has always struck true
because I am a son of Etza.
Wake, blowpipe! monkeys are coming;
be still, quiver! or
the monkeys will be frightened away.
I am a son of Etza,
my blowpipe will always strike true.

## SONGS OF DANCING WOMEN
## PERSONIFYING BIRDS

I

Being the wife of the cock-of-the-rock,
being the little wife of the sumga,
I jokingly sing to you thus:
Cock-of-the-rock, my little husband,
wearing your many-coloured dress of feathers,
graceful in your movements!

I know I am useless myself,
but still I rejoice,
for I am the wife of the sumga—
So I jokingly sing!

II

Great pheasant, great pheasant,
pheasant with the long hair and the big tail,
my little son, whom I have intoxicated with the beer!
I have made myself like the pheasant,
putting on me your long tail
and dressing myself in your brilliant feathers—
So I jokingly sing.

**Quechua**    PERU

## DANCE SONG

This princess who does not know love,
We will throw her in the sweet water of the lake;
There, there she will learn,
Drinking that sweet water,
That I am to be loved,
That I am to be cherished.

This woman who does not know love,
We will throw her in the barren field of snow;
There, there she will learn,
With the white snow chilling her,
That I am to be loved,
That I am to be cherished.

This girl who does not know love,
We will drag her to the bridge and throw her in the muddy stream;
There, there she will learn,
Drinking the muddy water,
That I am to be loved,
That I am to be cherished.

# LULLABY

My mother begot me, amidst rain and mist,
To weep like the rain, and be drifted like the clouds.
You are born in the cradle of sorrow,
Says my mother, as she gives me the breast.
She weeps as she wraps me around.
The rain and mists attacked me,
When I went to meet my lover.
Seeking through the whole world,
I should not meet my equal in misery.
Accursed be my birthday,
Accursed be the night I was born,
From this time, for ever and ever.


# SONG

As is the apple of my eye, beloved one!
You are dear to her who loves you.

Mountains that divide the land! take pity!
Make the road to turn, that I may find him.

Heart of my love! The mighty rocks,
Stopping up the road, hinder me.

Flowing from village to village, the great river,
Increased by my tears, hinders me.

As is my eye, so are the waters of yon cloud,
They encompass me, as I wait for my love.

Lend me your wings, O falcon!
That, rising in the air, I may see a welcome sight.

When the rain falls, or the wind is high,
My love resting under the shade of a spreading tree.

## GIRL'S SONG

Little willow, green branch,
Color of my hope,
It is my own doing
If I am weeping in your arms.

Some one wants me to die,
I am not dead yet,
I have not felt
The poison I have been given.

Someone wants me to go,
I have not left yet,
I have not found
One to take me home.

## SONG

When you find yourself alone on the island in the river
your father will not be there to call to you
*alau,* my daughter!
your mother cannot reach you with
*alau,* my daughter!

Only the royal drake will be there to court you,
with rain in his eyes,
with his tears of blood;
rain in his eyes,
tears of blood.

And even the royal drake must go
when the waves in the river
grow wild,
when the waters of the river
rush headlong.

But then I will go to court you,
singing:

"I will carry off her young heart in the island,
her young heart
in the storm."

## SONG

Today is the day I must leave,
I will not go today, I will go tomorrow.
You will see me set out playing on a fly-bone flute,
carrying a spider-web for a flag;
my drum will be an ant's egg
and my hat! my hat will be a hummingbird's nest.

## ELEGY

A tree's sheltering shade,
A road of life,
Clear crystal of a waterfall,
These you were.

In your branches
My heart nested,
In your shade
My joy thrived.

Can it be that you are going
All alone?
Will you not open
Your eyes again?

What road must you take,
Leaving me behind,
Not even opening
Your lips?

What tree now will give me
Its shade?
What waterfall will give me
Its song?

How can I bear to be left
All alone?
The world will be a desert
For me.


**Mapuche**    CHILE


## ASSEMBLY SONGS

### I  *Complaint of a Young Wife Whose Husband Is Sexually Overactive*

I dreamed of a lapwing a long time ago, and now I am like a hen under the wing of a rooster.


### II  *The Husband's Reply*

Wife, dear wife, it would be better if you went more slowly and did not talk so much, or else there may be someone else asking for my favor. If you feel the same love for me that I do for you, just be quiet. Don't set people talking about us; this is our own affair.


### III  *The Wife's Counterreply*

Husband, dear husband, what you have said shows that you just jumped at conclusions. I wasn't speaking seriously.


## MAN'S ASSEMBLY SONG

Only with one eye do you glance at me at present. When you hide your face, I might as well be dead.

**Choroti**     GRAN CHACO

## SONG OF A VISITOR TO
## A STRANGE VILLAGE

Now I have come, now I have come, to see my brothers.
Now I have come from far away to see my children.
Now it is well with them.
They shall not see enemies.
Now it is well with them, with me.
Now I have come to see my brothers.
Enemies shall not kill them.
Now it is well with them.


**Kaingang**     SANTA CATARINA, BRAZIL


### KEENING

I am remembering my mother. I want to call her mother. I am remembering my mother. I am the one who called her mother, but now it is all over. I am remembering my mother. When my mother would look at me she would remember that my father had seen me and she would weep—now that is all over. I am remembering my mother. I and my children used to call my mother mother—that is all over. I am remembering my mother. I want to see my mother. When my father would return after leaving me he would think of how I suffered, and he would weep. Grandmother, whose name I bear, would think of my sickness and suffering.

**Carib**    SURINAM

## WORD OF THE THUNDER

I am the Thunder, the terror of the earth reflects my oneness.
The earth I do vibrate, I the Thunder.
All flesh fears, that reflects the oneness of the Thunder.
I pass along my field.
With swiftness all must move out of the way.
The lightning precedes me.
The thunder-axe I have made, I the Thunder.

**Bush Negro**    SURINAM

## LOVE SONGS

I

When you sleep, dream of me, many thanks.

II

When you lead me to deceit I will not follow; such things you should
not teach me.

**Town Negro**    SURINAM

## RELIGIOUS SONGS

I    *Adyanti Winti*

Tell all the women for me,
I am not dead yet;
Tell all the women for me,

*Word:* "The *Aula* (or 'Word') of anything is its life description, its being" (A. P.
and T. E. Penard, as cited, p. 258, n. 1. See Sources and Permissions).

I live, I am not dead.
But let go of my neck,
And clasp my back;
When I am in my hour of passion,
Loosen my head.
Hold me by the neck,
Loosen my back,
When I am in my hour of pleasure,
Loosen my neck.

11    *Akantamasu*

*Ye-a-o, mia, mia, mia,*
To my very lair my dead trouble me-o,
I am *Kantamasi-o*
I am *Kantamasu,*
But human beings trouble me,
It is well, too
Since I am a good person
To my very lair, my dead trouble me,
I am a good person.

# INDEX
# OF PEOPLES

# INDEX OF PEOPLES

* For the Eskimo of Greenland and Canada, see *The Unwritten Song*, I, 3–32.

† For the Malay of the Moluccas, see *The Unwritten Song*, I, 177.